## BOOKS BY JOHN D. SPOONER ("BRUTUS")

The Pheasant-lined Vest of Charlie Freeman
Three Cheers for War in General
Confessions of a Stockbroker
Class
The King of Terrors
Smart People

# SMART PEOPLE

# JOHN D. SPOONER

# SMART PEOPLE

## A USER'S GUIDE TO EXPERTS

Little, Brown and Company — Boston – Toronto

Library of Congress Cataloging in Publication Data
Spooner, John D
    Smart people.
    1. Success. I. Title.
BF637.S8S66        640        79–16067
ISBN 0–316–80740–0

BP

Designed by Susan Windheim

*Published simultaneously in Canada
by Little, Brown & Company (Canada) Limited*

PRINTED IN THE UNITED STATES OF AMERICA

*Smart children are special too:*
*For Scott, Nicky, and Amanda.*

All my Smart People are based on real people and I want to thank them for their contributions to this book, and to my life. But except for the names and descriptions of the famous, all the characters in this book are fictitious. The situations, while they are derived from my own experience, have in every instance been deliberately altered to confound, confuse and otherwise render identification of the principals impossible.

After all, I want to keep *my* Smart People on my team and not have them enticed away by *you*.

# CONTENTS

# SMART
# PEOPLE

# 1 RECRUITING THE TEAM

You have waited in line to get into a restaurant or theater or disco. You have waited, trying to make conversation with your friend or husband or wife, feeling frustrated and annoyed by the delay, feeling like one of the herd, helpless to do anything about it. Suddenly you see a couple walk completely past the line, ignoring you, ignoring everyone. They go to the front of the line, confront whatever authority waits at the door, and are immediately ushered inside. *You* continue to wait your turn, frustrated, still ignored. We all know someone who is always ushered to the front of lines. Think about this person — because he can do a lot more than be ushered in front of you in line.

He can get a bigger discount from his stockbroker.

He can be welcomed in private clubs around the world.

He can get Superbowl tickets when they're presumably unavailable. Or seats to a sold-out Horowitz or Neil Diamond concert.

He can be invited to play in the Bob Hope Desert Classic or the Alan King Celebrity Tennis Tournament.

He can get cleaning help and baby-sitters and plumbers who will come on a few minutes' notice.

He can get legal assistance without having it be the worst experience of his life.

He can buy jewelry, designer clothing, home furnishings, and appliances at stunning discounts.

He consistently gets moved up to first class from tourist.

He has a doctor who makes house calls.

You also know the person who accepts the fact that he must wait in line forever to get seats behind a post, the person who brings his car in for a tune-up and ends up paying for a valve job.

This is the person who buys jewelry only at Tiffany's, at the highest retail markup, who buys clothing just *before* everything goes on sale, who pays a local contractor up front for brick work because the contractor demands it.

This is the person who gets bumped off the overbooked flight.

He is the guy whose reservation the hotel cannot find. He is the person who pays a scalper *double* for difficult-to-find tickets and who tips a maitre d' at a top restaurant and finds himself at a table in Siberia anyway, still ignored.

This is the person who is seen by his regular doctor's new associate, because the regular doctor is busy.

This is the person who had an amicable divorce in his pocket until his lawyer stirred the situation into a disaster. He is now in litigation up to his ears.

This is the person whose water pipes burst during a dinner party and who ends up holding two galvanized pieces together for the night until the plumber arrives at eleven the next morning.

What is the difference between these two characters? The difference is Smart People.

A brokerage-house boardroom is a mirror of the soul. The clatter and the action grab at the emotions. The atmosphere makes people greedy, it makes them hopeful, it makes them afraid. It also makes them reveal themselves. "Things are complicated," a client said to me recently. "From the time I was eighteen, people have been trying to complicate my life. Machines confuse me, marriage and children exhaust me, expenses and taxes wear me down. I can't get a plumber when I need one, and I know the kids' orthodontist has got me on the string like an annuity. I need help daily in a hundred different areas, and I get gouged and overcharged everywhere. What ever happened to barn-raisings? You know, neighbors helping neighbors . . . one guy with a hammer, the other guy with nails, and the women baking cakes and making meat pies. It just cost me a *hundred and thirty dollars* to have a carpenter put up a basketball backboard for my boy. Lumber? Gotta be three dollars. Hoop? Five bucks. *Tops.* Labor? One hundred twenty-two, and my first running right-hander from the key pulled the whole thing down into the driveway. The middle class today is screwed at every turn."

My client was hysterical, but essentially correct.

We are surrounded by high-priced incompetence. We do not have the time or ability to shop price or quality. And self-improvement is not the key to survival in a society in which we have lost control of our own destinies.

By ourselves we are isolated. Society is complicated, it is over-crowded, it is indifferent to the individual, however self-reliant. Your government, your society have turned you into a number, and the numbers game has become increasingly impossible to escape. How do you become a nonnumber and transform yourself into a person again? Screaming and complaining can't do it. The world is too indifferent. What *can* you do?

The key to a successful adult life lies in surrounding yourself with experts, a master person for every need. We have gone beyond taking care of ourselves. We need others to care for our medical, legal, financial, emotional, and even our bodily survival. Most of us blunder about these tasks like the balls in a pinball machine. We are aimlessly buffeted, taking our chances and paying the bills. In these times of instant communication, when a top-level hernia in the Middle East can produce a selling panic on Wall Street, when most Americans' nervous hysteria is close to the surface, we need help. This book is about building your own

King Arthur's Round Table. This book will help you to find and recruit Smart People.

My own life would not be possible without my team of experts. I run a large stock-brokerage business with several thousand customers. I write articles for national magazines and do a great deal of lecturing. I have had six books published in the last twelve years, books that have been through several paperback editions and have been translated into foreign languages. I have been married to the same woman all that time and have three children. I have a house in the country and a house by the sea. My annual income is in six figures. *None* of this would have been possible unless I'd learned to make people responsive to my needs. Without *my* Smart People, the organization of my life would be in tatters; my parallel careers, parallel disasters.

The patriarch of the famous Guggenheim family, Meyer Guggenheim, gathered his five sons together years ago. He held up six sticks, showed them to his sons, then broke them, one by one. "You see how easily they snap," he said. Then he took six unbroken sticks and tried with all his strength to break them at the same time. He was unable to do it.

"You see," Meyer said, "individually, we snap easily. Together, *nothing* can break us."

This principle holds true for all of us. But we each have to build our *own* family. We need Smart People.

I know the stories of more people than do most doctors, lawyers, or psychiatrists. Mine is a psychiatric profession. People reveal to their broker more of their true selves, more of their real emotions in relation to their money than they do in years of therapy. The average doctor with a successful general practice has about five hundred families on his patient roster. I see almost twice as many people as that. People tell me what they're afraid of; they tell me what they desire; they tell me who they are. Thus, as you will see, *Smart People* is a book about a kind of therapy.

You can receive more help from people who understand the human condition from a practical standpoint than you can from years of sessions with doctors who know the jargon of their profession but don't necessarily know how to live successfully in the modern world. *Smart People* will tell *you* about your money and managing your debt. It will give you secrets about household help and divorce lawyers, travel agents and surgeons. It will tell you how to get a literary agent, how to deal with superstars, carpenters, baby-sitters, policemen, and maitre d's. It will tell you about people and things you may be curious about but have never encountered: cocaine dealers, loan sharks, Middle East oil entrepreneurs, inventors, hit men, sex therapists, the very rich.

The book will also tell you about many of *my* Smart People — how I discovered them, what they do, and what they advise *me* to do with problems of all dimensions. I will also tell you about Smart People whose names you will recognize and whose advice you may profit from. The important thing to remember, however, is not how smart these people are for themselves, but how smart they can be for you.

Most of all, this book will help you build your own cadre of experts, people who care about and will respond to *your* needs. Smart People *can* simplify your life. They can make you wealthy. They can find you bargains. They can give you pleasure. They can clean your house or apartment. They can make you laugh. They can set you free. They can make you happy. And best of all . . . they may make *you* a Smart Person.

All of us are faced with the same kinds of problems. How can we make out on what we earn? How can we afford to educate our children? How do we prevent people from taking advantage of us?

What do you want out of life? Respect, admiration, power? A six-figure income? Would you settle for only a fair deal, or do you want the most for your money? Achieving each of your desires, fending off the people or things you fear may require different forms of expertise, expertise you do not possess. But somewhere out there is someone who can help you . . . *if* that someone wants to help. Somewhere out there are people who can solve any of

your problems. How do you find them? And if you do find them,
how do you make them respond to your needs? One thing is
certain. You must make others recognize you as an individual, not
a number. Once you make others do this, they're stuck with you;
they must deal with you as a human being.

I have carved out simple principles for getting others to respond to you, whoever you are, wherever you are. These principles can work for you regardless of your tax bracket. The examples
you will read in this book are from my life and experience.
But you can relate them to your own experience — regardless of
where you live or who you are, regardless of age, sex, or race.
Smart People surround you. I'm going to teach you how to find
them, recruit them, and use them to make your life better.

First of all, think about your life. Like everyone, you have
stories about yourself that you remember with pain, with pleasure, with amusement. Most of these stories involve both you and
other people. I'm going to tell you many stories in this book,
stories that will illustrate how I have recruited Smart People.
Similar smart people can be recruited by you and kept on your
side. The principles are the same and can be used all your life.
Remember, all of us need help. You cannot do it alone. You need
allies. *Smart People* will show you that you may already have the
essence of your team in place, without ever having realized it.

The first Smart People Principle is

*Use People from Your Past*

Few of us can resist the chance to reminisce with someone who
shared a part of our childhood. Most of us are suckers for nostalgia, retaining memories of what has been when times were
simpler and we were smaller. Try to maintain friendships from
the past. And do what can be more important: keep high school
yearbooks, Sunday school pictures, college yearbooks, club or fraternity directories. Never disdain school reunions. In these books

and pictures and at these events you'll find key smart people who will simplify your life, who cannot resist helping you, because they all shared past experiences with you.

Respond to high school reunion questionnaires. Respond to college reunion questionnaires. People I once considered "cool" would never consider replying to these inquiries. They would never consider going back to look over or be looked over. But those people are fools. There is no bond as strong as the past. And it becomes more important as you grow older.

When I moved to my new town several years ago, I consulted both my high school and my college directories. Sure enough, Jackie Ritter lived in the town, and Jackie Ritter had made all of my manual-training projects in seventh and eighth grade — the birdhouse, the writing desk, even the envelope holder in the shape of a cranberry picker. Jackie was the town plumber, and, although we hadn't seen each other in years, he dropped several projects to fix pipes, redo bathrooms, and check heating systems for me when I called him.

What did I say to him?

"Is this Jackie Ritter, maker of the best birdhouses in the Mason School seventh grade?"

"Who is this?"

"Is this Jackie Ritter who couldn't go to his left for ground balls in the hole at shortstop?"

"Who *is* this?"

"Is this Jackie Ritter who saved my ass in grammar school and who is going to save me again when my bathroom drain clogs? This is John Spooner, Jack, how you doin'?"

"John Spooner," he said. "God, didn't you ever learn how to fix *anything?*"

Reminded of his past triumphs, he couldn't wait to save me again.

But remember, you must call *your* Jackie Ritter *before* your bathroom drain clogs, *before* your pipe bursts, *before* your hot-

water heater explodes. You have to set up your team in advance
of emergencies, not *after* they occur.

I jumped to the head of the line with Jackie Ritter in ten
minutes of memories. Every time I see him, a few old stories
ensure that I stay at the top of the list.

And it doesn't matter if the people from the past were old
enemies. Old school enemies can, in fact, work particularly well
for you. At my twentieth grammar school reunion, several years
ago, I spotted Enid the Amazon. And she was gorgeous. I had
given her the name "Enid the Amazon" in the third grade when
she towered over all the boys. She hated me. I embraced her at
the reunion, and she rushed me over to her husband.

"You traumatized Enid's youth," he told me. "She's told me
thousands of times about her nickname and how she'd love to get
back at you." We were adult now. Childhood antagonisms were
childish. We were both big enough to forgive. I told her how
terrific she looked and how wonderful it was for a woman to be
tall. Enid and her husband run one of the largest ticket agencies
in New York. Now whenever I need impossible-to-obtain seats, to
a Neil Diamond concert, or *A Chorus Line*, or the World Series,
Enid the Amazon comes through for me. She had remembered
me as making fun of her. But then at the reunion I praised her.
She had made it as an adult, and I was living proof that she had
changed. She *was* better. She cannot now refuse the human contact of someone from childhood, some strong association with
friend or foe that reaffirms the past, that, in fact, makes the past
better.

You have to make the effort to stay in touch. If you do, people
will not resist. And they don't even have to be people you know.
Club and fraternity directories often list members by cities. I
have called members of associations or clubs or high school
classes of mine in places like Watsonville, California, Memphis,
Tennessee, and Panama City, Panama, and have been given the
best of those towns. I have called these people and said, "Hi, I'm
John Spooner. I grew up on your block years ago. I lived next to

the Hathaways. Remember, they were the ones who put the cat in the washing machine? I'm in your city for two nights, and I wonder if you can give me a steer on restaurants?"

The technique is to ask for something they can readily give: information. This approach also flatters them. *They* are asked *their* opinion. They will give you some ideas and then very probably will give you some more. The surprise technique works better than writing a letter ahead of time. It gives the people you call no time to make up advance excuses about their availability.

This technique will work for you the way it does for me. People care about shared memories and experiences: the old block, the games, the teachers. Out of thousands of people you've remembered *them*. They're flattered. This obviously makes them feel special.

*Use* the people from your past. They'll prove to be Smart People for you.

The second Smart People Principle is

*Have Something to Trade.*

You cannot, of course, deal constantly with people from your past. Probably you live far from the places of your childhood. You therefore have to find new people to help you. You must always have something to offer these people in return for their help, something that will make you special to them. I give autographed paperback editions of my books to people who do various jobs for me. A paperback costs an author fifty percent of the retail price of the book. I order them by the case and give them away to prospective customers and prospective Smart People, as gratuities for services rendered or in friendship. It's a cheap way to have people remember me. They may even read the book. And the whole enterprise is deductible.

But most of you will not give away books you have written or paintings or other work of your own hand. By "something to

trade" I really mean advice, services of your own, or referrals of
new business for the person you want to recruit.

Even small touches can be effective. For instance, if you have
workmen at your house — movers, carpenters, plumbers — offer
them a beer at the end of the job. Whether they take it or not,
they will remember you. The next time you call them they will
respond with more personal attention to the task. Little touches
that you offer to trade can bind others to you.

Inflation is with us for the rest of our lives. Goods and services
are escalating in cost at runaway rates. And the amount you pay
seems to have *nothing* to do with the quality of these goods and
services. So you must have a specialty to trade that transcends the
money involved. If you are a professional — lawyer, doctor, scientist, musician, athlete, banker — offer this information to people at the beginning of your relationship. Don't wait for the
tradesman's bill to inform him of what *you* can offer. "Before you
start the job," begins one of my warm-ups, "I want to let you
know something. This isn't just any set of gutters you're about to
clean and oil. These are *magic* gutters."

Usually the contractor will nod. And inside his head he is jumping up and down, itching to get back to his office and tell his
buddies about the crazy guy with the magic gutters.

I show the contractor into my studio (you show him into your
house), and I pull out my private phone directory, studded with
hundreds of names. (For practical purposes, I keep this private
telephone directory *full* of names, addresses, and phone numbers.
Absolutely full from A to Z. It always impresses tradespeople.
Even if it contains names and addresses from other places, other
years, this magic phone book never fails to make your magic
gutters.) "You see this book?" I say, asking the contractor to riffle
through it. "Almost every name represents a potential customer
for you. Everyone in this book at one time or another looks for
gutter cleaners. If my wife or I recommend you, you can increase your business dramatically. If we have reason to complain,
we will also have reason to mention that to all of our friends. And

they'll mention it to others we *don't* know." This method works
wonders, and we do bring significant business to all of our best
service people.

This may sound like a threatening technique. It may sound
abrasive to you. But, particularly if you are a woman dealing with
service people at your home or apartment, it can be extraordinarily effective for you. If the people who perform services for
you perform well, there is a bonus in it for them: more business.
Smart People techniques produce organic results. More business
for your service people brings *you* better service. Home service
people are impressed by efficient women. And you will have bargaining power because you have something to trade. The dividend of trading is that it makes you more interesting to others. It
makes *you* a character to remember.

Having something to trade also means being able to offer your
specialty in exchange for service. You can and should develop a
specialty for barter, even if you are not professionally trained in
anything. Americans living in our anonymous, mobile society
desperately hold out their hands for touches of humanity. Learn
about all factory outlets in the vicinity of your home. Know about
effective tennis pros and skating teachers. Know about obscure
restaurants, about housecleaning people, about screen and storm-
window installers. Know about baby-sitters. Have collections:
paintings, sculpture, stamps, Oriental rugs. Others love to learn.
Have something to teach. If you always have an ace in the hole,
something you can trade, you will forever be interesting to others.
And, what is even more important, you will forever be interesting
to yourself. One of the great problems in America is loneliness,
the affliction of the single, the divorced, the aged. If you develop
a hobby, an interest in something other than television, you need
never wonder what to do with yourself. You need never lapse into
self-pity.

Having something to trade recruits Smart People. And it is
essential to remember this: the process is organic. It goes on and
on. People recruited for your team will find other effective team

members for you as the years go on. The buck never stops for you. The methods explained in this book, once mastered, will have the same ripple effect as pebbles tossed in a pond. Your Smart People team can grow as large as you want or as large as you need.

The third Smart People Principle is

*Make Yourself Memorable.*

None of the Smart People Principles can be mastered overnight. It takes time and thought to assemble people from your past if you have never concentrated on it. If you have no special skill or hobby or talent to trade for service, it will take time to acquire it. Making yourself memorable seems the easiest of Smart People Principles. But, like riding a bicycle, it takes practice. Once learned, as in riding a bike, it should be second nature.

Let me give you an example of how one of my Smart People made herself memorable.

Lisa Fairburn is a lady lawyer who specializes in tax problems. She is particularly effective in fighting Internal Revenue Service audits for her clients. In conversations with the IRS she always finds a way to bring up this story about herself:

"I am devoted to people," she says, "to my clients, to my husband. Do you know the greatest tribute a wife has ever given her husband?"

"No," says the IRS.

"Well *I* do," Lisa says, "because I've given it to *my* husband. He's a Republican and always has been. His name is Arthur. Last year he had his fortieth birthday and, as a surprise present, I took myself to Providence, Rhode Island, and had tattooed on my left buttock an elephant holding a banner in his trunk. Written on the banner in red ink is 'Arthur turns forty.'"

"Let's see it," says the IRS.

Lisa never shows the tattoo. But she once climbed bare-bottomed onto her firm's Xerox machine and now carries in her wallet the photographic proof of the deed. Lisa the Lawyer's elephant tattoo never fails to get a reaction. She is always remembered with a smile. And those smiles have brought her clients rebates and favorable treatment, as well as bringing her continuing business from clients who appreciate her style.

A tattoo is an extreme example of making yourself memorable. What is important is working on yourself to become someone whom *others want to help.*

Remember also that little touches can separate you from the mass of other people. Most people in the world who serve you think that you don't care if they live or die: locker-room attendants, newsstand dealers, shoeshine boys, toll takers, window washers. Show them they're wrong. Be cordial. Life pays dividends in surprising ways. And remember: By paying attention to these people you're also making *yourself* memorable to them.

For instance, call a cab driver by his first name when you enter his taxi. Every cab license shows a picture of the driver and his name. "How you doing, Harry?" will melt all but the chilliest New York cabbie. In an overcrowded world, everyone wants to be treated as a human being. Another effective touch that I use you can use also. Probe people's Secret Life. Ask others who may be serving you in various ways, "What did you want to grow up to be when you were a child?" This question always elicits a response. It also makes people want to perform for you, because you took the time to ask something no one ever asks. It helps to make you memorable.

You especially need to make yourself memorable if your genes have not endowed you with the personality of a Bill Cosby or the wit of a Joan Rivers. Don't be afraid of gimmicks, even if they aren't subtle. *Embrace whatever works.*

Men used to wear a flower in their buttonhole. Now either florists don't sell boutonnieres or clothing manufacturers don't make buttonholes on lapels. I wear a small, rainbow-colored enamel heart on my right lapel. No one can resist commenting on it. "Wearing your heart on your sleeve?" they say. "What's that for, the Heart Fund?" they say. "I see you've got your heart-on today," they say, and then become embarrassed. But they continue the conversation. My little heart has never failed to get me quickly by secretaries and receptionists who guard their bosses like eunuchs guard the harem. Everyone remembers the rainbow heart, and everyone who sees it wants one. But when you select your attention-getter, make it unusual. Make it your own. My editor thought the rainbow heart was nonsense. "It's a pretty ornament," he said to me, walking through the Boston Public Garden one day, "but who pays attention to ornaments? Every woman wears earrings. You get so used to them, they're like part of the ear. I don't buy the heart-pin story." Yet within ten minutes a gallery owner, a literary critic, two teenage girls, a maitre d', and a bartender at the Ritz-Carlton Hotel *all* commented on the pin. It is an attention-getter and has become a trademark.

"The rainbow," people ask, "what's it mean?"

"It's what's at the end of it," I tell them.

"A pot of gold?" they say.

"A pot of gold."

And they're right. Because the pin has brought me both service and business. Getting a foot in the door is what *your* attention-getter will produce. *Then* you can deliver the goods.

Most people don't have this chance to get a foot in the door. *Anything* giving you an edge is fair. You have to be able to advertise yourself without wearing a sign on your chest. If something distinctive makes people remember you, then use it to your advantage.

In recruiting your Smart People team, you have concentrated on people who can help you from the past, and you have developed something to trade for the services of others. Now you are also on your way to making yourself memorable.

As we move on to advice from Smart People in different professions, expanding upon the basic Smart People Principles, you must understand that there are distinct types of people you will need to recruit. You will need experts at every level of life, in every profession, to take care of your needs — physical, spiritual, emotional, financial.

Since Smart People exist at every level of society, I have separated into classifications the types necessary for your team. You will readily recognize the people available to you from your experience, from your own lives.

It is not enough for you to have a tax attorney. You need the lawyer who can get your cook a permanent resident's visa and get you a patent on your invention. It is not enough to have a surgeon. You may also need a heart specialist or an allergist or a child psychiatrist. It can be as important to you to have a sympathetic policeman on your side as to have a good stockbroker. *Smart People* will tell you whom you can use, whom you will need, and how to keep them with you.


## THE ROUGHRIDER

Roughriders are the *street-smart* Smart People. They may lead lives no one would wish to emulate. They do not respond to problems in the conventional manner. But if you have Roughriders who are responsive to *you*, you may never again get traffic tickets, fear enemies, buy diamonds in a jewelry store, buy clothes at retail, wait in line at restaurants, search in vain for concert tickets, or worry about taking an exam. Get the picture?

Kurt the Cutlass is my Roughrider for doing the outrageous. He is called "the Cutlass" because his approach is similar to the ferocious slashing attacks of that particular sword. He achieves results by overkill. He is controversial and amusing, and, even if not always successful, he prides himself on at least having answers, very often good ones. Kurt the Cutlass intimidates. He is physically large, with a shock of very blond hair that he parts in the middle like a gigolo from a musical of the 1930s. Kurt manages money for heavyweights who like secrecy, for people with large ordinary incomes, like athletes and actresses and rock stars, and for businessmen who generate chunks of money abroad and somehow find themselves with undeclared cash of various currencies.

I met Kurt flying first-class to Los Angeles when an engine flamed out over Denver. He taught me lessons right away. The first-class section was full, and everyone was terrified, fearful with typical airplane dread. No one dared tell his neighbor that armpits were sodden with anxiety and toes were squeezing against the ends of shoes with fright. Kurt the Cutlass jumped to his feet. "All right, you bison." (Kurt has a language all his own and refers to people, individually or collectively, as "bison.") "This aircraft has four engines and can fly perfectly well on one. The plane has such sophisticated gear that it can land itself, so I would suggest you all take an extra drink, relax your stomach muscles, and thank God that you're in first class. If you want to take your mind off the situation further, I can organize us into three sections to sing 'Rock, My Soul, in the Bosom of Abraham,' the greatest round since 'Row, Row, Row Your Flagetta.'" ("Flagetta" is another of Kurt's words. He uses it strictly as a noun.) By this time, everyone in first class was amused, and Kurt the Cutlass was in control.

Later, in Denver's airport lounge, Kurt let me in on some of his secrets. "I'll tell you, bison," he said, "sometimes you have to force yourself to be onstage, just to get what you want. No one's going to notice you, especially these days, unless you make sure they notice. You want to make business deals, have connections? One essential thing: on business trips always fly first class. On holidays with your wife, always fly tourist."

"I would think you'd care more about comfort on vacations."

"Wrong" he said. "R, o, n, g. You want to *save* money on holiday, you want to *make* it on business. I've made so much more money flying first-class, I can't tell you. Because you always meet people when you travel, especially if you make the effort.

And the people you meet flying first are the people who count. Whoever I sit next to, I wait for the champagne. Then wherever we are flying to or from — say, Cincinnati — I say to my neighbor, 'How long you been in Cincinnati?' This opens things up. It doesn't matter who you're sitting next to. Once from L.A. I was sitting with a ten-year-old girl. 'How long you been in Los Angeles?' I asked her. Turns out she was the granddaughter of the founder of a Big Board aircraft company. I kept her in Cokes and comics and attention all the way to Pittsburgh. Later I phoned the family and asked for the kid, the bisonette, and mentioned my kindness. Before you know it, I did a corporate finance deal in Paris for the company. No way *their* kid ever would have flown tourist. You fly first class because the heavies fly it. Maybe not the people so heavy they're reverse snobs, so rich they're pinching pennies or sucking around Ralph Nader. Those people you don't want to reach. They're too suspicious.

"Other megaheavies fly their own planes. That's why I have my pilot's license. That's why I knew what was happening with the engine on fire. If you know how to fly an aircraft you are interesting to anyone in first class. Because basically, almost everyone is terrified of flying. They love to be reassured. A big mistake that commercial airlines make: they never really explain anything or reassure *anyone*.

"The simple corollary is true about vacations," Kurt says. "Why pay the extra freight for six more inches of seat and a hot-fudge sundae when you have to pay for it yourself? With your wife, you're not going to talk to other people, certainly not to single businessmen. So first class is a waste of dough. Fly tourist with her. Talk to her. She isn't going to get you into the Gnomes of Zurich. She isn't going to introduce you to the Aga Khan. The whole thing is simple economics."

I recruited Kurt by referring someone to him, a man who manufactured shoes in Europe and needed help with certain banking connections in Switzerland. The arrangement was mutually satisfactory, and I keep Kurt interested in me with a promise that I may refer more people to him in the future. You see, I bind him to my side by *having something to trade*, something Kurt wants.

Another hint from Kurt: "What happens when you make cold calls to big shots? They're never in, they're indisposed. You never get through the receptionist. For weeks I used to call the governor in my state about a state policeman who had run me off the road. I had zero luck reaching the governor. Finally, exasperated, I said to the lady on the phone, 'This is Kurt the Cutlass. I'm returning the governor's call.' Two minutes later I had the old boy on the phone. It's a great lesson, one that's worked for me dozens of times. I place the call, tell the receptionist I'm returning the call of Mr. Big. Invariably I'm put right through and at least have a chance to launch into my pitch."

"Look," Kurt said, "anything you want, I can do. At upper levels. You want to get the best service in any restaurant, here's what you do. Take the maitre d'. They're the worst snobs, the biggest thieves in America. First of all, always pretend you are from out of town. It immediately sets you apart in a restaurant. To the maitre d' you say, 'My associates from Rome' (if it's Italian) 'have raved to me about your restaurant.' Obviously, it's 'my associates from Paris' if it's a French place, and so on. Then you slip him *one* bill. Make it a fiver. They never look. They just palm it and put it in their pocket and give you a great table. *Never* give a maitre d' more than one bill. More than one bill means *ones*. When you're seated, quickly estimate what the meal will cost. Then give the waiter twenty percent of that estimate *before* the meal and ask him, 'What's your name? Jerome? Okay, Jerome, here's something to get you started. We all enjoy ourselves and there's something on the other end, too. Can you dig it, Jerome?' Jerome always digs it. It isn't just the disbursing of money," he tells me, "it's the way it's disbursed."

Kurt the Cutlass is invaluable to me in other ways. One afternoon last January an unexpected northeaster tore into town with swirling snow and high winds. As is the habit in modern society, businesses shut down at two, people retreated home in panic, public transportation was at a standstill, and cabs stayed in the garage. Forced to work late, with no way of getting out of the city and covering the twenty miles to my home, I called Kurt for an idea.

"You got a parking garage or gas station near your office?" he asked.

"Both. About a block away."

"Go to the parking garage first. Then the gas station, if you strike out. These places always have more help than they need. Especially in lousy weather. For ten bucks cash money, someone will leap to drive you home." An eighteen-year-old attendant at the garage took his Volkswagen out into the storm and had me home in forty minutes. The ten dollars was well worth it.

Again, it is not money that is the problem. It is getting others to respond efficiently to the money, making sure that your dollars buy the best service and advice.

Remember: Roughriders, the *good* ones, can be difficult to find and recruit, either because they operate in shadows (and are gamblers, con men, enforcers, loan sharks) or because they mistrust most people in a position to pay them for their services. Roughriders have, in many cases, been trampled by society. It takes time to win their confidence. But once it is won, they can be extraordinarily helpful, if only to teach you how lucky *you* really are.

## THE MAVEN

The next classification of Smart People you will need is the Maven. The Mavens are your *everyday* experts: doctors, lawyers, decorators, carpenters, money managers, shopkeepers, plumbers, baby-sitters, cleaning help, the people who serve you and care for you and make your routine easier.

The derivation of "Maven" is from the Hebrew word meaning "connoisseur." Mavens provide the expertise that can cut through the nonsense and, on your behalf, *get things done.*

Here is how I cemented the relationship with one of my service Mavens:

I needed a new surface on my driveway. The old blacktop had cracked with the freezing and thawing of Northeast winters. I also needed gutter and roof work. And I needed my house painted. I called someone who did both driveways and roofs and was well recommended by friends.

"Dad, there's a couple of rednecks outside looking at the house," my eight-year-old boy said one weekday morning early. I went out to see what they wanted, dressed for the office in a three-piece suit, a velvet bow tie.

"I'm Jim Wilder," one of the men said. "You're expecting me. We're looking at your driveway. It's a big one and you know what's happened to asphalt prices."

"Then why are you looking at the house," I said.

"I ain't. I'm looking at the roof. Seems like you could use some work up there. Shingles. Flashing. Chimneys."

"Why don't we take it one step at a time."

Jim Wilder looked at my three-piece suit, my velvet bow tie, and quickly mentioned half a dozen things that looked like they needed repair or replacement. Of course, he was equipped at fancy prices to handle everything. Now was the crucial moment. Wilder had been recommended to me by a friend who prices all jobs down to the nickel. My friend had said, "If you can get along with Wilder, he'll do a great job. Otherwise, he's worse than a Mercedes mechanic. He'll screw you every step of the way." So I took Wilder into my studio and employed one of the greatest ways to recruit service people onto your team: the High School Athletics Gambit.

Before I had called Wilder to come make an estimate of driveway costs, I had found out where he lived. Many plumbers, masons, electricians, carpenters, painters, and repairmen live in the towns where they grew up, following their fathers' trades and staying with the comfortable, the familiar. And even if these people have moved from their birthplace, chances are they have children in local schools who play sports. Even if not, they gather in local taverns or clubs. They know what's going on in their communities. Sports are almost universally loved by these people. I mentioned several famous local athletes of years past to Wilder.

"How the hell do you know *them?*" he asked.

Casually I said, "I played against them."

He stared at me for a moment. "What do you know," he finally said. "Looks can be deceiving."

This is an example of *using people from the past.* Or rather, names of people from the past, to personalize the situation. It also illustrates how to make yourself memorable through the simple method of contrast: everyone is not necessarily what he or she appears to be. This technique can be very effective.

Of course, Wilder never checked my athletic credentials. But the mention of playing sports, particularly high school sports, gave me instant credibility as one of the boys. And it made my large house, expensive car, and well-tailored wardrobe acceptable. Jim Wilder now assumed that I had earned the money myself and had not had it given to me by daddy or daddy-in-law. By the end of our estimate session, Wilder had knocked two hundred dollars off his original figures for blacktopping the driveway. And he had volunteered two of his cousins for various assignments, one for masonry work, one for party bartending at bargain rates.

A potential problem with Mavens is in encouraging them too much. It is important to establish yourself as a hardworking, self-made person so that their code will not allow them to screw you. But a distance has to be maintained so you do not become responsible for their problems or get invited constantly to their town's high school football, basketball, or baseball games. "Maybe we can go on a junket together sometime," Wilder suggested repeatedly. "You know I got seven women living in my house. Mother-in-law, wife, five daughters. So I got a right to get away. I go on junkets, Vegas, Reno, Puerto Rico. Last year I went up to Vegas. Went to that Mustang Ranch with the legal hookers. I was so drunk, with three hundred stuck in my shoes, you know? I won three hundred at blackjack and I stuck it in my shoes. Well, I passed out in a tub at the Mustang Ranch. I got *nothing*. But the three hundred was still in the shoe. One of them tie jobs with little holes at the end of the toe. That's the important thing. Hookers you can always get. Even if they ain't Vegas hookers, who is usually special." I kept excusing myself from the junkets, pleading too much work.

Mavens feel sorry for you if you continually plead work. But they understand, and they believe you are not copping out on them. Mavens will be incredibly loyal to you, as will most of your Smart People. Especially *if you offer them something in trade,* either tangible or intangible. I gave Jim Wilder a paperback edition of one of my books, an adventure story, as soon as I was convinced that he did good work and that I could use him again. I also referred him to friends of mine, giving him access to business he would not otherwise have had.

## THE LAMPLIGHTER

Lamplighters are the third category of Smart People. These people can assist you more in psychic ways, ways that can be as important as getting you a stock that doubles or finding you Super Bowl tickets or telling you about an auto mechanic you can trust.

Your Lamplighters *inspire* you. They may never actually perform services for you. But by their advice or example or friendship they make life easier to bear. They may improve your soul; they may feed your psyche, they may provide for you an emotional place of peace.

Lamplighters give you pause for reflection upon yourself and a sense that your life can be *better*.

One of my Lamplighters is Raymond the Drummer. He is a person recruited from my past, a childhood friend. Raymond is a drummer in the traditional sense; he's a traveling salesman who goes about recruiting customers, selling a product by selling himself. Raymond is unique. His philosophies have been consistent since he was an adolescent. "I will see the world," says Raymond, "and I will never break my ass. It's impossible to starve if you have blond hair, blue eyes, and a willingness to lie down and watch the grass grow. In other words, not really give a damn." He has been a salesman for years. He has sold books, office supplies, advertising space, oil filters, and greeting cards and was the first boy I knew who lost his virginity — owing solely to the fact that he didn't care how ugly the girl was. One summer during college, Raymond and I worked as singing busboys on Cape Cod, earning twenty-five dollars a week salary and fifteen percent of all waitresses' tips. The tips, collected in change, we would scrupulously count out nightly on our cots in back of the restaurant after the last chorus of "When Irish Eyes Are Smiling" had died out in the lounge. We were off during the days, free to roam the beach, free to blanket-hop. Raymond would find groups of vacationing women: schoolteachers, nurses, secretaries. And he would always make a play for the most unattractive. His success ratio was unmatched in the annals of Hyannis, Massachusetts, and he kept a scoreboard on the wall next to his cot. His conquests. My conquests. Kept in check marks indicating second base, third base, and home. It was like comparing Warren Beatty and Don Knotts.

"I don't understand you, Raymond," I would say to him. "I mean, there is such a thing as *quality*. You've had the worst pigs in America this summer."

"While *you're* playing with yourself and reading *Sport Magazine*." He rested his case.

Some Smart People deserve the term because of their strong

sense of self-preservation. They react well to crises. Raymond the
Drummer always thought well on his feet. The restaurant we
worked in that summer had a moisture problem. The linoleum
floors sweated on hot evenings, making the footing hazardous for
the waitresses and for the two singing busboys with their Top-
siders and madras bow ties. One of our jobs was to liberally
sprinkle the wet corridor from the kitchen to the main dining
room with sawdust. George, the owner, would bellow at us several times an evening, "Sawdust, you knuckleheads. Good *Christ*,
sawdust for my floors." One Saturday night, with a particularly
boisterous crowd of vacationers scoffing down baked stuffed
lobster and butterscotch parfaits, the linoleum surface seemed as
if a Zamboni machine had hosed it down.

"Raymond, you moron," yelled owner George, "the sawdust.
You want my lobsters all over the floor? You want customers
slipping on butterscotch? *Sawdust.*" Raymond, seeing his fifteen
percent of the tips disappearing, raced to the storage closet and
found the sawdust bin empty. With the owner yelling for sawdust
and none available, Raymond grabbed an empty cardboard carton and poured into it five packages of Parmesan cheese. With
the frenzied approval of George, he proceeded to sprinkle it liberally on the restaurant floor. Of course, later in the evening, with
the Parmesan cheese providing no traction, sixteen dinners hit the
floor simultaneously, along with two waitresses and a weekend
guest of Morton Downey, the "Shortnin' Bread" man, who had a
house in nearby Hyannisport. George the Owner grabbed at his
heart, but he couldn't blame Raymond who, he believed, had
performed quickly and efficiently. "Sawdust is in the eye of the
beholder," Raymond said to me later, on the way to another
notch on his scoreboard with a dragon of a nurse from Aroostook
County, Maine.

You need people like Raymond, wherever you are. And you
should make time for them when they appear.

A year ago, Raymond the Drummer stopped in unexpectedly,

being in town for a booksellers' convention and being thrilled with the accommodations at a Holiday Inn. "You know," he said, "I need you as much as you need me. That's the real secret of a friend from the past. It's two-sided. We don't want anything from one another except the reassurance that we were both young and both somewhere else together."

Is Raymond the Drummer a Smart Person? He is true to himself and to his vision of the world. He also provides for me a noncompetitive place of peace, a reminder of playgrounds and auditoriums and beaches and friends long gone. Lamplighters do not provide goods or services for us. They provide messages and laughs and companionship and, by their example, inspiration. Raymond has the ability to make me relax and to make me appreciate that there can be happiness without anxiety, without constantly pushing. Raymond is a Smart Person because he can teach lessons about life. The fact that these are generally simple lessons about relaxation makes Raymond a special Lamplighter.

Remember: Lamplighters are not necessarily people to model your life upon, but rather people who can teach, people who pose no threat — but who somehow always make you feel better or more secure.

Also remember: Psychic lessons are a very small part of life. It is the practical side of life that drives most people to ulcers and frustrations: getting a child a scholarship, getting a favorable mortgage rate, getting a divorce lawyer worth his fee, finding relief from a back problem or a leaky roof or an ornery neighbor. These are the hard-core problems that lead us to need Smart People in the first place. Where do you place satisfying the soul in order of importance? In structuring my life I place the Lamplighters slightly to the rear of my Smart People hierarchy. I want my body and my pocketbook, my business and my family taken care of efficiently before I can allow myself the luxury of Lamplighters like Raymond the Drummer.

Finally, at the top of the pecking order, the kind of person you *must* know to be successful, is . . .


## THE SUMMA

Summas are the ultimate Smart People. They stand at the pinnacle of their professions. They attract service and attention by virtue of their own position or reputation or money. Summas do not have to actively recruit the best people in every field. Volunteers long to join the team of the Summa.

There are public Summas whose names the world knows. There are private Summas, perhaps known only to a community or to the fortunate people who benefit from their talent, knowledge, or power. Summas are Smart People complete within themselves. Their time is precious, limited. They are constantly sought out by others for advice, favors, and specific expertise. A Summa does not have to work routines to assemble his team; people flock unsummoned to Smart People of this type. Summas have more candidates for service positions than they have openings.

Finding examples of the Summa type is easy: any president of the United States, Henry Ford, Melvin Belli, Dr. Denton Cooley, Edwin Land of Polaroid, Barbra Streisand, Muhammad Ali, to name several from various fields. Summas are people with money and power and media clout who can recruit servants, advisers, protectors, and gofers merely by their presence. Often, the Summa is not what you might call a Smart Person. But Summas *are* smart in their radiation of power, in their ability to operate at the top of special worlds.

The people I have mentioned, and you can name dozens more, are the *public* Summas, the names everyone knows. I also have my *private* Summas, men and women at the pinnacle of their professions, who attract the best advice, the best service. The private Summas operate with a low profile, regionally, locally, often behind the scenes. They don't want *People* magazine interviewing them. They believe that privacy is the key to power.

The words of both kinds of Summas are listened to. They carry the authority of achievement. They can inspire fear, envy, or respect.

Recruiting Summas can be done with the three Smart People Principles: using people from your past, having something to trade, and making yourself memorable. You merely have to apply the principles harder.

How would *you* recruit a Summa? Here's something I did when I needed expert help:

For some reason, eye doctors seem busier than any other medical practitioners. Call an eye doctor whose name you have been given and inevitably the secretary tells you, "Dr. Murphy can see you at two-thirty on June 15." It is now March 11, and you have something stuck in your eye.

I had an annoying eye problem several years ago and was told that Dr. Wally Banks was one of the world's foremost retina experts, but that I could never get an appointment with him. I thereupon called one of our city newspapers and asked for the library. Every major newspaper maintains a library and cross-reference file for access to old stories, news items, and names of people in the news. Any locally famous person will have a file of clippings, available to anyone who is interested in seeing it. But you have to approach the library in the proper way.

"I'm doing a paper for a Ph.D. thesis on retina surgery, and I need clippings on Dr. Wally Banks. Could you possibly help me?" For seventy-five cents (for copying fees and mailing costs), the library was happy to mail me a folder full of copies of articles about Dr. Wally Banks. The articles told me more than I would ever want to know about him. What I *was* interested in was his hobbies. All of the articles written about Dr. Banks mentioned his interest in the satirical artists Hogarth and Daumier. I called the next day for an appointment.

"Are you a patient of the doctor's?" I was asked.

"No," I said.

"I'm sorry. The doctor is not seeing any more private patients."

"Please tell the doctor," I said, "that I have insights into the artists Hogarth and Daumier that no one in this city possesses."

"Kindly wait," the secretary said.

I waited. She came back after two minutes and said, "Would tomorrow at four be suitable?"

I saw Dr. Banks. Not until he finished examining me did he say, "I'm curious. Why do you, Mr. Spooner, know more about Hogarth and Daumier than anybody in town?"

"Because, Dr. Banks, I'm the only person in town who knows that the mention of their names can get me an eye appointment."

He is my Summa ophthalmologist, and I am now his stockbroker. Two phone calls and seventy-five cents recruited an otherwise unapproachable Summa for my team.

As I said, people pay attention to the words of Summas.

A friend of mine years ago was soliciting for a favorite charity. He approached Nelson Rockefeller, who was close to my friend's family. The more pleasant Rockefeller was to my friend, the less money my friend dared ask for. Finally, when the pitch was made, the request was pitifully scaled down, a pitch geared to friendship. Rockefeller immediately moved to the attack. "Never lowball," he said. "You insult me by asking for a pittance; you flatter me by asking for the moon. If you're looking for five thousand dollars, ask me for twenty thousand. In charity, always overstate your case."

If this advice came from Joe Ganella the Pontiac dealer, no one would pay any attention to it. The fact that it came from a Summa, a Nelson Rockefeller, gave it the unmistakable weight of gospel, the gospel of money and power. The maxim "Never lowball" has allowed me to raise thousands of dollars for charities when I never expected to obtain *hundreds*. It has also given me advances on books from publishers far exceeding what I knew (or thought I knew) they would pay. And following Rockefeller's advice has led me to another important lesson: People are contemptuous of what they get for nothing.

After my first novel was published, I was thrilled to be asked to speak to women's clubs, business groups, Rotary luncheons about books, money, the literary world. Not quite believing my good fortune at being a published author, it was my pleasure to gush for nothing. Although my reception was always polite, my talks were sparsely attended and a waste of my time.

One of my private Summas, a politically oriented lawyer, knew that my speechmaking often took me away from my office for two or three hours, sometimes for an entire day, when travel was involved.

"You get no fee?" he asked incredulously.

"But these appearances sell books," I said. "People hear me, see me, they go out and buy the books."

"Your royalty from a typical book is about a dollar, right? If you sell ten books from an average lecture, that's a lot. The only thing that sells books is word of mouth. Not advertising. Not talk shows. Only word of mouth. Unless the book becomes a movie or television series. I'll tell you something: you don't charge for appearances, you'll always be a small-timer. You charge, and you'll play to bigger houses and they'll buy more books. Remember this: Nothing for nothing in this world."

So I began to ask an arbitrary two hundred dollars per appearance. After my book *Confessions of a Stockbroker* became a bestseller, I raised my fee to five hundred dollars. Nobody blanched. Most groups paid the fee, although some, financially embarrassed, begged me to accept three or four hundred. I usually accepted, but with the stipulation that the difference be raised sometime within the following twelve months and given to a charity of their choice. That made my speaking engagement worthwhile, and also allowed me not to feel cheated. And it allowed *them* to think of me as extraordinarily decent and charitable.

All of you have Summas in the areas where you operate. I write books and manage money and have favorite Summas of my own. Ernest Hemingway was a literary Summa. Here's an example, using the principle of making yourself memorable, of how I got Ernest Hemingway to respond to me. Simple? It was just a matter of not letting a Smart Person pass me by.

It was Spain in 1959. The dangerous summer. Ordoñez and Dominguin, the world's premier matadors, were touring the country in a series of shoot-outs, *mano a mano*, pursuing ears and tails. I was pursuing a vision of the Lost Generation, hoping that it would all come true in Pamplona. Ernest Hemingway was in Pamplona, his first visit since he had written *The Sun Also Rises*. He was staying in a hotel, surrounded by an entourage, in as much splendor as Pamplona could offer. I was sleeping on the back seat of a shattered Fiat, rented and set afire for no good reason by several boys from Princeton. During the days, I stalked Hemingway, because the Silent Generation (mine) always believed itself to be the emotional incarnation of the Lost Generation (his). However, not having a war for an excuse, we traveled briefly, taking no chances, and remained expatriates only in our hearts.

After several days of running with the bulls, being drenched with wine squeezed from wineskins, and dancing in the streets with half the peasants in Spain and ten percent of the English majors at Smith College, I found myself standing directly in back of Ernest Hemingway, who was urinating next to a fountain off the main plaza of Pamplona. He was not alone. Waiting for him to finish were a journalist and a Smith girl. Too exhausted and hung over to be surprised or shy, I stepped next to Papa and unzipped.

"Mind if I whiz next to you?" I asked.

Hemingway looked at me. "Whiz is something women do," he said. "Men piss."

"You always piss with a crowd watching?" I didn't care. Just as long as I could keep the conversation going. He finished and stayed to observe me.

"Let me tell you something, kid," he said. "Everybody needs people." He indicated his companions. "And most of all, we need *smart* people. I need someone to adore me, someone who looks good, and someone to write down the things I say. Life should build toward the point where someone hangs around to write down the things you say. Have a good leak. Run the bulls." He laughed. "Men can also call a piss a leak." He laughed louder and left with his entourage.

That afternoon, a day that the sun was so strong it made you feel you had invaded another planet, I was sitting with two friends outside the bullring. They were drunk. Everyone in Pamplona was drunk. But my friends were the only ones in Pamplona getting their sneakers shined by three different shoe-shine boys. In three different colors. Hemingway walked by, surrounded by a crowd of college students, Spanish companions, and the same two friends of the morning.

"There's the whizzer," he called to me, instantly making his crowd jealous. "You have your tickets?"

"In the sun," I said.

"You never sit drunk in the sun at the corrida," he said.

"When your friends buy the tickets you do," I told him.

Hemingway looked at my friends, who sat staring at the murals being waxed onto their sneakers. They squeezed wine from their wineskins into their mouths, onto their shirts, onto the ground. Hemingway smiled. Irony and pity. He looked robust, handsome, bigger than the rest of his group. "I told you," he said. "Find *smart* people. You don't drink wine and sit in the sun. Goodbye, Whizzer." His companions were glad to have him back. They walked into the bullring, pushing to be near him.

I didn't need to be told to search for Smart People. But having the advice offered by Ernest Hemingway gave it, for me, the imprimatur. I accepted as gospel the need to begin building my team of experts early in my life.

Did Ernest Hemingway have better advice for me than the average waiter in a Pamplona cafe? Do celebrities have better advice merely because they are famous? The words they have for us may be wise or foolish. But the *telling* of their advice is everything. We enjoy meeting the stars because it makes us feel bigger, better. We can all bask in reflected glory.

Most of your meetings with public Summas will be one-shot deals. Take advantage of them. Don't let these people pass you by. Smart People can dine out on Summa stories for years.

Now you have four of your Smart People types in place: Roughrider, Maven, Lamplighter, and Summa. Recruit them, use them, and have them lead you to others using the Smart People Principles. These principles will be developed further as you read on, in chapters that cover most areas where you will need help in running your life successfully.

## THE PHILOSOPHER-KING

There is one more Smart People type you will come to know. People of this type will provide a Greek chorus through this book, as they have throughout my life. They have a special place in the hierarchy of Smart People. They are Philosopher-Kings — bookends, if you will, to what comes in between. Smart People have come and gone through my life, according to circumstance, location, and time. But there are two that I hold on to, two people who cross all lines and who spill over into every section. They are people who have opinions about every subject, useful opinions, practical ones, always worthy of thought and discussion. These two people are my sounding boards.

Why bother with Philosopher-Kings? There is philosophy in using Smart People as there is philosophy in the rest of life. In addition to getting practical advice, we all like to talk about problems, events, the meaning of our lives. We all philosophize, mostly without realizing what we are doing. It happens to me, you, all of us. And this book is about philosophy, a philosophy of simplifying your life through Smart People Principles.

Let's face it. There is no such thing as the perfect condition in life. There is always something missing, something we dream about. Plato believed in the concept of the philosopher-king, the rational, benevolent being who could rule with reason, common sense, and wisdom. "Behold," Plato said in the *Republic*. "Human beings living in an underground den. Like ourselves . . . they see only their own shadows, or the shadows of one another, which the fire throws on the opposite wall of the cave." My Philosopher-Kings meet very special requirements. They are eminently successful in their own fields, and they immerse themselves in hobbies, sidelines, pursuits of the mind and spirit, pursuits other than their primary professions. And I don't mean charities or boards of directors. I mean personal, selfish, Renaissance pursuits. Pursuits at which they excel. My Philosopher-Kings are very modern, and yet not modern at all. Your Philosopher-Kings must give you the impression that they would fit into any century. My Philosopher-Kings correspond to this Medici ideal; each is unique. One is a blond, one is a redhead. They are both men. One is a lawyer, a partner in one of the city's most prestigious law firms. The other man manufactures maternity dresses. He is the redhead, and his motto is "You knock 'em, we frock 'em." Henry the Red is his name, and he came to me as a client when he had heard from friends in the garment business that I had made a big score in Simplicity Patterns, a New York Stock Exchange company and the leading manufacturer of dress patterns for the home-sewing market.

"Anyone who can make a nickel in the rag business, without being in the rag business, I want for my stockbroker," Henry the Red said. "Now here's where you made your first mistakes. . . ."

Henry the Red is constantly pointing out the weaknesses of others and the absurdities of the human condition. His role as my Philosopher-King is the essential one of forcing me never to take things too seriously. Henry the Red is one of the largest and most successful makers of maternity fashions in America. And yet he spends most of his day talking on the phone all over the world about some of his hobbies: medicine, Afghan hounds, coins, stamps, history, yachts, golf, birds, ham radio, and RKs (rotten kids — the children who grew up in America in the 1960s and were handed, in Henry's opinion, the world).

Henry the Red never travels the way most people travel. Wherever he goes, from the New York–Boston shuttle to the bazaars of Asia, he encounters famous people. And he always recognizes them, confronts them, and becomes their friend. Things happen to Red Henry because he makes them happen.

"First of all," Red Henry says, "I read everything. I watch everything. And because I do, I recognize everyone. But the key is to *talk* to them. If you approach celebrities as a typical fan, you'll be shut off immediately. Approach them as a character, or as an equal, and you may end up with a buddy for life.

"Let me give you an example," Red Henry said. "About ten years ago I was driving through France with my wife. She wanted to spend a day shopping in Paris, and I told her that I wanted to go into the country, perhaps take a spin out to Fontainebleau. What I really wanted was to find a golf game. It was the time when my number-one interest was golf. Sure enough, after I stopped enough people walking on the side of roads and yelled at them, 'Où est le club de golf?' several pointed me in a certain direction, yelling back, 'oui, oui, St. Cloud!'

"I found St. Cloud, parked in the lot, and wandered over to the practice tee. There's a fellow hitting shots with a five iron, spraying them all over the place. No control whatsoever. I'm wearing an old pair of corduroy pants, rubber-soled walking shoes, and a cashmere sweater with holes in the elbows that I had at the Wharton School years ago. Of course, I'm also sucking on my pipe as I'm watching the fellow spray his shots. After several puffs I say to the man practicing, 'Never in a million years will you be able to strike a golf ball with that swing.' He jumped around, not believing what he heard, and who is it? The Duke of Windsor. Not giving him a chance to be annoyed, I said, 'Shorten up your backswing, Your Highness. Think to yourself that you're only taking *half* a backswing. The difference in results will be astounding.' I took three puffs of my pipe indicating absolute authority, and the Duke said nothing. He hit three five-iron shots in succession, shortening his backswing. Each shot, moving with just a slight draw, went approximately a hundred and seventy yards. *Three perfect five-irons.*

"Within twenty minutes I was fully outfitted: shoes, clubs, even the cap off the head of the St. Cloud professional. (It was sunny, and sun bothers the ol' redhead.) We teed off in a foursome. Naturally, the duke is my host and my partner, and he tells me before we tee off, 'At first I thought from a distance you were part of the household. One of those cheeky second cousins from the Horse Guards who never amounted to anything.' Well, the story's not over. By the turn, we're best of friends and one up on the pro and the second or third richest man in France, an aircraft manufacturer who enjoyed bankrolling the duke."

Henry the Red went on, "I'm coaching the duke on his backswing and telling him more about America than he'll ever need to know. He's playing well, but I'm duck-hooking my tee shots and putting like a gorilla. Terrible. By the end of fourteen holes we're two down, and I'm beginning to worry about what we're playing for. All I have in my corduroys is five hundred francs, and I certainly don't want to appear to be a pisher in front of the Duke of Windsor, who, I'm sure, has *nothing* in the pockets of his plus fours. We halve fifteen and win sixteen, when the duke holes out from ninety yards off the green. Due to my instruction and his new backswing. So we're now one down with two holes to go. On seventeen, with the pro giving us all strokes, I get a par with a fancy twelve-foot putt downhill, and we're all even. The duke is ready to give me the Order of the British Empire but I'm terrified

of eighteen, a long par four, and the industrialist hates me because I've been needling him and I'm on to his social-climbing
game.

"All of our drives on eighteen are in the fairway. But the pro is
in super shape thirty yards ahead of the duke and me. Even the
industrialist is ahead of us, and I'm giving *him* a stroke. Luckily, I
had been talking a lot of medicine to the others during the match.
You know, giving them tips on good health and diagnosing their
various ailments. I'd told them about my session in medical
school that was interrupted by the war and how afterwards I had
to come out and save the maternity rag business. Well, we're
opposite a fairway sand trap, two hundred yards out, and I'm
about to hit my approach to the green, when suddenly my heart
accelerates like a dragster. I've got strange ailments. This is
paroxysm auricular tachycardia. The heartbeat goes to a hundred
eighty beats per minute and I've got to slow it down to seventy.
I've got to lie down with my legs elevated for about five minutes,
hold my breath, and put pressure on the vagus nerve.

" 'Excuse me, Your Highness,' I say to the duke. 'Hit your shot
and don't worry about me. We're gonna win this match.' They
can't believe it when I go over and lie down in the sand trap, my
legs resting higher than my head. They're terrified. Of course,
everyone thought I was going to croak, and the pro from St.
Cloud was particularly concerned about the club's liability. They
all hovered around me in the trap. 'I'm going for my personal
physician,' said the duke.

" 'I can phone my surgeon,' said the industrialist. 'He can be
out in a helicopter from Paris in fifteen minutes.' The pro signaled
two foursomes to play through while I told my worried partner,
'It's almost passed. The heart regulates itself this way rather
quickly.' After six minutes I jumped up and, refreshed, hit the
fringe of the green with the four wood. Our opponents, in a hurry
to be rid of me before I died, shanked their shots, the industrialist
hitting his out of bounds. The Duke of Windsor and I won the
match. I gave him my cashmere sweater with the torn elbows,

and our opponents gave me two thousand francs, my share of the match stake. I took the francs, about five hundred U.S. dollars and my hand was cool. But Jesus, what if we had been playing for *thousands*. What if I *lost?* Anyway, the duke asked my wife and me to call on him and the duchess in St. Moritz. And the two thousand francs almost paid for the Balenciaga my wife had bought that afternoon."

"I wonder," I asked Red Henry, "if I would have told the duke to shorten his backswing?"

"Always have an opinion in a strange situation," Red Henry snapped. "And deliver that opinion with absolute certainty. It also pays to look like shabby gentility. Remember, part of my creed is 'Look British. Think Yiddish.' "

Red Henry's value to me is that his stories always have a lesson, a moral. If *you* recruit Philosopher-Kings, their stories also should provide lessons in life. This way, the Smart People way, you waste no one who can be important to you.

My other Philosopher-King was lifted from the ranks of my college classmates. Like other Smart People, he was recruited from my past. His name is Mather Stevens, and the world at large has viewed him, without really knowing him, as the consummate snob. His credentials seem to support that view: St. Paul's School in Concord, New Hampshire; Harvard, where he rowed and was a member of the right clubs; Harvard Law School and the proper Wasp-dominated law firm that has traditionally managed the money and the lives of his city's most venerable names. But where Red Henry is a cynic and an upholder of the conservative ethic, Mather Stevens is a liberal, a humanist in the true sense: "Someone who has a strong interest in or concern for human welfare, values and dignity."

Mather Stevens is a people's lawyer the way Fiorello La Guardia was a people's lawyer, with humanity at the center of his concern. If the profession of law is ever given a good name, especially in our bureaucracy-laden democracy, it is attorneys like Stevens who are responsible. The first time I saw Mather Stevens

I knew, even at eighteen years old, that he was a winner. He was holding forth in a locker-room discussion about classes, about women, about history.

"The conventional wisdom," he said to a group of cronies, "only means something in a meaningless exam. The things that are important are questions like 'Where was the first railroad in the United States?' "

Of course nobody knew. Mather looked superior, which was something he was wonderful at. "Quincy, Massachusetts, to Neponset. Three miles."

He went on, "No one will ever forget you if you know things nobody else knows. Even if they are trivia. Cultivate the obscure and you will have better friends than anyone else, because people who cultivate the obscure will band together and reject the ordinary."

I became a friend of Mather's through a superficial trick that I knew would work. Although I lacked sophistication, although I was not smooth, although I was not chic, although I was not rich, I nevertheless was years ahead of Mather Stevens and his friends because I had gone to a large public high school. Which is to say, I had had early knowledge of women. Stevens and I began our friendship through my use of the Smart People Principle of making yourself memorable.

I gave Mather a ride from the crew boathouse to his dormitory with my then current girlfriend. She always picked me up after practice in her father's be-finned pink Eldorado Cadillac. I knew Stevens would never forget that car. And he never has, because he grew up in a world where a ten-year-old Plymouth was considered the proper vehicle for anyone.

The girl is gone. The pink Cadillac is gone. But the result remains, and Mather Stevens is firmly in place in my life as a Philosopher-King.

He says things that other people quote for years. This is just one of his uses for me. His lines are unique. For instance: Stevens is happily married, but damns the sexual revolution of the 1960s in which he did not take part. "Christ," he complained to me, watching two comely paralegals from his office go by, "the world is *four billion* years old . . . and I was born *five years too soon.*"

So now the three Smart People Principles are in place. Your Smart People types — Roughrider, Maven, Lamplighter, and Summa — are waiting to help you. The Philosopher-Kings are keeping things in perspective. You are now ready to see how the principles and people operate together in different areas. You are now ready to see how they can make your life easier and more successful.

# 2 THE GOOD LIFE

The good life will mean different things to different people. For you, the Good Life may be cruising off Tahiti, or it may be lying in a hammock with a portable radio and an iced tea. It doesn't matter whether you search for the perfect wave or the perfect martini, the Good Life for all Smart People is being pampered in settings you enjoy the most. It is living out fantasies. You can have your own Good Life using Smart People Principles. For me the Good Life involves travel.

When you do travel, be aware of the principles that can turn the odds toward your pleasure. Here's how I recently used one of my Good Life Summas to ensure hospitality:

"Signor," a uniformed motor-launch driver said to me, "I am to take you to the Gritti Palace Hotel."

He said it all, "Gritti Palace Hotel," as if it were a sin not to include the entire title. My wife and I had never cleared customs at the Venice airport. No passports had been stamped, no baggage inspected, no lines endured. The Motoscafi driver had poured us each a glass of chilled Corvo, a dry Sicilian wine of good flavor, had escorted us to the launch's mahogany-paneled salon and punched a button on a portable radio, surrounding us with Puccini. Racing through the channel markers from the airport we could see Venice coming at us like the opening credits of a James Bond movie. At the Gritti dock the launch barely scraped the landing. The concierge was waiting. The porter was waiting. The polished wood lift hummed us to the top floor and the double bedroom with double windows looking out onto the Grand Canal and the Cathedral Santa Maria della Salute, built in the seventeenth century to celebrate the end of the plague. The room was filled with roses, on the bureaus, on the writing desks, on the night tables. The small refrigerator contained two splits of champagne, two bottles of mineral water (both with and without gas), six Tuborg, minibottles of Glenlivet, Beefeater, Galliano, Remy Martin V.S.O.P., two Schweppes, and two small cans of Heinz tomato juice. There was a card from the management: "Compliments of the director. All friends of Ned Fairbanks are friends of ours."

Ned Fairbanks is my secret Summa in the pursuit of the Good Life.

"No one knows me," Ned says, "except for people who count: golf pros, tennis pros, concierges, maitre d's, dog men, white hunters, bandleaders, club stewards, and chairmen of the board. When my father got out of college in 1937, *his* father gave him a choice: Harvard Business School or a trip around the world, with the proviso that he not set foot in the United States for twelve months. He chose the trip around the world and saw revolutions in South America, the rise of militarism in Japan, Nazi youth marching bare-chested in the rain in Munich. The education he received in his travels taught him an important lesson. The world was changing, and it was no longer so important who your ancestors were. It was fine to be an aristocrat, but you had to be an aristocrat who got along with ordinary people. He hammered that into me, and, as I was growing up, I discovered two ways to succeed with people: music and sports. If you can play them both, you are made for life."

This works for Ned. It is not necessarily true for everyone. But you must have something, some other dimension that connects you to people. You can make the connection with interests in painting, in macramé, in collecting lead soldiers. But you must choose something that will intrigue and interest others.

Ned Fairbanks is one of the great salesmen of industrial machinery in the world. And although hundreds of people have the expertise and the high-quality equipment for sale, Fairbanks is remembered by everyone he sells to as being special. Ned Fairbanks shows his equipment nationally and he shows it abroad. He travels for business three weeks out of every month. He carries with him on all of his trips a simple Spanish guitar that cost him twenty-three dollars in a pawn shop near the middle of Barcelona.

"Part of this game was my grandfather's fault," Ned explains. "He passed along what seems to be the family motto: Work your ass off. And when you're not working, *play* it off. We had a compound in New Hampshire, on a lake. Seven houses, one for every uncle and distant cousin. Forty people worked the compound, which had fifteen acres devoted to farming. The place had athletic facilities you wouldn't believe: sailboats, canoes, kayaks, a bowling alley, tennis courts, one of the first squash courts in America, a skeet-shooting range. At two o'clock every summer afternoon, and this goes back to the early 1920s, all work would stop and all employees and relatives would report to the baseball diamond. The diamond was groomed as well as Wrigley Field. Everyone would participate in a seven-inning baseball game. But Grandpa would pitch for both sides. *And* umpire. He was a sports nut and a stickler for winning.

"My wrinkle is music," Ned continues. "I always sang in church choirs, and I took piano lessons for ten years. The old-fashioned disciplines: music lessons, sports lessons, summers in New Hampshire. I was shipped off to boarding school at age eleven and told to keep my shoulders straight. Later, Joan Baez was playing in coffeehouses in Cambridge when I was going to Harvard. She influenced me, along with Josh White, Leon Bibb, and, of course, Woody Guthrie. Then the real world. What do you do when you're grown up and working, selling on the road? The nights can be excruciating. Lonely hotels, lonely bars, films in foreign languages, sitting by yourself. The best restaurants, hotels, and bars in the world don't make up for the fact that you're selling industrial machinery, and you soon get the picture that nobody gives a damn about that."

That's when Ned Fairbanks bought a cheap guitar and began to carry it everywhere with him. First it was an aid to prevent the blues. Then it was an inspiration that has brought him service and attention wherever he goes, as well as a great deal of business.

Ned carried his guitar into Harry's Bar in Venice, one of civilization's great watering holes. Dining late, whether accompanied or not, Ned would have been dressed like an officer of a British bank. Roger, the barman, asked him, as bartenders all over the world had asked him in various ways, "You holding that for a friend?"

"It's my drinking companion," Ned said. As always happened sooner or later, he was asked to play, and he played "The Wabash Cannonball," his husky baritone sounding perfect in a room as small as the front room in Harry's Bar. By the end of the song everyone in the room was silent. Then they burst into applause. Ned quietly smiled and, sitting on a bar stool turned around facing the patrons, he sang several more ballads featuring beautiful ladies, easy chords, and places like Laredo, Abilene, and Sonora. Drinks could have been on the house after that, but Ned's style was to buy a round for everyone else.

Ned has worked his magic in bars all over the world. He is remembered everywhere with nostalgia because he sings romantic songs without being tedious. And his secret is being so unexpected. "Contrast is the key to having people respond to you," Ned says. "You give them something that is a total surprise, you have them for good. For one thing, no one expects someone who looks like he just stepped off the commuter special in Darien,

Connecticut, to play the guitar. And another thing, even assuming they *allow* you to play the guitar, they don't expect that you're going to be *good*."

Everywhere that we have dropped Ned's name we have been welcomed — with the "A" table in restaurants, with seats in bars where there were no seats, with complimentary wine, with suites in hotels for the price of rooms.

Whenever you travel, travel with the recommendations of a friend like Ned Fairbanks.

This is not the only lesson Ned has taught me. The most important thing he has done is to explain to me the Secret Life Syndrome. It is part of the secret of recruiting and binding Smart People to you. Here is what I discovered through Ned Fairbanks:


## THE SECRET LIFE SYNDROME

Everyone has a secret life that includes fantasies like those that lie within all of us. There is not an actress or judge or minister of state or corporation president or golf hustler who doesn't harbor longings to be something else, or to abandon work to take up a hobby, or to retire to the English countryside. Everyone has a soft spot, a nostalgic view of himself. And there is not a Smart Person I have met who does not respond to the mention of this. One example is the way I became a friend of Ned Fairbanks. It is an extreme example because it involves the saving of a life. But the method reflected in the incident has eased *my* life immeasurably and has both made and saved me hundreds of thousands of dollars.

After a six-month stint in the Army Medical Corps when Vietnam was a French problem and we fired at cardboard pop-up targets, I was in Europe for a brief vacation before going to Wall Street. Traveling through Italy with a friend, I stopped in Portofino to take a rest from museums, mosaics, and churches. We ran

into Ned Fairbanks, a school classmate of my friend, in a cafe.
We spent the day drinking wine and sitting in the sun. Aristotle
Onassis's yacht was anchored in the harbor, complete with winch
on the stern for his seaplane and a speedboat for waterskiing and
trips to shore for black-tie dinners. Winston Churchill was on
board that summer. So was Maria Callas. So was Onassis's wife,
Tina, whom we watched waterskiing that afternoon. She was red-
haired and graceful, slaloming behind the speedboat. "I'm in love
for the first time in my life," said Ned Fairbanks, full of Valpoli-
cella. The more he drank the more convinced he was that Tina
Onassis would love to meet him. "I'm going to swim out to the
yacht tonight," he said. "You don't refuse hospitality to the Ivy
League."

At seven-thirty that night, still in the cafe, we were all planning
to swim to the yacht, my friend to seek a job with Onassis, I to
have a brandy with Winston Churchill. At nine-thirty we stood on
rock stairs, twenty feet above the sea. The lights of the yacht
flickered at us from half a mile away. "The cocktail lamp is lit,"
said Ned. "Let's go." As he prepared to dive into the water, the
moon suddenly came out from behind the clouds, bathing us in
picture-postcard light. Fairbanks launched himself off the steps at
the same instant that I saw sticking up from the water a long,
thin steel pipe, looking like a sharpened tiger stake imbedded in
the harbor floor. I grabbed at Fairbanks's bathing suit; it ripped,
but I had held him back enough that he fell into the water
directly below. If he had dived out, with the full spring of his
legs, he would have met the steel pipe somewhere between his
stomach and chest. I ran down the steps as he broke water and
began swearing at me.

"What the hell's the matter with you?" he yelled. "You trying
to kill me?"

I just pointed in back of him at the spike. The shock sobered us
all. Tina, Ari, Winston, and Maria dined without us that night,
and Ned Fairbanks has remained a close friend ever since.

The next day I asked Ned if he had often done impulsive,

romantic things like swimming Portofino harbor at night while drunk to meet Tina Onassis. "No," he said, "but I sing and play the guitar." He told me about his grandfather then and about his childhood and family. And he admitted that he was concerned that the world of business would leave him no time for songs.

"Wrong," I told him. "They will be your biggest advantage whatever you do. Because they will make you different from anyone else you meet in your profession."

Fairbanks's guitar and voice have opened doors for me all over America and the world. At the Gritti Palace in Venice, I opened my complimentary bottle of Remy Martin V.S.O.P. and carefully poured it into a glass. The windows go down to the floor and look onto the Grand Canal. A gondola went by with a gondolier singing "Come Prima" ("For the First Time").

Ned Fairbanks had put me into that particular room. But the hotel room was nowhere as important as the lesson he taught me of probing for the Secret Life.

Fairbanks was recruited for me by accident. We will not all save people's lives. But what we can do, in order to find out Secret Life answers, is to *accept thanks* from people we *have* helped. Say yes when someone offers you something in return. If you assist someone, try the graciousness of accepting something in return. It helps bind others to you.

Ned has a list of questions that can help you probe the Secret Life of others. Use them to open doors for *you*. Ask *the questions no one asks:*

1. What was your childhood like?
2. Where were you in the service?
3. Did you play sports in high school or college?
4. What did you collect as a little girl?
5. Did you have a pet?
6. Did you go to Sunday school?
7. Was your mother a good cook?
8. Did your father spank you?"

Remember the two key ways to have people respond to you and to attain the Good Life:

*Probe the secret lives of others.*

And, *have a Secret Life of your own.*

Billy Morgan is my Good Life Maven. His only regret, apparent to anyone who meets him, is that he was not born in England, with a title, a hundred and fifty years ago. His friends call Morgan "Captain Money," and he plays the role to the hilt. He is a flamboyant figure, with hair that people dream about, thick and black and slicked back like the young Robert Taylor's. Billy Morgan does not care about adapting to the world as it is. He acts as if it *were* a hundred and fifty years ago. The shock of people's realization of this is marvelous to see. I could never get away with it. Most of us worry too much about people's feelings. Billy Morgan gets service because he commands it. People other than his social peers he treats as if they were the downstairs staff of the Bellamy household. He either orders people about or he ignores them.

I first met Captain Money at a coming-out party, in the days when parents threw away seventy-five hundred dollars on Lester Lanin, champagne, and the entertainment of several hundred people who couldn't have given less of a damn and lived to drink, destroy property, and lay rubber on early-morning roads in MGs and Chevy convertibles.

I had wandered into the kitchen at one point, looking for a stuffed egg. Captain Money was there with our young hostess, the debutante of the evening. She wore a long white dress and long white gloves. She was plump and blonde and could hit a golf ball like a man. "There's a great golf exercise," Morgan was telling her in his bored, superior manner. "Raise your arms over your head." The debutante complied, and as her arms reached for the kitchen ceiling, Morgan reached down and pulled up the hem of her long dress. He pulled it right over her head, revealing her in bra, girdle, stockings and white satin shoes. At this very instant the debutante's mother, carrying gin and tonic and a tray of petit fours, pushed through the kitchen door. Her daughter's head and arms were covered by the white gown, but she could hear the girl's muffled screams. Captain Money didn't miss a beat. He turned, pointed his finger at Mummy, and commanded *"Out,"* in a voice that would have frozen the maitre d' at the Tour d'Argent.

This kind of behavior instantly attracted me. Captain Money had a style that made him unforgettable. He was so outrageous that he got away with it.

Why do I need a Good Life Maven? Why does anyone need an impossible snob for expert advice? And expert advice about what? If Ned Fairbanks prepares the way for me wherever I travel, Billy Morgan provides me with entrée into places of privilege, places open only to members or only by invitation. We all harbor both secret and open desires to belong. Billy Morgan, Captain Money, belongs only to special places shuttered to the public. He gives me glimpses into areas most of us will never see, places that are fast disappearing because of inflationary pressures, inheritance taxes, and a mobile society that preaches equality but privately yearns for places of privacy and selectivity. We are all snobs under the skin. Morgan dares to flaunt it, something most middle-class Americans fear to do.

Why does Billy Morgan need me? Simple. It's the application of the Secret Life Syndrome. Years ago I said to him, "With all the places you've seen, the people you know, you should write a travel book."

"No one who read it," he replied, "would be allowed into the places I go."

That was the end of it I thought, until the next week when Billy came to my apartment with a briefcase full of typewritten poetry. Poetry different from that most amateur poets write today. The pieces were rhymed. "Free verse is for hippies who can't write poetry and wear their emotions on their jeans," he said. "They believe feelings are best expressed on bumper stickers. If you're educated and you want to write poetry it must scan as well as rhyme."

Billy was a secret poet. But everyone wants to write a book or meet an athlete or film star or be involved in political campaigns. Everyone has a Secret Life. Once you discover someone's Secret Life you have to become a good listener. Billy Morgan invites me to his clubs and his country houses to tell me his stories. He has the knowledge that the Good Life, as he knows it, is becoming a habit impossible to support. If he is forced someday to join a middle-class world he fears, he'd rather not do it completely cold turkey. So in exchange for letters of introduction all over the world, and invitations to his grandfather's ranch in Colorado, his club in Belgravia, his cousin's farm in the white highlands of Kenya, I read his poetry, listen to his tales, and watch a certain world disappear.

There is a Smart People technique that I have used with Captain Money. In fact, I use it constantly, and you can use the same device.

While listening to people and probing for the secret life, I always carry a small forty-cent notebook in my jacket pocket. If *you* carry such a notebook with you, and write down thoughts that pop into your mind or the special things people say and do, these will be some of the results:

1. You will have a record of the progress of your thoughts, an easy guide to processes of your mind.

2. You will have a time-consumer while you're waiting in airports or train stations, at checkout counters, or gas lines.

3. If you write down funny or clever or interesting or strange things people say, they inevitably think that *you're* interesting or strange — which can be even better.

"What are you writing in that notebook?" someone will ask you at a cocktail party.

"I'm writing down the story someone told me about Jimmy Carter's roommate at the Naval Academy" or "I'm taking notes for a novel" or "I've been given the name of someone great who'll put fabric on my walls." Everyone is curious about the notebooks. They set you apart, make you seem well organized and a student of human nature. They also provide an interesting record of your life, interests, and thoughts without the boredom of writing regularly in a diary. Keeping a small notebook in your purse or pocket makes you an instant journalist and will give you a glimpse of yourself over a period of time that can be especially informative.

I caught Billy Morgan involved in a deep kiss with the wife of his lawyer one night at a party. "Christ," I said later, "I can see the wife of your best friend, your neighbor, your broker. But your lawyer?"

"A gentleman," said Billy Morgan, "is never afraid of the consequences of his actions."

I immediately wrote that down in my notebook, and he, pleased with my Boswellian interest, invited my wife and me for a week of shooting in South Carolina.

J. B. Harper, the plantation manager, picked us up in the station wagon at the Charleston airport. On the forty-minute ride to Sweet Air plantation, fifteen thousand acres of live oaks, upland golden-grain rice fields, timber, swamp, meadow, and trail, he told us stories of the people who had visited the plantation. "'Course General Sherman paid us a visit in 'sixty-three. Burned all the way to Chee-Haw Neck. Fought the battle of Honey Hill. Then turned around and burned his way back to Charleston."

I asked him about a former secretary of defense who had been a frequent guest. "Was he a good shot?" I questioned.

J. B. Harper spit out the window of the wagon, then pressed a button and slid it up again. "The secretary of defense? He couldn't hit the bull's ass with a bass fiddle. All he was good for was after-breakfast comments. He'd eat a huge meal, pick up a missile-system budget, head for the john, and say 'Gonna launch me a trophy.'"

Billy Morgan was waiting for us in front of the plantation house, a huge, sprawling antebellum mansion owned by people in New York whose ancestors found oil in Texas in 1919. They kept the house fully staffed from September until May, at which time the snakes and the bugs opened their acts and it became unfit for living. The New Yorkers used the place for five weeks and lent it to friends like Billy for the rest of the time.

Billy Morgan had shot Sweet Air every January since he had been eighteen. "Duck, dove, and quail. And on New Year's Day years ago, we used to invite all the folk from miles around for a deer hunt on the front lawn. Deer were so plentiful they'd just run by the house. Thinned the herds and was a great gesture for the community. Then we'd ride down to the old quarters and hear the Reverend James, who was one hundred and four, sing hymns with his congregation. I always wore my pink hunting jacket because Reverend James loved that jacket. Someday I may leave it to him."

Our room was a double with long windows looking over the back lawn bordered by magnolias, palmettos, and live oaks. At the end of the lawn was the trapshooting range, fronting the marshes of Sweet Air that looked as if all the duck in the world stopped there to catch their breath. In the distance the marsh ended at the sea. It was a view from *Gone with the Wind,* a view that Billy Morgan loved, but that he took for granted, a birthright.

Now maybe you would never hunt except with a camera. And there are people who would be uncomfortable in the mornings when a knock would come at the door.

"Fire?"

"Yes," we would say.

Two white-uniformed maids, with tiny white lace caps, would enter, both carrying small stacks of hardwood. With eyes averted from the beds, they would stack the wood in the fireplace, spray kerosene on the pile, and set a match to the bottom. They would leave as the flames shot up the flu and the heat moved in waves out into the room. Then coffee would be brought on a silver tray and left on a table. My wife and I would lie in our beds under quilted puffs that had been at Sweet Air for fifty years and wake

up slowly, watching the fire and saying to each other, "Do you
believe it? Do you believe it?"

The first breakfast was something out of the horn of the Ghost
of Christmas Past: fresh-squeezed juices, choice of eggs, hotcakes,
sausage, bacon, grits, fresh fruit, apple pie, beaten biscuits. And,
with every meal, special guava jelly from Lapham in Pompano
Beach, Florida. Billy Morgan sat at the head of the table drinking
from a silver julep cup that was filled with a combination of beer
and champagne. After breakfast, Billy rang the handbell and
Peter, the butler, appeared. Peter served each meal, mixed cocktails, cooked lunch in the field, and provided advice on every
plantation subject. He also anticipated any request, however
trivial. He was a tall black man with the dignity of someone who
knows he is indispensable. "How about the greeting song, Peter?
For Mrs. Spooner," said Billy.

Peter wore a white jacket and had been very stern while serving breakfast. At the request for song he began to smile. He stood
at the giant mahogany sideboard and looked at my wife. "Good
mornin', Missy Susan, howdee howdee do," he sang slowly.
"Good mornin', Missy Susan, howdee howdee do. Well, we're so
very, very glad to see youuu. Howdee, howdee dooo." The song
was sung as if at a campfire with a big moon playing tricks
through dark clouds. It sounded like "In the evenin' by the moon-
light, you can hear those banjos ringin'." Peter had his rituals and
they had to be observed. He had to sing the chorus for each
guest, while Billy Morgan drank beer and champagne and put his
booted feet on the table and thought about hunting and drinking
and war.

Spending the week with Morgan, you get sucked into the action. It's like playing cops and robbers as a child, or playing
cowboys and Indians. Sucked into the ritual we rose at eight,
breakfasted at eighty-thirty, shot trap or relaxed until eleven-
thirty.

"Pull," Morgan would yell, precisely at eleven-thirty, and one
of the guests would release two clay birds from a spring-

powered trap machine. Shooting double birds, Morgan destroyed the clay Frisbee nearest to him, swung his Holland and Holland twenty-gauge over and under along the second pigeon's arc of flight and blew it to chips. "Time for a stirrup cup," he would declare, and off he would stride, across the front lawn to where Giles, the groom, waited with our horses. Peter, the butler, also waited beside a small table laden with pitchers of whiskey sours, pitchers of Bloody Marys, bottles of wine, a cooler full of Lite beer, and a quart of Wild Turkey. Morgan poured himself three fingers of Wild Turkey and toasted, "May the coveys be plentiful and the ride be fair." Then it would be mount-up time and a two-hour ride through cornfields, burned-out timber shoots, and along the marshes and shore, while Giles sang country songs and the January air smelled like springtime in other corners of the world.

While we cantered, Peter would be on his way to the predetermined luncheon spot in the Land Rover, which always traveled out of our sight and hearing. We would arrive famished at the picnic spot, perhaps a small bluff surrounded by oaks, looking down on a tidal river that flowed with the ease of the days when Indians fished there for trout. Anticipating our arrival, Peter would have set up tables and camp chairs, started a cook fire, set the table with silver and glassware and with linen napkins tucked under the forks. There were thermos jugs with hot soup and hot coffee. There would be shrimps and rice, just-baked cornbread, a salad of spinach and Bibb lettuce.

Billy Morgan would cook the quail, shot the previous day and cleaned by the kitchen staff. Morgan did the quail in an iron pan in which a pound of bacon had cooked. Quail are small, slightly larger than your fist, with tiny bones and succulent dark meat. Morgan did them in bacon fat and beer that he alternately drank and poured upon the sizzling birds. Whenever anyone in the party raised a hand into the air, Peter would slap either a chilled Tuborg or a glass of chablis into the waiting person's grip. The quail were eaten by hand, the bones thrown over our shoulders into the bushes. The conversation was of other hunts, the Civil War, the sensation of being lost in time and space, and Sweet Air plantation.

Bob, the dog man, appeared after the third beer or the fourth glass of chablis, with his three hunting spaniels in a cage in back of his pickup. After lunch we mounted up, our shotguns secured in scabbards attached to cavalry saddles. The saddles had the stirrups covered with leather patches because so much riding at Sweet Air was done through brambles and brush, country that would snag ordinary stirrups.

Billy Morgan put on a Cincinnati Reds baseball cap, spit into the brush, opened a Tuborg with a church key tied to his saddle. "Only people who don't know any better use zip tops," he would say, ignoring the zip top on any can he used. Bob, the dog man, nodded, spitting his approval, and loosed his animals — Dandy, Doll, and Alice. "Hi-yoop," Bob yelled. "Find 'em, Dandy; find 'em, Doll; Alice; hi-yoop. Find 'em."

We shot in pairs. When a dog would find a covey of quail and would go on a point that made him look as if he were stuffed and set in a natural history museum, Bob would signal two of us down from the horses. Billy Morgan can flip shotgun shells from his hunting-jacket pocket and slide them into his twenty-gauge faster than Clint Eastwood can draw in a spaghetti western. The quail would come up like skeletons in a carnival fun house, suddenly, without warning. Double roar from shotguns, and Bob moved the hunt on. "Find 'em, Dandy," he'd chant. "Daid, daid. Find 'em, Doll."

The dogs moved to the dead birds, as Bob signaled the shooters onto the quail's next hiding place, through woods and brush, cornfields and pine scrub. When our limit was taken and the sun about to disappear, Bob would call in the dogs, and we would race back to the plantation house, with Billy in the lead, pretending to be a cavalry officer.

"When you're Captain Money," he explained, "you can be a cavalry officer or a tank commander. The secret is to be yourself as little as possible." He would stand up in his stirrups, give a yank at his Cincinnati Reds cap, and signal. "By the gallop, yoooo. Burn, rape, and pillage as you go." And he would gallop down the road with his lady of the moment, who always tried to keep up with Captain Money — which she could generally do, if it were only for a week.

At Sweet Air house, Peter, the butler, would have tea ready in the living room, with a fire large enough to roast Joan of Arc and Savonarola standing side by side. After half an hour, when the day's hunt had been examined and reexamined and the shotguns had been cleaned, the two maids in lace caps would quietly arrive and announce to my wife and the other women, "The baths are poured. Hot, waitin'."

Back in the rooms, evening clothes would be laid out on the beds. "We dress for dinner at Sweet Air," we had been told. My wife had casually mentioned earlier that she smoked Merit cigarettes, and there was a carton waiting on her bureau. On my bureau were a bottle of Dewar's White Label, a bottle of Harvey's Bristol Cream, ice, a carafe of water, and two glasses.

"Can I marry Billy Morgan?" my wife asked.

"You don't marry Billy Morgans," I said to her. "You don't want to get close enough to see what happens after the guests leave."

We would dress and go on to cocktails, ritual Gibsons served with oversize supersweet cocktail onions from Charles F. Cates and Sons of Frison, North Carolina.

After dinner, Morgan didn't have to ask Peter to bring the port and to pass cigars. Captain Money was the master. Sitting by the fire, he wore velvet foxhead slippers with his dinner jacket, and he snipped the end from his cigar with a silver snipper from Dunhill on Jermyn Street. "You know what's wrong with society?" Morgan asked, as secure in South Carolina as in his high chair. "It's middle-class morality. George Bernard Shaw said, 'I have to live for others, not for myself.' That's middle-class morality." He crossed one leg over the other and pulled on his cigar. "I live for myself. But I want others around to take note of it."

Knowing himself, and fearing his own obsolescence, he wanted witnesses. Billy Morgan, my Good Life Maven, gave up his Secret Life with great reluctance. I found that by being a listener and asking him questions no one had asked him before — about his sensitivity, about his hidden artistic ambitions — I had a person smart for me, one who could provide glimpses into worlds most people only read about in six-hundred-page romances, where all the men are dashing and all the servants know their forks.

The prejudices of snobs can be as interesting or dangerous as the prejudices of anyone else. Billy Morgan, over the years, has defined a gentleman according to this set of observations:

1. A gentleman stirs his drinks with his finger.

2. If buttons appear on a gentleman's sleeves, they must always be accompanied by real buttonholes.

3. A gentleman's parents should be divorced.

4. A gentleman wears boxer shorts.

5. It is *never* so warm that a gentleman wears a short-sleeved shirt.

6. A working-class person grinds his cigarette out with his heel; a gentleman, always with his toe.

7. A gentleman never wears ready-made bow ties; he always ties his own.

8. A gentleman never wears loafers to work. When he does wear loafers, he never wears socks.

9. A gentleman always wears braces with three-piece suits.

10. Formal clothes are never referred to as a tuxedo. "Dinner jacket" is the customary nomenclature.

11. Patent-leather pumps are worn with a dinner jacket unless the evening is at home. Then, velvet slippers are appropriate.

12. A gentleman must know his way around a golf course, a tennis court, and, most especially, a sailboat.

13. A gentleman never buttons the bottom button of his vest.

14. A gentleman rides. And if he doesn't now hunt, at one point in his life, he should have.

15. A gentleman should have a grandmother who lives in one of the following places: Southhampton, Long Island; Montecito, California; Northeast Harbor, Maine; Charlevoix, Michigan; or Upperville, Virginia.

Holidays are lonely for Billy Morgan, and we can always count on some glorious invitation prior to times of the year when families gather. It is June 7 and the phone rings.

"You guys free July Fourth?" is Captain Money's opening line.

"Just a clambake," I told him.

"I've got seats six C and D, seven C and D on the Concorde to London. And tickets to Neil Diamond at Woburn Abbey, Robin Tavistock's hangout."

"Who did you call first, Billy?"

"You. I called *you* first. I've written a novel, a first draft I want you to take a look at." In truth, our bags were already half-packed. We were only waiting to see whether we should include sneakers and rackets in case tennis were to be on the program.

On the Concorde, Captain Money handed me a telegram from Henry Maxwell, his bootmaker at 177 New Bond Street. "I had an appointment this afternoon for a fitting," he said. "This came this morning."

The telegram. It was from Robert Giddon of Giddon Ltd. Clifford Street — Captain Money's Saddlemaker. It read, "Your Bootmaker Henry Maxwell, 177 New Bond Street. Prefers to see you tomorrow, Friday. Feet may not be normal on the day of your flight and therefore measurements erroneous."

Morgan was smiling. "Some things never change," said Captain Money, pleased beyond reason.

The weekend cost us one meal, a late supper at the Dumpling Inn in Soho. Neil Diamond had done two encores of "Sweet Caroline."

The Good Life can mean many things to you. But my research into the lives of Smart People constantly reinforces the fact that people love to retell stories of their past. The Good Life is not just of the moment. We revel in others' tales of their exploits, of their triumphs and luxuries. My Philosopher-Kings underscore the lessons they give in life with stories from the past.

"The Good Life is realizing fantasies," says Red Henry, my Philosopher-King. "And you can do it if you believe that everyone is going to have a good time with you. Then you won't hesitate to approach strangers or celebrities or to call people in different towns whose names you're given.

"An example of fantasies coming true: It was 1954, springtime in New York. I was there seeing the buyers from Saks and Bloomingdale's. Having a drink at the Four Seasons, I notice a couple sitting at the table next to me. She is pregnant and wearing one of my designs. Naturally I go over, comment on the goods, ask her for suggestions about fit, color, styles for next fall. They ask me to pull up a chair and join them. Turns out that he is one of America's premier sports writers. He's with Time-Life and about to leave to cover the Masters Tournament in Augusta.

"Well, all my life I've wanted to see the Masters, so I fix up the man's wife with an invitation to my showroom the next day to pick up some dresses at the right price. Then I tell them about famous characters I've known on golf courses, including my friend Zuffy Hoffman who putts with a three wood and who has tufts of hair that grow out of his ears so thick that no one will ever dance with him because he tickles their cheeks. Sure enough, the writer invites me to the Masters, to all events including the big Calcutta the night before. Naturally I go.

"The ol' redhead is soon drunk as a skunk with Jimmy Demaret in the lobby of the Bon Air Hotel in Augusta. Two hours before they tee off I never saw anyone as polluted as Demaret. Morning comes. On the tee. I'm watching Demaret, wondering how he can stand upright. 'Boom' he hits his first drive right down the middle about two ninety. 'Snap' he hits a six iron better than I ever saw anyone hit a six iron, three feet from the cup. 'Bang' he cans it for a birdie. *I'm* the one who can't stand up. *He* makes birdie as if he had had twelve hours sleep after a glass of warm milk.

"Nineteen fifty-four was the year that Billy Joe Patton, a country boy from Kentucky and an amateur, led the Masters for three rounds. The Masters Tournament was something before television brought the crowds. People came who loved golf, good manners, and the beauty of Georgia. It was Bobby Jones's show, his tournament. And it was like the South before the Civil War: live oaks, great service, pretty ladies. I followed Gene Sarazen one day, Hogan and Snead another. On one fairway I snuck under the ropes, right next to Hogan and Snead. There's Snead hitting a shot. 'Beauty,' says Hogan. That's all he'd ever say. Hogan hits a shot. 'Beauty,' says Snead, a tough guy.

"There I am. Hogan and Snead striding down the fairway with me striding between them. The sports writer I came with can't believe his eyes. Me, Henry the Red. 'You knock 'em we frock 'em.' The Masters at Augusta with the bourbon and branch water. That's the Good Life. But there's an expression from the Talmud that's part of it. And I say it every day, a loose translation. 'We pray to God that our station in life not be reduced.' "

My Good Life Lamplighters I discovered one lunchtime. They are an inspiration and an example, and a rarity today. They are a happily married couple. Despite the incredible divorce rate in this country, we remain a marriage-oriented society. Because a happy, successful marriage seems so rare, this chapter, concentrating on the Good Life, should contain an example of the genre for you to emulate, perhaps, but certainly to stop and wonder at.

Eric and Cinda Slater own a boutique on one of New York's smartest shopping streets. They sell dresses, shoes, accessories, and household objects at fancy prices. They travel a lot, stay incredibly thin, eat fruit and cheese for lunch, drink white wine or Perrier, smoke dope and do cocaine. I'm not advocating the taking of drugs or equating the Slaters' habits with achieving a successful marriage. But I do believe that, if you are going to criticize society or its institutions, it is best to do it from the inside, belonging to clubs or having tested the prohibited stimuli. The Slaters' use cocaine or marijuana in amounts probably not equal in ill effect to your smoking or my use of crunchy peanut butter. The Slaters are successful and smart. They have overcome one-dimensional, rigid, albeit privileged, backgrounds. They have created a style and a caring for each other that is equally inspiring to people who know them well and to strangers who shop their store, My Cup Runneth Over.

"What did I know about anything when I got married?" Eric asked me. "I was from Shadyside Academy in Philadelphia; Cinda was a Jewish princess from the five towns of Long Island. You know what I thought was fun? Horror shows. Destruction. Fernanda Wetherill's coming-out party, hanging from the chandeliers breaking Mumsy's Waterford. That was fun."

Eric was the first person I knew who wore collarless shirts, black tie with jeans, camel's hair when it was unpopular, white flannel pleated pants when they had been out of style for years. He was the first person I knew to spot the Beatles, to let his hair grow to shoulder length in the 1960s, to cut it short in 1974. Eric has a knack for trend-setting, for perceiving style before others know it exists.

"I met Cinda," Eric said, "when I was in law school finding out that being a lawyer was not my route. She was incredible. We were erotic fantasies for each other — the aristocrat Wasp, the Jewish princess. Christ, they hadn't even made *The Way We Were* yet. She taught me how to love. And not to be afraid of taking a chance. I mean, you have to understand, wearing engineer boots to a deb party, mothers of girls thought I was an anarchist at best. Turns out I was a designer; I had style. You know what it's like to be copied? Everyone, all my friends used to wear what I wore. Cinda set me free."

Cinda told her side: "You think it's wrong of me to say that I've got the brains, he's got the taste? All I can tell you is that the big lesson in life is, Whatever works for you, *do it*. We met at a speech by William Kunstler, the activist lawyer. Eric and I were on the barricades in the sixties, anti–Vietnam war, pro-environment, free Bobby Seale, the whole banana. I knew I was committed, but at the Kunstler speech all I could look at was Eric. It was what he was *wearing*: a three-piece seersucker suit over a Lacoste pink shirt with a panama hat. He was a dude. I walked over to him during the speech and tapped him on the shoulder. He turned and I handed him a piece of Bazooka bubble gum. 'There's white wine and pâté when you finish that,' I said.

"The unexpected always works," Cinda told me, "when you want to meet someone. I've given away tons of Bazooka gum to strangers. It's a sure thing."

Eric left law school and Cinda left a women's magazine where she wrote a shopping column. They had a romance where they couldn't leave one another alone, and they decided that with their discoveries about each other they should start a business. They were married in a field in back of a friend's house on July Fourth. There were two short ceremonies, one performed by a rabbi, one by a Unitarian minister who smoked pot and coached youth soccer. Stereo speakers played a tape put together by Eric and Cinda. It included "Amazing Grace" played by bagpipes, "Holy City," and the "1812 Overture" complete with rockets and cherry bombs at the finale. Dancing followed the outdoor service. The impression of the guests was that a peace had been signed between two warring armies, two armies now drunk and exhausted but sure to fight again in the future.

Eric and Cinda opened their boutique. They stocked it with European fashions, housewares, and accessories bought on a honeymoon/shopping tour that lasted almost three months. The boutique caught on and prospered, becoming a mecca for the chic, the gay, the young marrieds with money. My Cup Runneth Over, the name of the shop, sold pasta machines, beach chairs, and corkscrews along with Italian clogs, Scandinavian jerseys, skirts from Greece, floppy hats from Yugoslavia. The music sys-

tem played Bach and James Taylor. Eric and Cinda dispensed
wine and cheese and advice to the patrons who sought friendship
as well as style, at fancy prices but in the lowest of keys.

Why describe Eric and Cinda's backgrounds? Why are they
Smart People? A good marriage today seems the most difficult of
achievements. Cinda and Eric had almost every obstacle set in
the way of happiness. Theirs is a mixed marriage, with all the
pressures of dissimilar family and background. And they work as
well as live together. Spending twenty-four hours a day with
one's spouse provides no safety valve; there are too many decisions together, too many possibilities for failure. But they keep
the marriage going, full-time, with children (a boy and a girl),
and they amaze everyone who meets them with their talent for
patience, humor, and love.

What are the secrets of successful adaptation to marriage?
Many of the lessons we can all use, regardless of where we live or
what we do. Cinda told me long ago, "The essence of a good
relationship consists of two things, a sense of humor and the
ability not to get bogged down in trivia. We have a game we
devised years ago called Espionage. We play it everywhere we go
when there are people around us, in restaurants, in theater lobbies, on planes. We listen to other people's conversations, and,
whenever we do, we find the incredible petty problems, annoyances, and trivia that drive others crazy. The world is one big
Woody Allen movie or Feiffer cartoon. Tell people this and they
nod. 'Yeah,' they say, 'we fought about overcooked broccoli last
night.' It's part of life but *such* a bore. Espionage gets us silly,
and laughter takes us out of ourselves, lifts us away from playing
other people's games."

Cinda continued, "When one of us is annoyed with the other,
or has the blues, the one who's up will tape our breakfast or
dinner conversations. Playing it back makes us realize how foolish
and small we are. That's Espionage. But the salvation of our
marriage is constantly remembering *why we got married in the
first place.* Most couples completely forget their courtship. We

want to remember the reasons we were first attracted. We remind each other constantly of events from the past, our foolishness and discoveries. Sexually, it is a reinforcing theme. Tales of the passing years, places, people seem relaxing for us. Memorable lovemaking stories give us memorable lovemaking now.

"There's another important aspect of successful marriage," Cinda said. "You should take trips. You must get perspective on your job, your home, your children. Even if it is only for twenty-four hours, an inexpensive night in a hotel in your own city. Get away several times a year, a weekend if you can't afford a week. It doesn't matter where. But *don't* take your children. Be by yourselves and remember why you got married. You can make it successful by stepping away from reality. The loneliness of the divorced person is hell on parents, worse on the children. It means that marriage was a waste of time."

Wherever I've worked, I've always wandered at lunchtime. My Lunchtime Therapy promotes mental health and provides a necessary break from the routine and pressures of workdays.

Try this: Walk into any city street at noontime and sit by a fountain or on a bench or on the library or courthouse steps. Watch the crowds — business people, lawyers, secretaries, police, derelicts, schoolchildren. Instantly you will see people you will the ugly, the ignorant. You will see nervous people, hurrying to wolf down a tasteless sandwich without appreciation. Five minutes of Lunchtime Therapy and you will immediately feel good thank God you are not. You will see cripples and winos, the blind, about yourself. You will feel lucky. Self-pity will disappear when you look around you and say, "Look at all the poor, miserable bastards in the world. I can see. I can stand. I can appreciate beauty and hear music." Watch the panorama wherever you are for several minutes each day. The comparison with your own life will make you feel a lot better. Lunchtime Therapy works, and it makes you notice the world, not just pass through it with your thoughts turned inward on your own petty problems.

My Lunchtime Therapy always includes wandering into shops near my office, or into art galleries if they're in the vicinity. I do this for two reasons: First, to get a feel for business in the community, with an eye to relating it to stock-market activity, in retail areas. And second, small entrepreneurs, if you become friendly with them, can often offer services and advice that do not come with inquiries into the Yellow Pages.

Sometimes during my Lunchtime Therapy, my strolls into shops and galleries, I stop into My Cup Runneth Over and see Eric and Cinda being harassed. People are demanding service, clothes are out of stock, suppliers have been slow in deliveries, the air conditioning is broken, and shoplifters are on the prowl. I catch Eric's eye. "You keeping it all together?" I ask him, nodding at the chaos in the shop.

He stops for a minute. "There is no real life without chaos," he says. "There is no business without its own particular problems. But if you're healthy," he says, "it's all just part of the game. You don't run away from these things. You've got to stay with it. Little daily things. Let them slide off you and away."

That's a big lesson from my Lamplighters. They are people who always leave you feeling better. And it doesn't cost you anything more than observation.

Sandy Baron: Roughrider.

Sandy Baron has a beard the color of broom straw. He shaves his head, leaving broom-straw stubble sticking up. After several days without shaving, his head looks as if it could brush off the shoulders of your blue blazer.

Sandy is an independent travel agent who works for various local organizations like Kiwanis, the Knights of Columbus, the University Club. He is my Good Life Roughrider, a hustler without malice whose search in life is for the perfect pub in Cornwall or the perfect five-day tour to Mount Kilimanjaro for under three hundred dollars a head. Whenever I need perspective on my life (which is often), I can call Sandy and ask, "What can you do for

me over a long weekend?" He never has to call back; he always
has a special. "Jamaica for one forty-nine fifty. Three days on the
beach, two meals, your own Sunfish, five complimentary planter's
punches. You got to be a Jesuit priest, but no sweat. The church
is changing every day, more liberal. So you turn your collar
around, big deal. You can't go to the bathroom these days for a
hundred and forty-nine fifty. If you've got five days I can get you
Mexico City for three and a quarter. The Hellenic Society."

I've been to Hong Kong with Hadassah and Hawaii with the
Veterans of Foreign Wars. And all for a fraction of what the
trips would ordinarily cost. But what kind of accommodations
and what kind of company are you pressed into with deals like
these? You get the best treatment and the best accommodations *if*
you know the person who arranges the tour. In my case, I know
Sandy Baron.

Sandy was recommended to me by a friend. She said that
Sandy could find the best and cheapest trip to the Greek islands
for a professional society to which I belong. I trusted the friend,
but I don't like to take chances. I think it is imperative to use
a travel agent who understands or even anticipates your taste.
Therefore personal contact is essential the first time you book a
trip with any new agent. Here is what I said to Sandy Baron:

"Mr. Baron, I hope we do business for many years. But it's
important that I ask you what you know about these three places:
the Dormey House in Broadway, the Cotswolds, England; the
Cavalier Hotel on Wilshire in Westwood, Los Angeles; and the
rooms above the fifth floor in the Miyako Hotel in Kyoto, Japan."
These places I have always considered special for different and
perhaps obscure reasons. The places also are not known to the
average tourist or the average travel agent.

Sandy Baron knew them all. "Do they still serve fresh Danish
at the Cavalier for breakfast?" he asked. "For free?" Sandy clearly
would have a very good idea of what my travel preferences
would be. You should test agents this way with *your* favorite
places.

I asked Sandy if I could make an appointment, and he came to see me in my office. I had him come in immediately and wait while I talked on the phone. One of my pet peeves is any reception room. I dislike waiting on a couch, reading magazines while the receptionist hired for her breasts works on her nails and talks on the phone to her mother.

I always have visitors ushered in to see me immediately. I enjoy watching them while they think I am occupied with something else. I also can set up my visitor by what I am saying to the person on the phone, making my delivery humorous or gentle or authoritative according to how I want to prepare the person who is waiting.

While Sandy Baron listened to me, he looked through my telescope at the harbor. Tugs were escorting an incoming cruise ship, white against the deep-blue winter sea. The ship seemed to come into the harbor reluctantly, as if February were a cruel joke played on a tanned visitor from the Caribbean. I got off the phone. The telescope had made Baron thoughtful. "I'm not really a travel agent," he admitted to me. "I'm a sucker. I can't stay in one place long enough to accumulate money. I should build a business, get an organization, delegate authority. But I'm compulsive about seeing the world. I have to go on the trips myself. I see that ship and I think about the Virgins, St. Thomas, Gorda Sound, Jost van Dyke."

"You've been to Foxy's?" I asked.

"Foxy's? I worked for him for four months. Washing glasses, slicing limes, making nice-nice with people off the boats."

That was it. The sparring to make the connection, to find the item that triggers response from someone's past or from the secret place in their hearts. Foxy's Bar on the island of Jost van Dyke, and Foxy himself, an island institution suitable for a Hemingway novel. Foxy, the irreverent bar owner, sarcastic, difficult. The ogre with a heart of gold, who had received more invitations to society weddings and debutante parties than Meyer Davis's orchestras.

Maybe you've never been to Foxy's. But the principle is the same. Find the Secret Life Syndrome. Search for the spot that will make others respond to you.

From that moment on, Sandy Baron took care of me. He became more than a travel agent. He became an adviser, a counselor, because he thought I appreciated special places, the ones you save for yourself. I had something to trade with Sandy. I not only could find customers for him, but I could find special places as well. People take care of those who feed them either business or information.

Later that year I was on a jaunt to Las Vegas with Sandy, a long weekend and a freebie at that. The plane was loaded with shoe people, traditional high rollers, who had to buy three hundred dollars' worth of gambling chips in return for everything else being on the house. Sandy waived my fee. He had me along as consultant, which meant I was to stop him from having Scotch sours for breakfast and silver bullets, otherwise known as martinis, for lunch.

Sandy juggled hair appointments for wives, private gin games for husbands, tickets to Sammy Davis, arguments with pit bosses and hookers, gratuities for dealers and maids until he couldn't stand it any longer. Then he discovered chemin de fer about two in the morning, in a crowd that included Alan King, two sheikhs from Abu Dhabi, and a godchild of Franklin Roosevelt. Sandy won twelve hundred dollars in forty minutes and accepted six stingers from a waitress in hot pants. A woman in a long green jersey dress pressed herself against his arm after his first hundred-dollar bet. She kept whispering, "I like your style," every time the dealer tapped the shoe, every time Sandy took a stinger and slipped the waitress a ten-dollar chip.

When Sandy moved away from the chemin de fer table he was doing the gay fandango and singing "What Is This Thing Called Love?" to the woman in the green jersey dress. Pulling me with him, he left green dress waiting outside the men's room. Inside he did a little jig of joy, brushing his teeth with tap water, liquid soap, and his finger. "Oh, I'm in paradise," he yelled. "A fistful of money and a beautiful woman." Babbling with glee, he pulled off one tasseled loafer and began stuffing bills into it. His money was spilling all over the floor, and he dropped to his hands and knees to retrieve it, calling me to help. "It's a two-loafer night," he yelled. Off with the other shoe, stuffing it with bills, spreading the excess around to his pockets. "I had them give me tens," Sandy said. "Tens make sense, tens make people stand tall. How many tens for green dress?"

He lurched from the men's room, limping noticeably from the wadded money in his shoes and gently took green dress by the elbow, steering her toward the elevators. About that time one of his junket shoe men threw up into a roulette wheel in the main casino and ruined the roll, particularly for the wife of a high-placed loan shark from Jersey City. The loan shark knocked the shoe man onto the seat of the blue pleated slacks he had had made in Milan. The wife of the shoe man bit the loan shark somewhere on the side of his body. Sandy Baron was stopped at the elevator by eight of his tour guests, hysterical over the fight, just as green dress had leaned over Sandy to press the button for his floor. An hour later, after green dress was long gone, order restored to the casino, the loan shark mollified by Asti Spumante, and the shoe manufacturers safe in their beds, Sandy and I had a nightcap in the lounge where the organist drank Canadian Club and played to an empty house.

Sandy was hung over beyond the point where liquor made him feel anything more than lost. "I could have kept going in the elevator. But no, not me. You want to know why I'm a travel agent? Two things: I'm naturally flirtatious, with both men and women. And I enjoy being a mother. Glad-handing as I walk down the aisles of planes, greeting my charter people, coming in to breakfast in foreign hotels where anxious faces greet me, grab me, waiting for assistance with language, shopping, sightseeing. My father was in the retail business. He worked six days a week. On the seventh he was too exhausted to do anything with his family." Sandy sighed. "So I determined to concentrate on leisure time. And my family is many families — all the people I parade around all over the world. The ironies of life."

A woman came up to us. Everything about her was dragging: her dress, her hairdo, her face. She was the wife of the man who had thrown up into the roulette wheel. "I wanna thank you, Sandy," she said. "Saul isn't like that. You handled the whole situation like a truly admirable person. My whole Community League girls will know about this when we get back."

Sandy thanked her.

"No, I really mean it," she said. "By the way, do you think any Chinese restaurants will be open at this hour? Saul says a little egg foo yung he could keep down."

Sandy beamed. He knew the answer.

"A great place at the end of the Strip," he said. "Open twenty-four hours. And the owner always gives me group rates. Of course you may have to have the whole dinner."

Being a Roughrider, Sandy Baron has given me various hints over the years that have eased the pain of traveling. They are unconventional hints. But Roughriders court the unconventional. It is their specialty. In Sandy's words, here are some of the ways he cuts down the odds against travel horror stories.

1. "My first rule, not only of travel but of life: Always act as if you belong wherever you go, and as if you know exactly what you are doing. The army taught me this. It works particularly well at private beaches or at clubs where you don't belong.

"Whenever I've been a guest, or spoken to groups, or solicited tours in any club anywhere in America, I ask to see their library or reading room. I always put in my briefcase a sampling of their stationery and envelopes with the club letterhead. Sometime during the meeting I ask my host, 'Do you have reciprocal rights with many clubs abroad?' Most good city clubs in America have reciprocity with the finest clubs in Europe and Asia, giving temporary membership privileges to Americans with introductory letters. I get a list of the clubs abroad and, armed with my stationery, I wait for my next trip to Dublin, Paris, Singapore, or wherever. For instance, the Garrick Club of London has exchange privileges with the St. Botolph of Boston where I had dinner recently. Knowing I was going to London in the near future, I took some St. Botolph Club stationery and wrote 'This will introduce Mr. Alexander Baron, a member in good standing of the St. Botolph Club. I would appreciate your extending to him all the guest privileges in accordance with our reciprocal agreement. Yours truly, Ebenezer French, Secretary.'

"At the Garrick in London, I was served before-theater dinner in splendor. I had champagne, roast beef, strawberries and cream. My waiter bowed and scraped. 'Yes, Mr. Baron,' he said. 'Will that be all, Mr. Baron? Call a carriage, Mr. Baron?' Christ, a carriage! As if I were Lord Upthine of West Sussexshire. I pay cash at the Garrick. The club picks up a little change they wouldn't have had, they toss out the note when I'm gone. Nobody's hurt and I've had sniffs and tastes and nibbles of the best. I've done this all over the world, been treated like a prince. And without paying a nickel in club dues. The secret is to always act not only as if you belong but as if you're on the goddamn board of governors."

2. "If you visit Iron Curtain countries, customs can be murder. Slip the inspector, male or female, a *Playboy* or a *Penthouse* or any semipornographic magazine. You'll be whipped right through customs before anyone else. And they may not even open your bags. A *Playboy* is the best bribe for Communists, particularly the women inspectors in Rumania."

3. "Always carry a small travel bag that stays with you on a plane. Have in it a change of clothes, your money, and some toilet articles. It's incredible how often luggage disappears or is misplaced when you travel abroad."

4. "On planes the food is usually terrible, whether the flight is international or domestic. There are several things you can do about this, things of which you may not be aware. Order a di-

abetic meal, which usually consists of a small steak or broiled chicken with several vegetables. It is much fresher than ordinary fare and, in some cases, even delicious. Order the seafood platter, also diabetic, which could include shrimp, lobster, crabmeat, and fresh vegetables. On morning flights, to avoid cold eggs and artificial sausage, order the kosher meal. Bagels and cream cheese with coffee can be much better than gooey sweet rolls with soggy bacon."

5. "Carry a silver-headed cane and limp slightly. The cane is a conversation piece and can get you special service from cabin attendants. The limp will get you preferential seat selection because of your physical limitations (gout, arthritis, an esoteric sporting injury from polo or court tennis)."

6. "Always try to have a name at your destination, someone to call who has local knowledge. Using this reference can lift a trip out of the ordinary. Check your college or school alumni records for old friends who live in your destination city. Check professional societies to which you belong for similar societies abroad. Above all, always consider yourself a *treat* for others, so that knowing *you* will be as interesting for them as it is for you to see their city or country with the help of their local expertise. A new acquaintance abroad or an old friend called out of the blue can turn an ordinary vacation into the trip of a lifetime."

7. "A hint that will get you service and attention whenever you travel abroad: Have a catch phrase in every foreign language, a phrase that may be nonsense but will immediately tickle the funny bone or the curiosity of the natives. In Italy, I say to the concierges and waiters and shopkeepers, 'Non che rosa sensa spina, non ch'amore sensa fina.' It means 'There is no rose without a thorn, there is no love without an end.' It stops 'em dead in their tracks every time. Then they laugh and give you special attention, thinking you are either very funny, very romantic — or nuts.

"In France, I use 'Il pleure dans mon coeur comme il pleut sur

la ville.' 'It rains in my heart like it rains on the city.' The French
love it and they embrace you. Sometimes I also use 'J'entre dans
la salle de classe. Je regard autour de moi. Je dis "bonjour" au
professeur. Je prends ma place.' That's the first lesson American
kids used to be taught in basic French. When you say it in
France, they *know* you're nuts. But they still pay attention because they don't want any trouble. I've got phrases like that in
every foreign language. They always work."

Sandy Baron will continue to provide me with inexpensive
travel because I appreciate his routines and I let him know that
*he* is appreciated. But more than this — I continue to feed him
customers and the names of special places. With my travel
Roughrider, I always have something to trade.

The Good Life has many meanings, some intensely personal.
Some people need hard work first to enjoy leisure later. For others, hard work is poison. My Philosopher-Kings often point out
differences in life-styles, to let me know that my definitions are
certainly not the only ones.

For instance:

"You know the true meaning of leisure?" Mather Stevens asked
me one day at lunch. "People like you and me are missing the
boat. I was in Nassau at the Lyford Cay Club last month, and I
entered a big backgammon tournament. The entrance fee was
two hundred dollars, and the winner would take home ten thousand. I was knocked out in the third round, took two hundred
and fifty, but it's the characters I want to tell you about. There's a
whole group of people you never heard of who travel from watering hole to watering hole and play backgammon for big money.
You know I talk while I play, probing for possible weaknesses in
my opponents. In the third round I'm playing a guy who is the
spitting image of David Niven: ascot, blazer, slightly bored and
aristocratic. In trying to break through his calm, I say to him at
one point, 'By the way, what do you do?'

"He looked at me as if I had absolutely no business being across the table from him.

" '*Do?*' he said in a loud voice. Then louder, '*Do?* Oh, my dear chap, I'm not pushy at all.'

"He proceeded to wipe me up, and left me with the knowledge that the rich are *still* different from you and me."

# 3 CELEBRITY AND THE INSIDE LIFE

The more our society tries to turn us into numbers, the more we long for heroes. The more we are forced to be anonymous, the more we hunger to see celebrities, to be close to celebrities, to have something of them rub off on us. Most of us are on the outside looking in, longing to be insiders in the world of politics, sports, big money, show business. This is a democracy.

At the same time, we don't want to believe in heroes anymore. But despite the fact that we probably need Joe DiMaggio and Clark Gable more than ever, our all-pervading media coverage of everything diminishes celebrity to the size of our own boring neighbors and friends. We don't want to believe in heroes. But despite ourselves, whoever we are, we do.

It is difficult, in two hundred years as a nation, not to lose innocence. It can take four hundred years to lose naiveté, but innocence seems gone. Publicly, it seems also that we have lost our belief in heroes. I say "publicly" since the media — films, television, newspapers, magazines — strip overachievers down to the comfortable size of everyone else. Models in advertisements stress the common look, politicians are universally scorned, the popular writers are more tax-shelter seekers than personalities, our screen actors and actresses are usually smaller and uglier than you or I. The term "superstar" as applied to practically every journeyman athlete and rock performer is ludicrous. Line up a hundred musicians and a hundred hockey, baseball, and football players and you'll have roughly twenty thousand pounds of so much muscle and callused guitar fingers. Indistinguishable from stockbrokers, lawyers, plumbers, steelworkers, and waiters. Just the variables of clothing and hair, a little factor of fat. And yet, despite our tendency to pay up for the mediocre, despite having every community in America able to have its own Dustin Hoffman look-alike contest, we all want to believe that people in the news, people in the NBA, people on the screen are grander, larger, luckier. And even though television series and movies so often fail to offer anything to anybody, we still have a love affair with show business.

What makes our celebrities important is that they can make people *respond* to them by the mere factor of recognition. People *know* them in bars, restaurants, on the street, in theaters. You may not realize it, but what *you* want also is recognition. *You* want the Inside Life. You may not be able to hit a baseball farther than anyone, or break a crystal goblet with your voice, or bring home a Middle East peace treaty. But you can use Smart People Principles to brush the celebrity world and get your foot in the door of the Inside Life.

Tops among my heroes are writers. And tops among my living writer heroes is John Fowles, author of *The Magus, The French Lieutenant's Woman, The Collector,* and other best-sellers. All of his books have been critically acclaimed, as well as avidly read by the public. I wanted to write to John Fowles because of a peculiar series of events in my life.

When my wife and I were dating, the special tension of courtship resulted in small lessons. She was a model and taught me about beauty. I was a writer and I gave her reading lists. She taught me about designers and fashion and makeup and physical conditioning. I taught her about vodka martinis and gave her sheets from legal pads listing such titles as *The Painted Bird, Heart of Darkness, The Alexandria Quartet, Passage to India,* and

*The Magus.* At that time in my life, my emphasis was heavy on appearances and reality. I adored the games of John Fowles and, for various reasons, I thought what he was saying about love was just right.

My wife-to-be would burn my reading lists. She would mail them to me, shredded. She would serve them to me in ham sandwiches.

"Give your reading lists to your mother," she would say. "Improve *her* mind. She's the one who needs lessons on appearances and reality."

So *The Magus* remained untouched by her until months after our marriage. Then, one rainy Sunday afternoon in Boston when you could imagine that Beacon Hill was Paris, she picked up the book and thumbed through a few pages. Two hours later, enthralled, she was still at it. At midnight, when I turned out my light, she was sitting up next to me, refusing to go to sleep, the book propped up on her knees. I awoke some time later, aware that I had rolled over and been smacked in the eyes by electric light. She was still reading.

"What the hell time is it?" I demanded.

"About one," she said. "I'll turn it off in a minute."

I sneaked a look at the clock. "It's two-thirty, for chrissakes," I said.

Then I was fully awake, in the middle of marriage's most frustrating component: the pointless argument. Several weeks thereafter, my wife announced that she was pregnant. She pinpointed the night of conception as that Sunday night. And we blamed it completely on John Fowles and *The Magus.* When our son was born, we named him Nicholas, after the hero of the novel. A year later, with an impending trip to London, I wrote Fowles, telling him the story of Nicholas and offering to buy him dinner, lunch, or a drink. Disappointed that I received no answer, we left for London, vacationed, and returned to find a letter posted from Greece.

"Dear Mr. Spooner," it read, "I am somewhat embarrassed to

find that I now come within the same category as the famous East Coast blackout of a year or two back — I believe that did something for the birthrate also. The book was full of metaphorical conceptions, of course, but I didn't mean it to go further than that. Anyway I wish infant and progenitors all happiness.

"I've been away from England these last weeks, which is why I am late in replying; and now have to go away again, which is why I must postpone the pleasure of meeting your wife and yourself. I hope you enjoy London. I expect I shall be in Boston again fairly soon and then we must have a drink. Best wishes, John Fowles."

Some time later, we received an autographed copy of *The French Lieutenant's Woman*, which I have had boxed and bound for Nicholas, anticipating the time when he becomes involved in appearances and reality.

How did I get Fowles's address? How do you get any famous person's address? It was easy:

We are all star-struck. We lust over stories of the rich and famous, feeling better about ourselves if the celebrated are revealed to be somehow diminished. If *you* feel compelled to write to people you admire, you will find that the real ones will almost always respond. Addresses of home or agent or office will be in *Who's Who*, which every library has. In the case of authors, a call to the publicity department of the publisher can usually elicit the author's mail drop, or even the phone number. I called Little, Brown (Fowles's publisher) and, when connected with the publicity lady, said, "This is Rick Epstein, from Universal Studios television." I let that sink in. "I don't believe in having secretaries call for anything, do you? You want to be big-time, you take the trouble to do it yourself."

"You need some blurbs?" she asked me.

"Blurbs I got," I said. "What I need is John Fowles's address. We're making an offer for several of his stories. His agent is away and the English prefer dealing directly anyway."

"I don't know if I'm authorized to . . ."

I interrupted. "Just have the call transferred to the president's office. We discussed this in New York. You heard my name? Rick Epstein?"

Two minutes later I had John Fowles's address.

Henry the Red, my Philosopher-King, gave me the Rick Epstein routine. "A fraternity brother from Wharton," he said, "used to see how far he could go with this. He'd cab at lunch time to Chauveron, '21,' Sardi's, Four Seasons, the Algonquin. He'd have a three-and-a-half-hour lunch and sign the tab 'Rick Epstein, CBS' or 'Rick Epstein, NBC' or 'Rick Epstein, ABC.' No one ever questioned it because my friend claimed it was the perfect producer's name. So on occasions when you feel like being a producer, be Rick Epstein." I wrote it down.

You think my John Fowles story was a fluke? People respond to the unusual. Here's an example of how Smart People can occasionally recruit *you*. Especially when they are seeking celebrity status and the Inside Life.

My wife and I several years ago were dining in a Hungarian restaurant. We were talking about a book of mine that was about to be published. "Pardon me," a man seated next to us said, "but do you know how to make a Hungarian omelette?" He was speaking in a Balkan accent when he said it, and he didn't wait for my answer. "First steal three eggs," he said, and pulled his chair right up to our table.

It seems that he had been working on several books, couldn't help overhearing our conversation, and was very curious about how to get a publisher, how to get an agent. He was charming and funny and told us stories in accents that alternated among French, Yiddish, Chinese, and Italian. You see, he recruited *me*.

You have to be open to this recruitment experience because others are going to seek you out. It's part of always having something to trade.

The next morning the fake Hungarian appeared at our house with a manuscript. Believing that one should pay the piper for services rendered, he juggled bottles for the children, made a curry with some shrimp we had in the freezer, played the Trumpet Voluntary on the push-button phones, and gave us a fifteen-minute accented dialogue on the nature of man and religion, between a Jewish rabbi, an Irish priest, and an Episcopal bishop from Greenwich, Connecticut.

I steered this new friend to an agent and encouraged his progress, and within the next year, he wrote a book that was a best-seller and a Book-of-the-Month Club main selection — *The Making of a Psychiatrist*.

David Viscott is the name of the man who wasn't afraid to believe in himself enough to come on strong. "How many writers do I sit next to in restaurants?" he said. "You get a chance in life, jump on it. Don't worry about people's privacy. Let *them* worry about that." His advice and common sense can be found in his books and magazine columns and on television talk shows.

What are the rewards for me, or for anyone who plays the Smart People game? The chance to help someone, of course. But, in addition to the obvious, for me in this case it was acting out the God role *and* having someone very valuable on my team, a free shrink. Perhaps even a resident genius. And, on the page opposite the copyright of *The Making of a Psychiatrist*, a dedication, "For John Spooner." And in the author's handwriting, "I thought about writing something profound, but that would be out of character; of saying something funny, but that would be easy. It's very hard and not a little embarrassing to say thank-you to someone who helped me find myself and who matters so much and in so many ways." That is enough reward for reading two thousand unpublishable manuscripts — and the reason for you to bug an author if you want to be published.

What does all this do for me? I have a special book sitting in my library with an inscription addressed to me by one of the most famous writers in the world. I have a book dedicated to me with my name on the third page that sits in hundreds of thousands of homes and libraries. How does this pay off? Even if I'm the same guy as yesterday, these items make people curious. If they're curious, they are going to remember me. Your job in recruiting Smart People is also to make others curious enough about *you* to respond to your needs, whatever they are. Remember: Smart People Principles are organic. They keep bringing in new members of your team, who in turn will recruit others.

You think these stories smack of hero worship or name-dropping? You're right. But name-dropping effectively can be one of your best methods of recruiting Smart People and of living the Inside Life. We are all conscious of celebrities. We would all be thrilled to shake the hand of Reggie Jackson, Muhammad Ali, or Jane Fonda.

You might think that Cambridge, Massachusetts, home of Harvard, would be a tough town to crack, an aloof audience, indifferent to celebrity. It's a town once defined by a friend of mine as "a place where the women have all gone to seed by thirty and their cars — BMWs and Volvo station wagons — are all broken down by the side of the road." After several Cambridge dinner parties featuring the sentiments of the *New Republic* coupled with droplets from Britain's Labour ministry, one gets the impression that a parade featuring O. J. Simpson and Farrah Fawcett-Majors would play to empty streets. But I have a story that proves we are truly a celebrity-hungry nation. This *is* a story about Cambridge, the town that has been home in recent years for Henry Kissinger, Peter (*Jaws*) Benchley and Erich (*Love Story*) Segal.

There are various levels of celebrity, and, when my wife and I were invited to a black-tie dinner dance on Brattle Street honoring John Updike, everyone I talked to who was going said, "I suppose we'll go, but we'd much rather stay home. We *hate* parties with themes." But this was the year that *Couples* was at the top of the charts, and when the guests arrived, all the women at the party flocked around Updike as if his public interest in infidelity would feed their own private moistures, their own private pockets of need. The men guests were law professors, English professors, partners in investment firms, architects of experimental communities, supporters of McGovern and little magazines. And all of *their* conversations took place with one eye watching Updike, watching their wives surround Updike with adoration scented with last year's Norell and lit by the glint of their mother's jewelry.

At the black-tie dinner dance all the men *were* in dinner jackets except the host, who wore a blue blazer. Dirty pool. But he was an orthodontist and presumably had not received an invitation himself.

"When is the band arriving?" I asked my wife at ten-thirty. She was the only woman there who was paying any attention to me. She shrugged.

At eleven I asked my host, "When does the band arrive?"

"No band," he said. "Records."

At eleven-fifteen he moved us all to the old windup Victrola. "Bouzouki records," he said, "brought back from Greece, from Mykonos. John and Mary [the Updikes] can lead. They're the ones," he said with huge delight, "who got us turned on to bouzouki in the first place." Thereupon thirty of the great liberal minds of the East crossed hands, and, with Mr. and Mrs. John Updike in the center of their circle, people began to dance to the bouzouki. The author and his wife were terrific, authentic. They had recently been to Greece and had the movements down pat. Everyone else watched them and imitated them with concentration, envy, and lack of coordination. The circle of people moved to the music, drunk people, kicking themselves, falling, concentrating. As the tempo picked up, the dance became everything. The guests turned from watching the Updikes into their own interpretation of the Greeks. Suddenly Updike and his wife were gone, out of the circle, out of the door, out of the party. But the other guests were now oblivious, kicking each other with relish, playing Zorba, no longer mesmerized by *Couples*. The host in his blazer wound up the Victrola again and the dance went on.

Our attention span may be short, the public may be fickle. But we do hero-worship. And we do love to hear stories about the famous and the celebrated. Perhaps you haven't had any books dedicated to you. Perhaps you haven't been to a dinner party with John Updike. What can you do to link yourself with the world of the celebrity, to be known as someone who gets close to the stars? You can use social situations to set yourself off as a special person, to make yourself less anonymous. You can do this by a technique I have used for years.

Smart People can dine out forever on celebrity stories. The stories should be part of your process of attracting people to your team *and* of making you a character in the eyes of people around you. You must learn the After-Dinner Gambit, which involves two parts: the Celebrity Game and the Joke.

## THE AFTER-DINNER GAMBIT

Calm usually descends after dessert at dinner parties, the calm around a table of people who sigh and say, "What next?" This is the moment for the Smart Person to rap on his or her wineglass with a spoon. It is the time for a story or a toast, and the time to separate *you* from the other guests. The toast is a custom that should never die. It honors your host and hostess; it establishes the fact that you are a gentle person who appreciates hospitality and who understands the Good Life.

> *Here's to the maiden of bashful fifteen;*
> *Here's to the widow of fifty;*
> *Here's to the flaunting, extravagant queen;*
> *And here's to the housewife that's thrifty.*
>     *Let the toast pass —*
>     *Drink to the lass;*
> *I'll warrant she'll prove an excuse for the glass.*

It may be Richard Brinsley Sheridan, but it never fails to get others to their feet. Be the first to toast; you'll always be invited back.

The Celebrity Game is the first part of the after-dinner gambit. It calls attention to you and establishes you as someone comfortable with the rich and famous. All of us grew up with someone who turned out to be Bette Davis or John Wayne or Jimmy Carter or Bob Dylan. Use such information about yourself shamelessly and, when asked "What was she like as a kid?" have a good idea of what may be special, salacious, or fascinating. It is important to know stories no one else has heard — except from you. Here are several examples of little-known show-biz tales for after-dinner Smart People recruitment:

No group of people in America was more powerful than the old Hollywood producers, the moguls like Louis B. Mayer of MGM, Harry Cohn of Columbia Pictures, Samuel Goldwyn of Goldwyn Studios. They lived like royalty, and, if they didn't expect the sea to part for them, they did expect total obedience from their personnel. Sam Goldwyn had a way with words, was famous for his abuse and misuse of the English language. And yet he gave audiences such classic films as *Wuthering Heights*, *The Squaw Man*, *The Best Years of Our Lives*. Goldwyn was unusual in many ways. He was able to surround himself with efficiency because he was tough; people feared him. They might not have wanted to respond to him, but they felt forced to. There are very few Sam Goldwyns today who are able to compel service through fear or intimidation. But it worked for Goldwyn. In his studio, his will was supreme.

No one dared laugh in Goldwyn's face when in 1932 he bought the film rights to a controversial novel about lesbians, *The Well of Loneliness*. The book was a best-seller, but everyone at the studio was shocked that Goldwyn had been suckered into buying it. At that time in Hollywood, censorship was rigid. Sex was only hinted at; homosexuality on film was verboten. We were coming into the era of *Francis the Talking Mule*. It was clear that Goldwyn had never read the lesbian novel. It was clear that he had made a major error. A nervous junior producer was chosen by lot to confront Goldwyn with the impossibility of making the film. Anticipating the worst, the junior producer tried the direct approach.

"Mr. Sam," he said, "you can't make *The Well of Loneliness.*"

"Why the hell not?" asked Goldwyn.

The junior producer blurted out, "You can't make it because it's about two lesbians."

Goldwyn sighed. He relaxed and tilted back in his swivel chair. "No problem," beamed Goldwyn confidently. "In the movie we'll make 'em *Americans.*"

You all like country and Western music. And if you don't, you're un-American. Tammy Wynette is one of the most popular women country singers, and her song "Stand by Your Man" is considered a classic. Her house in Nashville has fancy grillwork covering the windows, grillwork shaped into notes and scales. A friend of mine, visiting Nashville, asked about the fancy grillwork and was told, "You read the windows clockwise. The notes spelled out in the grillwork are the notes to 'Stand by Your Man.'" A new high in Americana.

Well, that's a little-known fact about a celebrity, but to prove what a down-to-earth good old gal Tammy Wynette is, you've got to know the heartaches she lived with on her way to the top. One of her husbands had two passions, fast automobiles and drinking. Usually in combination. One night, to ensure that he stayed home, Tammy gave the keys to all the family's half-dozen vehicles to her mother. Tammy and her husband spent the evening together, and then she went to bed. Tammy was sure that with no access to automobiles there would be no drinking, no driving, no scenes in the roadhouses outside of town. All the vehicles' keys were safe with her mother. At three-thirty, Tammy woke to find her husband gone. In a panic she called her mother who, with her choice of automobiles, jumped in the T-Bird and scratched gravel all the way to her daughter's house. Together they toured the gin mills and roadhouses, finding Tammy's husband, belligerent and well lubricated, at the fourth stop.

"How the hell did you get here?" Tammy demanded, leading him out to the T-Bird.

He looked at her triumphantly. "It's only fifteen miles honey," he said. "I took the lawn mower."

A celebrity's ingenuity is turned into *your* triumph.

The second part of the After-Dinner Gambit is the Joke. As it helps if you develop a certain style, so it helps if you become associated with a classic joke, a story you have told so often and so well that your public demands it, the way saloon audiences demand that Tony Bennett sing "I Left My Heart in San Francisco" or the way Hoagy Carmichael would be asked to play "Stardust" if he were spotted by conventioneers in a lounge.

"I'm always asked for the same things," Mather Stevens says, "two jokes, virtually the only two I know. 'Bad Mouth Schwartz' and 'Archibald S. Holbrook.' 'Bad Mouth Schwartz' is a terrible joke. But 'Bad Mouth Schwartz' is such a terrific name that, after dinner everywhere I go, people get their coffee and automatically yell ' "Bad Mouth Schwartz," "Bad Mouth Schwartz" ' until I have to get up and tell it. Can you believe I got a client last year, a man wanting a divorce, who called and said, 'Mr. Stevens, you don't know me. But last year at a club function I heard you tell "Bad Mouth Schwartz," and I thought, "If he could talk that well after dinner, then he could talk to my wife in court." ' That divorce brought me three trusts, four wills, and a merger."

"What about 'Archibald S. Holbrook'?" I asked my Philosopher-King.

"It helps even more than 'Bad Mouth,' " he said, "because I'm the only person in the East who can remember it when drunk. Any of the really famous jokes — 'Pierre LaFrance, the Great French Aviator,' 'The Long Island Duckling,' 'The Suffolk Downs Story,' 'The Probably Caper,' 'Six Black Hens,' 'Homer, the Horny

Frog' — all of those are easy to remember and can be told by anyone. But 'Archibald S. Holbrook' takes an intellectual to tell it."

You have to picture Mather Stevens in black tie and dress shirt, standing at a long dinner table. His fine blond hair is parted in the middle, his gold watch chain is shining on his belly, the links sparkling with reflected candlelight. Women in long dresses look up at him feeling like part of a secret. Men in dinner jackets look up at him, refilling their wineglasses, wondering if they also dare tell a joke. Stevens waits until he has them all and he begins. . . .

But, like most classic jokes, Mather's joke defies print. You must hear it told, with asides, dialect, and tone of voice. Stevens tells this joke as a command performance each time he and his wife are asked to dinner.

He finishes to wild applause, looks at his audience, then says "Coffee and brandy," and walks from the room. He gives no one else a chance.

Keep a story in your memory bank; have a joke at your disposal. People who say "I never can remember jokes" are seldom remembered themselves.

What else can you do to acquire celebrity stories or to get glimpses of the Inside Life that you can trade off for help in areas where you need it? One thing you might do is to go to any cultural center or arts group in your town or city. Go to any symphony or museum or performing center or repertory company and ask if they need help. All of these places need volunteers. All of them have the support of committees. If you get involved, you will meet Van Cliburn at a reception after he performs; you will meet Helen Hayes after a play; you will meet Andy Warhol after an opening. Famous people out of their own towns are tickled to meet local fans. They are pleased to meet people who make them comfortable and treat them to hospitality they would never know merely viewing the local scene from their hotel.

There are many ways at local levels to connect yourself to the arts. Smart People Principles remain in force. You will never know the Inside Life if you stand patiently in line, on the outside, in the cold. You can raise money for the ballet or the symphony. You can work for museums or little theaters. Your social standing will be enhanced, and you will pick up stories of celebrities, stories you can trade for the services of others.

There are whole areas of the Inside Life that the average person can enter only with difficulty. I am talking about businesses that carry a mystique for the general public. But you can approach sports, show business, and the arts with Smart People techniques. I can't tell you about ballet and Nureyev, but I can tell you about publishing. Again, the key is finding someone who responds to you, finding that Smart Person.

## GETTING PUBLISHED

I receive, unsolicited, about fifty manuscripts a year: poetry, screenplays, short stories, novels. Beyond the manuscripts I receive I must get a hundred phone calls or letters from people who want to get published, who want to find an agent or an editor or a producer. Regardless of your idea, the merits of your project, or your talent, there is only *one* way to get yourself launched. Your work must have a champion, and that champion, someone who believes in you, must be in a position of leverage, a position to get you accepted.

I had an older cousin who was a writer and a Yale man. He always seemed to me to be posed with ascot, pipe, and very dry martini, straight up. He was my Maven in the world of creativity, and his guidance and clout got me access to agent and publisher. My cousin had written a best-seller, *The Interns*, at an early age. "My ambition," he explained once, "was to be published before twenty-three, which was when Scott Fitzgerald was first in print." He would never tire of telling me how he worked, when he worked, why he wrote. He would quote John O'Hara's introduction to the Modern Library edition of *Appointment in Samarra*: "I am putting this down because it answers the kind of questions young writers always ask and because I like to read this kind of stuff myself." Everyone who has ever wanted to write loves that kind of stuff.

Composing, sculpting, painting, writing are solitary pursuits. You have the silent piano, the block of marble, the blank canvas, the empty page. People who do not face the problems of creative isolation can never understand them. And people who do face them have pitifully few friends or acquaintances who have been through it or can offer help. My cousin Richard was a bachelor who had made his money early. People who make money early tend to think it will go on forever, and he used his to enjoy life. He dabbled at architecture, painting, designing. He built his own dream house in Peterborough, New Hampshire, a redwood-and-glass monument to the single life.

When I told him that I wanted to write, he invited me to spend a weekend. "Bring some stuff I can read," he said. "Short stuff. Nothing in the first person. All you kids begin by thinking you can do *Catcher in the Rye*. Writing in the first person only *seems* easy. But bring some stuff."

So I would drive up to Peterborough, and my cousin would let me play with his toys. I could shoot his pistols and fish in his stream. I could listen to his records and tapes. I could admire his paintings and sculptures and his thousands of books. But mostly he would talk to me about writing and writers, about people he had known, like Robert Penn Warren and William Styron, about the time he worked on *The New Yorker* and lost a Thurber story down an elevator shaft. And he had marvelous stories.

"You know the one about Thomas Hardy, don't you?" he asked. "Every day he wanted to begin by putting words on paper, priming the pump. But a writer isn't always productive. One day Hardy got up early, looked at his blank notebook, and neatly began a paragraph with the word 'The' in bold, big letters. Unable to write anything else, he got dressed, had breakfast, and went out for a stroll. He had lunch at an inn, met friends, spent the afternoon in conversation. One of the friends asked Hardy home for dinner, and the great man accepted, staying late over brandy and more talk. Arriving home in the young hours of the morning, Hardy sat at his desk and stared for a long time at his notebook, open to the page he had stared at when his day began, naked save for that one word, 'The.' After long moments he picked up his pen, furiously writing for a brief moment. After that word 'The,' Hardy wrote 'hell with it,' and went to bed."

Spending time with my cousin I was always drunk before the cocktail hour, before I ever tasted a drop. To talk with a writer when you want to write is like wanting all your life to play baseball and having Ted Williams hit you grounders. My first weekend in Peterborough I brought up two short stories, written in college, and the beginnings of a novel about young marriage, first jobs, and New York. "You watch the fire," he told me. "I'll go into the study and read your stuff."

My cousin at length came from his study and carefully mixed himself a martini made with Gordon's gin and Lillet. "The worst people to give you an opinion about writing," he said, "are friends and relatives. These people, if they love you, may praise regardless of what they really think. Or they may offer what they always call 'constructive criticism,' picking you apart under the guise of help. Showing something you have done to friends or relatives, even ones who ordinarily have opinions about nothing, makes them instant experts on literature, art, and the cinema. Subconsciously, either they want you to fail or they are suddenly reminded of their own shortcomings: the painting *they* never painted, the book *they* never wrote." He took a long gulp of his drink. Then another one to make sure.

"Despite what I said about relatives," he smiled, "I can be honest. I'm rich and I'm a pro. I'm going to tell you something a cousin of mine told *me*. He had written a best-selling nonfiction book and a long-running play on Broadway, *The Tender Trap*.

He said to me after reading my stuff, 'God help you, you're a writer.' That's what I'm telling you," he said. "God help you, you're a writer."

Those were the greatest words I had ever heard. I sat in a daze as my cousin took his drink into his bachelor kitchen and began cutting up fresh vegetables for his own special boeuf bourguignon.

My literary Maven had me as a guest for many weekends. He was always encouraging and always generous. When the moment was right, he got me an agent and handed me a piece of Corrasable Bond with two numbered items on it. Number one was "Stay in the mainstream." Number two: "Work at it." And so I left New Hampshire to try it on my own, without a monthly pat on the rump and sips from the Maven's Gordon's and Lillet.

Remembering everything that has been done for me, I can never say no to people who bring in their "stuff" for appraisal. Even when their writing is atrocious I encourage them to keep producing. Most budding novelists will give it up in one failed shot, discouraged by their prospects and the lonely time it takes. The writing that indicates talent and the willingness to persist I pass on to my editor. He can usually tell after several pages whether the writer has the knack or not. Very occasionally, I will pass on someone to my agent, not the people who have only the ability to be published, but the few who have the goods to be commercially successful, to make big money.

Most creative people really need agents for one big reason: to talk about them and their projects at lunches in New York and Los Angeles. You can't always be in these places humping for yourself. You live in Little Rock or Sarasota or Minneapolis or Portland, Maine, where they don't have agents and there's nothing on the other end of your mailed manuscripts but a secretary from Vassar eager to be an editor and to reject *you*. If your manuscript comes to a publisher from a reputable agent, at the very least it will receive a good, honest read. And you'll have a chance at a contract.

Literary agents get ten percent of everything, well worth it if they are making deals for you. And if they aren't, it's not costing you anything but heartache. It is an agent's business to know editors, producers, directors, and television packagers (people who "put together" series, specials, movies made for television). It is also their business to be creative in relation to their clients, matching your ideas and manuscripts with the person most likely to buy.

In the summer of 1970, Wall Street was on the verge of collapse, and purchasers for stocks were as easy to find as Sano cigarettes. Since I had nothing to do with my days, I thought I'd make an outline for a book. It turned out to be an outline that my agent loved. "The timing is dead right," she said. "I'm going to work up the salivary glands of a few publishers and ask seventy-five thousand dollars."

"You don't think that'll scare them away?" I asked. "It's a lot for an outline."

"We sell the sizzle," she said, in her British accent that always bristled with the authority of a brush set from Mason and Pearson on New Bond Street. "And if we settle for fifty thousand, you wouldn't be too upset."

"Hell, I'd kiss Truman Capote in Bonwit's window for twenty-five thousand," I said.

"Everything's relative," she said and rang off.

The next day she called near the close of market trading. "Are you sitting down?" she asked.

"I'll take the fifteen thou," I said.

"You know what they've offered?" she said.

"All right, I'm sitting down. I'll take the ten thousand."

"I've taken the liberty," my agent said, "of accepting their offer of seventy-five thousand dollars."

Since it is always much easier to talk about other people's money than your own, it is sometimes better to have others negotiate in your behalf. I can afford to be the nice guy as long as my agent is hard-nosed. And her fee of seventy-five hundred was well earned, over vodka gimlets and antipasto at lunch where she made the deal. The business of publishers, agents, producers, and editors is done at lunch, when zeroes tend to lose their meaning.

Should you have an agent? Yes. It increases the leverage in your behalf. An agent can split your project into a dozen parts, market them all, and collect fees from all. An agent can work magazine serializations, foreign rights (every country where you're published is a separate deal), and radio, television, and movie sales.

What's the best way to get an agent? You're not going to get one by writing a letter. Instead, *bug an author!* Bother him. If you don't know one, write to your favorite. Writers always respond to fans, because in their books they speak to empty spaces, hoping someone is there. Most people will respond to persistence. If you believe in yourself, the persistence is justified. And according to the Smart People formula of getting responses by making yourself a character, the edge is yours. Getting authors to write you is easy. Just quote from *their* books in your letters to them. They can't resist immortality, not to mention the idea that they may someday be in *Bartlett's Familiar Quotations.*

Of the hundreds of budding writers who have sent me poems, novels, and plays, only two have ever really broken through. And they are the only two who played on their personalities as well as on their writing skills. Several years ago a young man of high school age came to see me, referred by the Big Brother Organization which said, "We don't know how to deal with him. We think he's a genius and he wants to write. But he's difficult." I saw him. He went to high school in a big city where most of the kids lived in run-down triple-decker apartments and played games in black-top playgrounds with steel nets on the baskets and broken bubblers set into cement. He was sixteen and was wearing chino pants and a velvet Edwardian-cut jacket with a carnation in the lapel. In one eye he wore a monocle.

"I am the reincarnation of Oscar Wilde," he said to me. "And no one I know has my talent. I have with me an operetta. Just the libretto, which compares favorably with *Ruddigore* and *The Pirates of Penzance*. I am working on an epic poem concerning the history of the Victorian era. Do you happen to know the stars, director, and writer of *Dinner at Eight?* Or the names of all the novels of Anthony Trollope? I do." I hated the little bastard instantly. But as his story progressed — orphaned at six, bounced from state homes to distant relatives — he seemed a character out of Dickens. And you could forgive the arrogance, the bravado.

"I knew my father wasn't dead," he told me, mellowing. "Once when I was nine I was watching television. It was New Year's Eve and they were showing the crowds in Times Square. All of a sudden, a black Packard convertible was pushing its nose slowly through the thousands of celebrators. Standing up in the back seat of the automobile was my father. He was dressed in white tie and tails, very aristocratic. And he was pouring champagne on the heads of the crowd. They never noticed, and he was above it all. Disdainful, proud."

My precocious Victorian was named James Sullivan. He graduated from high school the following year and went to New York, insisting that people call him Adrian Trilby. He affected a cough and told anyone who asked that he was the male Camille, doomed to break hearts and die at a young age. He had talent, and his personal style was so unusual that I was able to get a major publisher to give him, at seventeen, a thousand-dollar advance on his potential. But Adrian Trilby, after the money was paid, disappeared. He has never communicated with the publisher or with me. But every New Year's Eve, if I'm somewhere where I can see Times Square on television, I watch to see if a black Packard convertible is nudging its nose through the crowd with my boy Adrian Trilby spilling champagne on the heads of the proletariat.

If this isn't a true success story, it does show the effectiveness of achieving results through the unorthodox. As an ordinary young aspiring writer, Mr. Sullivan/Trilby would have been politely rejected wherever he went and told, "Keep trying. It will come with age."

A positive attitude can carry its own strong lesson. The most successful person I know in terms of attitude is a Lamplighter for everyone. He works in one of the most difficult professions of all in which to succeed — film producing. My Lamplighter of the movies hasn't made it yet. But he will.

You've all read stories of the big Hollywood producers, the famous names of the past: Selznick, Mayer, Goldwyn, Harry Cohn. And the modern gossip magazines titillate us with news about the new breed of successful producer: Robert Evans, Richard Zanuck, Tony Bill. My Lamplighter in the world of Hollywood is a producer who has yet to produce a film. But his life is an inspiration to all who believe in themselves with the dogged, gutsy certainty that they will succeed. My Lamplighter is waiting in the side streets of Beverly Hills to burst onto the sound stages of Burbank and Century City and, when the shooting day is done, to buy a little white powder for the entire company. His name is Paul Lipsitz. He has integrity and soul.

"You're going to write a film for me," he said in my first conversation with him. "I can tell from looking at your picture on your book jacket that you're hungry, and you want to be a star. There's a book about money I've optioned, and I want you to adapt it. Never mind no experience, you got Lipsitz for a teacher."

"You're a great judge of character," I told him. "You've got yourself a deal."

He sent me a first-class ticket to Los Angeles, and the next week I was there to consult about my Hollywood career. That I had never heard of Paul Lipsitz the producer didn't worry me. There are hundreds of independent producers today, all hungry to option books (referred to as properties) and package them — that is, find stars, writers and financing — for feature-film production.

I expected a young man in baby-blue jeans with an Indian cotton wedding shirt open at the neck to expose a dark hairy chest, where a Coptic cross of gold would rest. The inscription on the back, I was sure, would read "Baja — September '73, Bambi." I knew he would drink white wine, if he drank at all, and would offer me a joint from a case of six that he had had rolled specially in the back of a record store in Westwood Village. But I saw no one answering that description in the TWA waiting room. Figuring that I'd be paged, I was about to sit down when a voice boomed at me.

"Hey, cutie, welcome to real life," and I was lifted off my feet and subjected to a bear hug and wet kisses on my cheek. When the man put me down he apologized. "My emotions hang out of me," he said. "When I feel good I let the world know. We couldn't wait for you to arrive. I am Paul Lipsitz."

He was jolly, like the Ghost of Christmas Past. He was a Zero Mostel with a head of black curly hair. He carried all of my bags out to his car which was not, as I envisioned, a Mercedes limo, but a leased Volkswagen, its clutch pedal held together with friction tape. It was midafternoon in February, about seventy degrees, and the sky was the clear, cloudless blue that only winter seems to bring to Los Angeles. With a love that is demonstrated only for an adopted country, Lipsitz chugged me around the city, from Marina del Rey, with its thousands of masts choking off the sight of water, to Malibu. Then on to Chinatown and Watts, and finally to the canyons of the stars.

"I used to drive a cab," he explained to me, "when I first came out from New York. People would say to me 'Drive me around and point out the sights.' I'd drive and talk nonstop and plenty of times I'd pause at a light, still talking, and the guy would have fallen asleep, sprawled across the back seat. This is a big town, man. It's the new world."

That night we went to dinner, to a Mexican restaurant where I had my introduction to another Southern California institution, a pitcher of margaritas. We had stopped at three supermarkets on

the way there, where Lipsitz introduced me to the Feeding the
Scriptwriter game. This consisted of cashing small checks, no
bigger than twenty dollars, on three different checking accounts.
"They never question twenty bucks," he explained. "And I have
IDs in all those stores entitling me to twenty, no questions asked.
Suddenly we got sixty dollars. Enough for several pitchers of
margaritas and enough tacos for you to do your writing in the
john for a week."

"Why three checking accounts?" I asked him.

"For the gifts, man," he said. "The piggybank, the basket of
fruit, the Rams tickets. The banks all give prizes for opening
accounts. You think this ain't the promised land?"

"We couldn't get away with that in Boston," I said.

He looked at me as if I were crazy. "This is L.A.," he said. "You
can't mess around with our freedom in L.A. No helmets on mo-
torcyclists; no restrictions on God. We didn't invent freedom in
L.A., but we sure as hell brought it up to date."

My producer has one ambition in life, one obsession, one
dream. He wants to make feature films. He had been trained in
the army, on Governor's Island with secure civil service employees who did not feel threatened by a talkative corporal from
Jersey City. He learned every aspect of filmmaking and the guts
of every machine from cameras and sound equipment to mixing
and editing equipment. And he had his religion, did Paul Lipsitz.
It was Subud, an import from the Middle East that changed his
life.

"The key to Subud is the Ladyhan," he told me, "the chanting
of the mantra that eventually summons up vibrations from way
down in your soul. The more you do this, the more your intuition
and personality change. You work from within in Subud. It's the
theory that man is so screwed up that outside influences have no
meaning to him. We become numb to the conspiracy of the
machine. Technology brutalizes us. We need to free ourselves
from its vibrations."

"What has all this to do with filmmaking?" I asked him.

"Well, it mainly has to do with life," he said. "But this business is the only one in the world where friendships mean nothing. As a matter of fact, all your friends are out to *kill* you in this business. Not to mention the strangers who are ready to cut your nuts off at the earliest possible moment. Let me tell you, Judaism isn't *strong* enough to allow you to survive in the film industry. Plus, the *big* bonus," he said, dipping into the enchiladas with frijoles refritos, "Subud allows you to change your name."

"You mean you changed your name to *Lipsitz?*"

"No," he said seriously. "You get to change your *first* name. I was Stephen and I was miserable. It was logical. Most people have always hated their first names. Suppose you never felt comfortable with John. Kids always teased you about the toilet. Suppose you always felt you were a Clyde type. And suppose you joined Subud. If you seriously wanted to become Clyde, you could write the Grand Master in Indonesia and say to him 'Grand Master, all my life I've been uncomfortable as John. I never felt I was John. In my soul I'm not a John. But I feel in my soul that I am indeed a Clyde.' Then you wait. And fast. And pray. If you're lucky and sincere, after seven months or so you get a letter from the Grand Master. The letter starts off 'Dear Clyde.'

"Of course," he went on, "in my case it started off 'Dear Paul,' after Paul of Tarsus. I cover all the bases. It's another thing that helps you in the film business. You can never have too many gods."

Later that night he nursed the Volkswagen up to the top of Benedict Canyon and pulled to a stop in a vacant lot between two half-million-dollar houses. "Look at this," he said. And we got out of the car. Stretching out in front of us, seeming to go on as endlessly as the sea, was Los Angeles. A great system of lights winking on and off like the biggest airport in the world. He led me to the edge, where the canyon dropped off to dirt and scrub. The stars and planets blinked a counterpoint to the grid of lights below.

" 'If the moon and stars should doubt,' " Lipsitz quoted,

" 'they'd immediately go out.' That's William Blake and that's what I believe in. I have this fantastic religious certainty in my own destiny, and I'm going to build a house up here, or in another canyon, and I'm going to make films that will stamp my style on the world. And there isn't a shitheel in the business who can keep me away from it."

This complicated man lived in a one-room apartment with a hot plate, one narrow couch, and a beautiful dark-haired actress who loved him and believed. Lipsitz optioned obscure books about gambling and money and about cowboys and hardhats and life against odds. He charmed authors into free options; he promised writers rewards on the come, pieces of the action *if* the films were made. He fasted for days on end, not just because fasting is a tenet of Subud, but because he had no money. Any money he *did* have he spent on writers and options. Lipsitz had credit cards from every conceivable organization. He'd applied to American Express, Husky Oil, BankAmericard, Hertz, Farmers' Market. He'd make up names of references, giving his own phone number.

"Hello," the credit bureau would say. "I'm inquiring about a Mr. Paul Lipsitz, film producer. He's given you as a reference, Mr. Holton-Jones."

Lipsitz would be there as Holton-Jones. "Mr. Paul Lipsitz," Lipsitz would say, "made several industrial films for my oil company, and as far as I'm concerned, I can't believe he's not the best risk in Southern California. Punctual. High integrity. And a money-maker."

"Thank you, Mr. Holton-Jones."

The cards would come through promptly, and Lipsitz would pay the minimum five to ten dollars a month on every card. "I've got three secrets to living life to the fullest," Lipsitz would tell me. "One, subjective reality is more important than objective reality. Two, keep your center; stay collected. Three, get *your* money fast; pay them *their* money very slowly."

And Lipsitz taught me how to write films, how to define character through action and not through dialogue. He taught me how to see.

Few novelists or writers of nonfiction ever successfully make the transition to movies. One big reason is that films are a collaborative effort. Someone always has an opinion about your script: the producer, the director, the star. A film is a movable feast and a constant frustration to the writer whose ego must be sublimated to everyone else's. This is a bitter pill for writers of books, who ordinarily labor alone, achieving triumph or disaster on their own hook, with an occasional cautious editorial suggestion or pat on the rump. A further reason why book writers never make a successful transition to film is that screenplay writing is another discipline entirely. Good dialogue does not make a good film. It is the action and the silences that are important.

Lipsitz would assign me a problem in the evening. "Write me a girl of Hollywood Park," he would say, "who wins the daily double but who so excites the crowd that she is trampled to death in the winner's circle." I would write the scenes in the morning at my motel (which Lipsitz paid for by personally servicing the owner's Mercedes 300 SL). Lipsitz would come over at noon with corned-beef sandwiches provided free by a delicatessen owner whom Lipsitz had promised a walk-on part in one of his films. We would sit by the pool with our feet in the heated water, while Paul critiqued my writing until late in the afternoon. Then we would leave the motel to see a film at the Directors' Guild, where Lipsitz was a member, his dues paid by an aunt in Mississippi who also believed. Then we would have dinner in one of any number of good, cheap restaurants from Malibu to Westwood where one credit card after another would be produced for the bill. At dinner, Paul would critique the film from the points of view of cameraman, producer, actors, actresses, editor, and director. Then he would give me my assignment for the next day. "You're a woman in love with the Prince of Wales and you know he's coming to visit your local museum. You also know there is a robbery scheduled at the museum at the same time and the Prince may be in danger."

After dinner he would ride me around and show me the Los Angeles that I should learn to love. He had been in California for seven years and he still treated the city as if it were a new playroom he had had installed in his house. He would walk me down Hollywood Boulevard, pointing out the stars' names set in the sidewalk. He would drive me by the old studios of the thirties and forties. He would give a better tour of Brentwood and Bel Air and Beverly Hills than any organized bus company could ever provide. And through it all he talked only of films and what could be possible with the right scripts.

One night he took me to the cemetery in back of the Avco Cinema on Wilshire in Westwood. He led me to a corridor of cinder block construction where plaques marked the tombs of people set into the wall, row on row like wall ovens. He stopped and pointed at one for me to notice. There was a plastic cone stuck into a metal ring, above the plaque marking the occupant. Several wilted flowers, dried and dead, hung from the cone, a cheap vase in an impersonal wall of the dead. The plaque marked the burial spot of Marilyn Monroe. The flowers were sent daily by Joe DiMaggio. But it was eleven at night and the flowers had died.

We left the graveyard and walked around the corner. The UCLA kids were lined up for a block waiting to get into the late show of *The Lords of Flatbush*. Lipsitz had been quiet for a long time. He stared at the kids in line.

"What's real for them," he said, "is that both the Fonz and Sylvester Stallone are in *Lords of Flatbush*. What's real for them is not what's in Marilyn's cinder block but what's painted on the screen. And I'm gonna give it to them."

After our nights out, Lipsitz would drop me at my motel and give me a can of Coors from a six-pack he kept in his trunk. "A nightcap," he would say. "Writers can't work without their nightcap." That was the Lipsitz crash course in film writing from my Lamplighter.

After he dropped me off he would drive to the corner of California Street and Sepulveda Boulevard and pick up two hundred *Wall Street Journals* from a news dealer and deliver them between midnight and four in the morning to subscribers in Bel Air. Lipsitz did this for survival money, for ninety dollars a week. Up the canyons of Bel Air, *Wall Street Journals* for Jerry Lewis and Frank Sinatra and Ringo Starr and Kirk Kerkorian. When it rained, each *Journal* had to be individually packed in a plastic bag, making the job twice as long.

Paul Lipsitz, formerly Stephen Lipsitz, maneuvers around midnight walkers, stray cats, occasional coyotes from the bush of the canyons. He falls asleep at the wheel, narrowly missing trees, phone poles, Japanese bridges that cross streams to million-dollar fairy-tale castles. He delivers *Wall Street Journals,* laying wet printed capitalism through the iron gates of the rock musicians, the skin-magazine publishers, and the plastic surgeons of Bel Air. And while he does it, he fashions films in his mind, rolling down both front windows of the VW so that the wind will keep him awake.

At home, whenever I feel that goals are impossible or that the demands of others are keeping me from accomplishing anything, I call Lipsitz.

"What are you doing?" I ask him.

"Still pushing the peanut," he says.

"Any money in the kick this week?"

"This week I'm eating homemade yogurt. I laid out a thousand I didn't have to option a book about the old traveling carnivals. Most of the check is no good."

"How can you keep paying out money for properties and scripts and not have food for yourself?"

"A man's gotta take a stand. I'd rather not eat if I can make films. And remember, 'You never know what is enough unless you know what is more than enough.' That's William Blake again. We keep coming back to him."

It may be in show business, it may be in the League of Women Voters, it may be in the emergency room of a hospital. But the Smart People concept of a better life has to include someone who never quits and whose belief in what he does lifts him above the petty complaints of most of us. "If the sun and moon should doubt, they'd immediately go out."

# 4 SEXUAL SMARTS

Sex is different from money. This chapter will not tell you how to seduce or how to increase potency or how to achieve the perfect orgasm. It is a chapter that will assist you to get honest information that may help. Not information from manuals or from myth, but from other people.

Money and sex and good health. That's the order of subjects that sell the most books, that create the most interest, that move the most merchandise. For thousands of years there have been sex manuals, books that preach technique and teach positions. We are obsessed by sex. But our true obsessions remain mostly secret. Only our reading lamps know what we are absorbing.

What men display in public is locker-room talk, tales of their bravado, their successful exploits. For most of us, these exploits exist only in our imagination. We blow smoke at each other concerning our sexuality and the promiscuity of others. Locker-room talk goes on while we nurse our private anxieties.

Women, on the other hand, do not flaunt their own tall tales about sex. They read the books and the manuals and wonder privately about themselves. Along with the techniques and attitudes we read about, we are surrounded from birth by myth and misinformation. Almost from birth we're told that we'll be sexier if we use the right soaps, deodorants, cigarettes, automobiles. Advertising and the media have continually preached a sexuality available to all, which, in truth, is available to almost none of us. And these myths from childhood pursue us to maturity: "The sexual organs of blacks are larger than other peoples'; masturbation makes you go blind; oriental vaginas are horizontal; Mrs. Simpson nabbed the king with techniques she learned in the Far East." With all this myth and misinformation, how do Smart People deal with sex?

My Smart People questionnaire has elicited responses from all over the world, from hundreds of people, famous and obscure. The answers have been elaborate or careful or brilliant. But only one question has elicited dishonest replies in almost every instance. The question is, "Where does sex rank among the important things in your life—high or low on a scale of ten?" The answers in *all* cases have been either flip or exaggerated. Many of the respondents answered, "Fifteen on a scale of ten." You *cannot* get truth out of questionnaires. You need that human contact. You need people to talk with and listen to, in order to get at the truth as it applies to you. How will you know when you're getting good information? Sex is such a personal matter, you have to keep probing for the Smart People you trust.

"Three men who spoke with me recently," Mather Stevens told me, "all had problems with premature ejaculation. I told them all to think about Van Gogh paintings — or baseball or fishing — during intercourse. That same week, *I* thought about Van Gogh during intercourse and had a premature ejaculation. I made sure I avoided those three men for months."

You must trust your judgment in sexual matters and in the recruitment of your Smart People. Your characters will certainly vary in type from mine, as will your experiences. My stories can be used only as examples; I am giving no instruction here. The one thing to bear in mind is the infinite variety of approaches. There is no blueprint for sexual happiness. I can't dictate your tastes. But I can show you an assortment of solutions as revealed by my Smart People.

"Sex is mostly attitude," Mather Stevens always tells me. "Divorce cases over a twenty-year law career have told me more about the subject than most therapists ever hear. I am an expert on the subject, and I have to tell you that sex is ninety-nine percent mental.

"When I was young," he continued, "we all talked about sex constantly. But nobody ever did anything about it. That is, we didn't *really* do anything about it. Our fantasies were vivid. But most of them were wrong. But in high school, touching second base *outside* the sweater was nirvana. Now first base was kissing; second base was breast touching; third base, petting below the waist; and a home run, was, obviously, going all the way. There were more explicit terms like 'bare tit' and 'hand job.' But 'around the bases' was more genteel. If heterosexual sex was our goal and our obsession, homosexual love was considered a crime. 'Homo,' 'fag,' 'queer,' were dirty words, repellent. There's a story I recall about adolescent sex and the attitudes of the middle class of the time.

"One time, on Christmas vacation from school," Stevens continued, "I was invited to New York to stay with a classmate named Arthur. His parents were social, and much too busy for their prep-school kid. New York during vacations meant parties, dances, dates to go down to the Village, jazz at Eddie Condon's, getting drunk on screwdrivers, and hanging around the Latin Quarter trying to pick up a chorus girl. All very smooth, full of big ideas. Arthur's parents had an apartment loaded with guests with no weekend room for schoolboys. They were at 25 East End Avenue then. So guess what? They put us up at Cole Porter's apartment, in the same building. Cole was away for the holidays, and my buddy's parents, being good friends, had been given a key in Cole's absence. They would watch the place, water the plants, you know. I talk about Cole Porter as if I knew him, which I didn't. But when you're sixteen and privileged, you feel, or are made to feel, that staying in Cole Porter's apartment for the weekend is all part of the game. The apartment was luxurious, but I expected luxury. My friends were rich, and I figured that I would be also. A friend of Porter's was also staying there in his absence, a friend who was tall, slim, with soft wavy hair and a way of collapsing into furniture like a giant mantis. He seemed bored and most annoyed at having two prep-school boys for weekend roommates. We called him Blanche.

"Friday night we went to a dance, stag. Afterward we took two girls from Chapin to the Hickory House to hear Ahmad Jamal at the piano. My friend Arthur signed the tab, and one of the girls got sick in the cab all over me while Arthur laughed and the other girl kept saying, 'She never throws up from rye and ginger. Never!'

"The cabby screamed at us and dumped us near the Waldorf, leaving rubber as he roared off up Park Avenue. The Chapin girls, calling us rude, crude, and socially unacceptable, got their own cab home, leaving us helplessly giggling in front of the hotel. Drunk, and knowing that it was much too late to be cool, Arthur and I continued our hysterical laughing jag as we walked and ran and hooted our way back to East End Avenue.

"What do you do when you're sixteen, wearing black tie, drunk at three in the morning, and in possession of a grand apartment in New York? First you have a beer you definitely don't need, and then you thumb through phonebooks thinking of girls you can call. Finally, you strew clothing all over the apartment, fall into your bed, force the whirlies to go away, and pass out. Which we did. But I had the strangest dream that night. I dreamed I was asleep and that someone crept into the room and began masturbating me. It was so vivid that when I awoke, around noon the next day, I told Arthur about my dream.'

" 'Jesus Christ,' he said, 'I had the same dream.'

"We both ran around the apartment looking for Blanche, but he was nowhere to be found. All that day we plotted revenge, convinced that he had been the flogging night visitor. Late that afternoon, Blanche came back.

" 'Beautiful day, boys,' he smiled at us. 'I trust you had a lustrous time last night.'

"He swept on into his bedroom and shut the door. We heard him in the shower shortly afterward, singing 'Strange, Dear, But True, Dear, When I'm Close to You, Dear,' from *Kiss Me Kate*.

"Arthur and I took ourselves to P. J. Clarke's for hamburgers and planter's punches, and we plotted. That night, after Blanche dressed for dinner and went out, we rigged booby traps all over the apartment: full water glasses on chairs, waste baskets upturned, a silver dinner bell hooked to a doorknob. And everything placed in the path of anyone coming to us as a strange succubus.

" 'I'm gonna kill Blanche,' Arthur said.

" 'He'll never prey on unsuspecting boys again,' I said.

"We finally went to sleep, full of more anticipation than on any childhood Christmas Eve. And, before turning in, we tied a long string from Arthur's big toe to mine. If either of us was being violated, the other would be awakened and come to the rescue. We rejected the idea of tying the string around any other parts of the body. But we did think about it.

"Out of the deep pit of dreamland I could feel something lightly tugging on my toe. Slowly I awakened. The room was black, the middle of the night. Then a jerk of the toe and a steady pressure trying to pull me out of bed. I jumped up, tripped, and sprawled on the floor. Arthur turned on the bedside lamp, shining it in my eyes. He had dragged me out of bed. 'I couldn't sleep,' he said, 'so why should you?' I got up, broke the string that tied our toes, untipped the booby traps, turned off the light, and lay there unable to sleep. Thoroughly annoyed now, and listening to Arthur snore, I left the bedroom and wandered around the apartment. Blanche was gone, producing other dreams elsewhere. I looked at Cole Porter's books and his inscribed photographs on the wall. I played a quiet 'Chopsticks' on his piano. I can remember feeling sorry for Blanche and laughing to myself about the incident. So many things about sex are funny. I decided that then, and nothing since has ever changed my mind. I also decided at that time that probably any sex at all was better than none."

Mather Stevens emphasizes attitude, and the feeling that sex is fun. Everything in this book involves information you learn from other people. But sex is one area where most people *don't* talk. Your only help is to find people who will. Once you do, your job will be to recognize the people who are being honest.

Being in a psychological business myself, where I hear as many stories about people's lives as I do about people's money, I doubt the validity of surveys conducted by written questionnaire. The impersonal quality of paper, blank except for questions and spaces for responses, tends to make the respondent too anxious to make himself look good. Questions about sex produce dishonest replies. I have had hundreds of returned questionnaires from my Smart People and can draw only one conclusion from all of these thoughtful, interesting, and provocative replies: *Smart People do not put their feelings about sex down on paper.* They do not leave them lying around, recorded in their own hand. But they *will* talk about them in person. Enough so that perhaps my sexually Smart People can help you.

Maxwell Fine is my Lamplighter in the area of sexual activity and the pursuit of physical pleasure. He is a good man, and an unusual one in that his life appears to be centered on calling attention to himself. Yet there is no one I know more interested in other people. Because Max is interested in others, he takes the lead in relationships by talking about himself. One hint in discovering honesty in discussions of sex I learned from Max Fine. He is not afraid to discuss his failures; he is not afraid to be self-deprecating.

I met Max Fine on a shuttle flight to New York. He was sitting next to me reading *Clea*, the last volume of Lawrence Durrell's *Alexandria Quartet*. After several minutes in flight he slapped the book shut and looked at me. "*The Alexandria Quartet,* in my

opinion," he said, "is the finest modern fictional treatment of love.
*Read* it. It may change your life."

"I've read it," I said.

"You're not getting off that easy," he said. "What are the interesting places you can recommend in New York? Bars, restaurants, galleries, that sort of thing? I always ask strangers when I go to a new city, or to someplace I haven't been in a while."

Max Fine was going to a meeting of the New York League for Sexual Freedom, a dinner dance in the Empire Hotel.

"It's just like a cost accountants' convention," he told me. "Boring, like any gathering or association can be boring. I go hoping to be surprised. But I'm never surprised. Sometimes the best way to further a cause is through your own individual efforts, not through groups. Everyone wants to huddle together; I want to glorify self."

He had a sip of a vodka martini which he had brought along in a flask because no drinks are served on the shuttle. Then he took several pills. "B-1 multivitamins," he explained, "to counteract the alcohol.

"There are several keys to sexual success," he told me. "Be prepared to try anything and never be discouraged. I work to satisfy the woman, because in satisfying her I get the greatest ego relief and the greatest pleasure. Putting off pleasure, you know, is the ultimate release. I'll tell you a story about not being discouraged, then one about trying everything.

"At the Sexual Freedom League," he went on, "there are three favorite fantasies, at least for the male members." He laughed. "That was a little joke. But these were the leading fantasies, according to a poll. The first was to have interracial sex — you know, the *Mandingo* routine. The second favorite was to have someone perform fellatio on you while you were going through a tollbooth on the New York State Thruway. The last fantasy was to roger a mother and daughter — whether on the same or consecutive nights, it didn't matter.

"Well, I was on Martha's Vineyard last year on vacation for

two weeks. There is a nude beach on the Vineyard. Unfortunately, it's right next to a straight beach. A lot of creeps go to the nude beach to stand on the border waving their 'john thomases' at the old ladies and children in bathing suits on the other side. I'm an old nude bather. I've been bathing nude for years, for the health aspects. But I must admit I'm at *this* particular place to make a connection. I'm one of the few people on the nude beach with an all-over tan, so even without clothes I'm distinctive. I have no mark of obscenity, no band of white.

"Suddenly I notice a fantasy couple, a lovely mother and daughter. The daughter has to be around eighteen, the mother pushing forty from the right side. Up I go onto my hands and walk right up to their blanket.

"One of my secrets with women," Max went on, "is that I treat them romantically, from the first moment. I believe in courtly love. This means that you recite poetry. Women go crazy for poetry.

"Anyway, I walk up to the blanket on my hands, flip over on to my feet, and say 'She did not die from lack of love, as everyone supposes. The thing that really killed her was simply a lack of roses.' They were both amused. They sat up and smiled at me. They made no attempt to cover up. They sat up tall with their legs spread apart, curious and unashamed. I mention that because being unashamed is unusual in the Eastern part of the United States, even among nudists.

"'Do you mind if I sit down?' I asked them. They shrugged. But kept smiling. So I squatted down on the sand, introduced myself, and told them how much I admired parents who spent time with their children and vice versa. 'It's amazing,' I told the daughter, 'how like your mother you look. And how young your mother is. What did you do, have your child at fifteen?'

"The daughter blinked big hazel eyes at me and said, 'Would you let us cover you with sand? That's such fun. I haven't done that in years.' She asked me again, 'Could we cover you?'

"'I think the man wants to recite more poetry to us, darling,' the mother said. 'He's just getting warmed up.' The mother was delicious, ripe, attractive, with a wise look about her, a look saying to me that evening was just around the corner. I jumped at the chance to be included in their games. 'I haven't been buried in sand in years,' I said. 'I'd love to have you bury me. What shall we do, dig a hole and put me in to my neck?'

" 'Oh, no,' said the daughter, innocent as a child. 'Let's make it real fun. You lie on your back and let us cover you creatively. A sand sculpture.'

"I needed no more encouragement. I lay down immediately, submissive, arms folded in back of my head. The sky was unclouded and brilliantly blue. The sun was wonderful on me, especially on the parts where fools are covered with bathing suits.

"Daughter and mother giggled at each other and produced from a large picnic basket two small shovels, the kind used by children at beaches. They began covering my feet, my toes, my legs. They were very careful to avoid my 'john thomas,' most of which lay on its side getting tanned. 'Higgamus, hoggamus,' I chanted, 'woman's monogamous. Hoggamus, higgamus, man is polygamous.'

"While I sang songs and anticipated my reward, mother and daughter tantalized me with hot sand. Daughter made a funnel with her hands and began slowly pouring the tiny crystals over my sun-drenched organ. Having a mind of its own, it began to rise, seeking the heavens as it worshipped space. Mother joined daughter, and both began talking to me, tantalizing, enflaming.

" 'You like freedom,' the mother said. 'Your phallus,' she said, 'is straining to be free.'

" 'Can we take it home and play with it always?' the daughter pleaded.

"By now I'm completely covered with sand, except for my rampant erection which they are still teasing with dribbles of sand. Naturally, I'm going wild, and cannot believe my good fortune.

" 'You're ready then?' asked the mother.

" 'You're so ready?' asked the daughter.

" 'Oh God, fire at will,' I said, 'ready' being the understatement of the year.

"Daughter had disappeared from my sight for a moment, my head being constricted in its turning ability by walls of sand built around it. Mother leaned down very close to my ear and whispered once more, 'Ready?'

" 'Oh, *yes*,' I whispered back. Then the sudden shock of cold water poured all over my straining organ made me scream in surprise.

" 'Then go stick it in the sand, you lecherous old fart,' yelled the daughter. And peals of laughter followed as my insulted friend drooped back down to my body, all covered with soggy mudpack.

"It wouldn't have been so bad if we had not attracted an audience for the last fifteen minutes of my ordeal. I shook myself like a spaniel and struggled to my feet. Mother and daughter stood at the edge of the small crowd, watching my discomfort. They were holding hands in a very unfamilylike way.

" 'We're not mother and daughter, as you may now suspect,' the older woman said, 'and we were having a perfectly lovely time before you intruded.'

"I started to walk away, heading for the ocean where I could hide. The woman spoke at my back. 'My father constantly told me to remember two things in life,' she said. 'Remember that things are not always what they seem. And never throw a changeup to a lousy hitter.'

"I can remember swimming a long way out to sea," Max said, "then coming back, putting on my bathing suit, and leaving the beach.

"The next day," he went on, "I was back on the sand, giving the game my best shot once more. I try never to be discouraged in anything I do, particularly in my pursuit of sex."

When Maxwell introduced his sexual exploits with the story of a defeat, he kept me interested. I trusted his honesty enough to use him over the years as a sounding board and a source of information.

"The secret to sexual success," Maxwell says, "is this: You give pleasure to others and you get it yourself. But you know what makes me a sexual Lamplighter? I'm a widower. And a widower is entitled to *variety*. A widow also is entitled to variety. We're the survivors.

"There may be a woman in Kansas City happily married for thirty years who may be the greatest piece of ass in America. But like when a tree falls in the empty forest, who knows? Except her husband. *Maybe*. But what's he got to compare? *I* know because I'm not a kid. I'm fifty-four. And I can try 'em all or listen to 'em all. Men, women, teenagers, they all talk to me. *Because I am interested in people,* and I have *made* myself a curiosity."

Maxwell gets up in the morning and does yoga for fifteen minutes. Then he has strawberry yogurt sprinkled with natural bran and a cup of cappucino. He loads his folding twelve-speed bicycle onto the roof rack of his red Porsche and drives to work, where he is a principal in an advertising agency specializing in technical accounts. At lunchtime he puts bicycle clips around his pantlegs and pedals three miles to the Polar Bear Club, a section of private beach where old-timers, physical-fitness enthusiasts, and the unemployed sunbathe nude and swim in the ocean most days in the year. Max Fine is on the board of directors of the Polar Bear Club, and every New Year's Day he gets his picture in the papers and on television. He is shown plunging into the freezing waters of the harbor and frolicking in the snow with half a hundred other Polar Bears. "You know why I go swimming on New Year's Day?" he asks. "Of course, it's therapeutic, one of the best things you can do for circulation. But it also gives me an erection for twenty-four hours. I choose well my companions the first week in January every year. They never forget it; *I* never forget it."

"If it works that well," I asked him, "why not swim every week in the winter?"

"You give people caviar every night, pretty soon they can't stand the sight of caviar.

"But above all," he says, "remember that sex is mainly a condition of the head. *Getting there* is most of the fun. The chase is practically everything. Because you are pursuing pleasure, not exercise."

Maxwell Fine wears a handlebar mustache, and he uses it to advertise his availability. Meeting a new woman he is apt to say, "See how the ends of the mustache curl up? Beautiful lady, before I met you they were drooping sadly down. You make everything about me perk up." Then, while outrage or embarrassment sets in, he quickly kisses her hand. "Believe me, even Bella Abzug likes to have her hand kissed," he says.

Our dialogues continue, as yours should continue with the Smart People whom you find. These Smart People should *not* be people who are seeing you professionally. Your sexually Smart People should share ideas with you, as you may share with them. The key is an openness and honesty that emphasize how large a part the head, and not the body, plays in successful sexual encounter.

"You wanna know my view of life?" Maxwell asked me. We were sitting in his living room surrounded by walls loaded with contemporary art and framed photographs by Marie Cosindas. There was a bowl from Siena on a coffee table, full of lemons and limes. He plucked a lime from the bowl and sliced it in half with a small paring knife. Maxwell sucked on the lime, then he chewed the pulp, swallowing all of the fruit. "Life is like that lime," he said. "There are pips and juice and skin and pulp. You have to sample all of it, chew it, taste it, swallow it. And interaction with people is the key. Isolate yourself and you are lost. Lost is my definition of hell — the Irvington Rooms for Men. A boardinghouse. Alone. Where the accommodations cost two dollars a night, with a bar of soap and a towel."

"What are some of your secrets for achieving sexual happiness?" I asked him. "How do you develop women's interest in you? And what keeps that interest going?"

"First and most important," Maxwell said, "I express interest in *them*. And I ask their opinions about art, film, music, and literature. I never talk about politics or race relations or busing school kids. Those conversations do not lead to bed. I recite poetry, Sir Philip Sidney, Lovelace:

> Tell me not, Sweet, I am unkind,
> That from the nunnery
> Of thy chaste breast and quiet mind
> To war and arms I fly.
>
> True, a new mistress now I chase,
> The first foe in the field;
> And with a stronger faith embrace
> A sword, a horse, a shield.
>
> Yet this inconstancy is such
> As thou too shalt adore;
> I could not love thee, Dear, so much,
> Loved I not Honor more.

"I also use Bobbie Burns:

> O, my luve's like a red, red rose
> That's newly sprung in June;
> O, my luve's like the melodie
> That's sweetly played in tune.

"I sing songs in foreign languages," Max said. "'Autumn Leaves' in French is particularly effective. Also, 'Lili Marlene' in German. I talk about Freud's pleasure principle and I use one-liners like 'The only reason to put a woman on a pedestal is to look at her thighs!' No one is ever offended because I'm always flattering the woman I'm with. They believe, because of poetry and songs, that I *am* putting them on a pedestal."

"Another interest of mine is words and names," he says. "For instance, August Schoenberg was the Rothschild man in New York. His name meant 'beautiful mountain' in German, and he changed it to Belmont. Sounds more American, but it still means beautiful mountain, only this time in French. So August Belmont was one of our biggest financiers. Belmont Park, the racetrack, is named after him.

"Women love to hear about their names, where they came from, what they mean. I ask women their maiden name and then tell them its origin. You know Filene's, the famous Boston department store? It was founded by a man named Katz. He didn't like Katz for his store name. *So*, what is the French adjective for cat? "Féline." He switched two letters and called the store Filene's. And because of that no one has ever heard of Katz's Basement. Right?"

Max looked at his watch and stood up. "You know I go out socially a great deal. You don't find sexual adventures by waiting for the phone to ring. Luck favors the prepared mind. And while you're at it, don't forget to try anything. I have rubbed cocaine on the end of my penis and inside the vagina lips. I have used vibrators and cock rings and French ticklers. All with a view to satisfaction and experiment. If I could leave commandments behind for my children (if I had children), I would tell them these things: One, never look back, they may be catching up (a paraphrase of Satchel Paige). Two, exercise daily and enjoy. Three, freedom is necessity understood. Four, eschew obfuscation."

Maxwell Fine, my sexual Lamplighter, then stood on his hands and left the room, presumably to dress for dinner. Next to the bowl of lemons and limes on his coffee table lay an open copy of Proust's *The Past Recaptured*. Maxwell had underlined in purple ink several lines: "There is not a woman in the world the posses-

sion of whom is as precious as that of the truth which she reveals
to us by causing us to suffer."

I have a private Summa in matters of sex. He is a psychiatrist
by profession, an eminent psychiatrist whose original specialty
was neurology. We have lunch together once a month in the
Italian district of my city, a section my private Summa prefers
because he can wander after dining, savoring the sounds and
smells and tastes of Europe. And he can buy the homemade pasta
with which he breaks his perpetual diet.

We met at a cocktail party several years ago, in a time when
everyone was playing the stock market. "Dr. MacDonald Stone,"
we were introduced, "meet John Spooner. John's a hot stockbroker." Then my hostess warned me, "Careful, Mac Stone's a
shrink. He can have you committed."

"I don't think I want to meet a hot broker," the doctor said.
"From what I've seen, the temperature of hot brokers can go in
only one direction."

"Cold," I said. "Bite your tongue."

"You know the origin of the expression 'bite your tongue'?" Dr.
Stone asked. He proceeded to tell me that, in Saxon England, if
someone mentioned an event everyone dreaded — "You better
lay aside some sharp rocks for when the Normans invade" — the
peasants believed that if you bit your tongue immediately the
words would be called back and the event forestalled.

I told him my experiences in investing money for psychiatrists,
and how much emotional factors influence movements in the
stock market.

MacDonald Stone was utterly charming in the way older people can be when they listen to what you say. He was in his late
sixties, with pepper-and-salt hair looking like an oat field that had
been cut with a sickle by a demented farmhand. He believed in
exercise — for other people only. "I read and I write," he told me.
"And I think about what I've learned during the years. Exercise

takes time away from the books I may never read before I die."

"Ah," I said, "but if you exercise you may live longer and be able to read even more books."

"If your genes," he said, "and your past dictate that you will be a fat person or that you are prone to coronary heart disease or that you will be bald by thirty, then diet or jogging or rubbing gelatin on your head won't help. Americans are the greatest suckers in the history of civilization for believing that they can help themselves or help others or help the world. 'Every day in every way,' Norman Vincent Peale, Dr. Moon, *I'm Okay, You're Okay*, Canadian Air Force exercises, et cetera, et cetera. In our delusion, we try to change the genes and we lose the ability to be at peace. And what I mean by peace in our society is really privacy. Privacy is what we most desperately need and find most difficult to obtain."

I asked him several questions about his education, places he had lived, if he had known Freud.

"Freud was a genius, no doubt," said Dr. Stone. "But he couldn't know about America in the nineteen-seventies. We need a new language of the mind. Sex is a problem for ninety-nine percent of the married people I see professionally."

Since I had done something few people did, which was to ask him about his past, he invited me to lunch in the Italian district the next week.

How do you recognize honesty when you're recruiting people who deal with personal matters? Certainly you have to trust your own instincts. In the case of Mac Stone, I knew he was different. He has never suggested, in our years of friendship, that I become a patient. And I have never suggested that he become a client.

We have been lunching together for almost five years, meeting once a month over antipasto or mussels, veal, and a pasta of the doctor's choice. He knows that it's free therapy for me, and I enjoy the role of eternal son. We watch old men play bocce, talking to each other in the dialects of Sicily and Naples. I call our conversations the Piccata Dialogues, after the doctor's favorite entree. Twice a month I get lessons in behavior patterns from my private Summa, who has taught at Harvard Medical School, served at the Nuremberg trials in 1945, and wears a red velvet smoking jacket while seeing patients. The smoking jacket, lined with the MacDonald tartan, was sent to him by a niece of Neville Chamberlain.

The doctor is writing a book about the behavior he has observed during his thirty-five years of practice. He has had a continuing interest in my studies of how emotions affect investment decisions. "You scratch my back, Dr. Mac; I'll scratch yours," I told him, and he patiently answers my questions about society, love, marriage, and sex.

"Successful lovemaking can take many forms," he told me. "But successful sexual adjustment in marriage has two keys: tenderness and patience. Sex is ninety-nine percent in the head. It is important for any patient of mine, indeed for all people, to feel good about himself or herself. You know that every male ejaculation produces about two hundred thousand sperm. And that it fertilizes only *one* or possibly *two* eggs produced by the female. What are the odds that you're going to be a great left-handed pitcher or a soprano at the Met? or a Mongoloid? *One* sperm out of two hundred thousand makes it. And nature seals off that egg. You have to feel very depressed at this realization. *Or* you have to feel unique. Unique is how you *should* feel, and it is my job to make people accept this. You are a *miracle*."

"The major problem as I see it," Dr. Stone went on, "is that the civilized order of things has made us inhibited. Society demands remarriage, for instance. Samuel Johnson said that marrying a second time is 'the triumph of hope over experience.' George Bernard Shaw added that 'a man who marries a second wife didn't deserve to lose the first one.' Never forget that order has been imposed on us artificially. The more order, the more we get away from basic primitive things. But we *do* marry and procreate and stack inhibition on top of inhibition.

"A man was brought to me once by the police," Dr. Stone said.

"He was very respectable, a distinguished older lawyer. He had been picked up after complaints from women on the most fashionable shopping street in town. The elderly lawyer had taken a Kotex napkin, painted it with iodine, and was shoving it into the faces of well-dressed matrons. The policeman told me the story. 'We thought you'd want a look at him, Doc. See if you can get him put away. Looks like he's unraveled his spool.'

" 'Take him to a hospital,' I told the officer. 'He doesn't need a psychiatrist. He has a brain tumor.' "

"The diagnosis proved correct," Dr. Stone said. "We have reached a point in our history where only brain tumors can cause us to revert to primitive behavior."

Always our lunch discussions at some point turned to sex. Dr. Stone quoted Havelock Ellis to me. "The omnipresent process of sex, as it is woven into the whole texture of our man's or woman's body, is the pattern of all the process of our life."


## THE CHILDHOOD REACTION

It was Dr. Stone who turned me on to the Childhood Reaction, one of my methods for making people respond to me. This process involves briefly questioning new acquaintances about their past. The technique flatters people and binds them to you.

"Sex is the expression of the total person," Dr. Stone told me. "If a person is chronically unhappy, he rejects sex. To get at problems in therapy, or in life, one must get at the earlier life of the person. All solutions become apparent in the probing of early life. I believe that the most important training in medicine is getting a good history. But people don't give a history easily. It takes time. My approach to therapy is that attitudes can be modified. I want to effect changes in your perception. I want you to realize that growth in life occurs when you accept changes in your perception. Certainly what you say now may not be valid for you at age sixty. As to sexual fulfillment, your attitude should be that tenderness and compassion are the keys to this over the long haul.

"Remember also that nothing is perfect except in frozen moments; there is no coming to consciousness without pain. I have come to learn that platitudes depend upon who is mouthing them. We reject our friends' telling us that we had better lose weight for our own good. But the doctor who tells us that we have to take off fifteen pounds because there is too much pressure on our heart sends us into fearful reaction. There is no part of life that is more satisfying than learning lessons at the feet of the experienced."

When Dr. Stone served as a psychiatrist at the Nuremberg trials, he appreciated the sweetness of life for the first time, brushing as he did so close to the core of evil. "Teach sweetness to your mate," he told me. "Touch her in many ways. Teach her to touch you. Every relationship needs quiet, private moments. Schedule them if you have to. But have them."

One day after lunch we walked from our little restaurant to where the old Italian men gathered to play bocce and smoke their pipes. Dr. Stone and I sat on a bench next to a small withered man wearing a felt hat left over from the 1930s. He seemed to be quietly sobbing.

"Are you all right?" Dr. Stone asked.

The man looked at us with sad eyes. "My wife died ten years ago today," he said in speech still thick with the accents of Naples. "I come to places where we were happy together, and after a little while I feel better. It is not a bad thing to cry and remember."

We got up and walked quietly back toward the tall office buildings where we made our weekday homes.

"Remember," Dr. Stone told me before we parted, "something I learned from Karen Horney thirty years ago: 'Fortunately, analysis is not the only way to resolve inner conflicts. Life itself remains a very effective therapist.' "

Smart People, who are sensitive to life and its experiences, can often help you more than any professional, whose only credentials hang framed on an office wall.

Most people who read this book are not aggressive. Most people in *life* are not aggressive. They are not pushy or even secure enough to insist upon service, to insist upon being noticed. That's why they need Smart People. Because they are not going to become aggressive, no matter what they read, no matter who bullies them. *Smart People* is concerned with getting the edge, with getting others to respond to you without the court of last resort, which is to become a pushy, aggressive son of a bitch yourself.

My sexual Roughrider is someone in the minority, someone most of us can never become. I use him as a Roughrider because I am always amazed at his stories. And at the results achieved by someone whose philosophy involves total aggression. His credo is, "I may get my face slapped a lot. But I get laid a lot, too."

Buzzy Graham is my Roughrider for whom the birth-control pill represented a major setback.

"Hey," he told me, "all America today is a place where there's no more competition. I blame the myth that we're all created equal. For chrissakes, the government, the drug companies, everywhere you turn, they're trying to make the myth come true. And it doesn't mean being equal in getting opportunity, but equal in being boring, being assholes."

I'm sitting in a topless lounge at one o'clock in the afternoon with Buzzy Graham. He is eating oysters and has just told our waitress, "Hey, baby. You know what I had? I had a lousy meal here last week. I had a dozen oysters, but only ten of them worked." She didn't think it was corny because Buz Graham is big and aggressive and looks as if he will kick people in a fight when they're down. Which he will. And in the head.

Why have a sexual Roughrider? I believe that part of your

Smart People team should be made up of individuals who do not play by society's rules. *You* might call them *anti*–Smart People. They are valuable because they teach us about the dark side of the moon. Most of the time, Roughriders don't give a damn about the consequences of their acts. We may not like these people. But there are lessons to be learned from those who say, "To hell with convention. I just don't *care*." Very often you can learn more from the Roughriders than from any other sort of Smart People. Because they are *street* smart.

I recruited Buzzy in my network of the past. We worked together one summer when I was in college, as counselors at a boys' camp. At the time, Buzzy was heavy into exposing himself in unusual ways. For instance, we used to take nights off and hang around the outside porch of Howard Johnson's in Naples, Maine. It was a gathering place for the hundreds of off-duty counselors who worked in the children's camp circuit in the Sebago Lake region. Buzzy would pick a group of female counselors and ease into their conversation. Invariably, someone would ask, "Anyone have the time?"

Buzzy would say, "Sure," unzip his fly, and pull out his penis, around which he had buckled his watch. "It's nine-thirty," he'd say, and then stuff himself back into his pants. It would happen so fast that the women sometimes weren't sure that they saw what they saw. But it was a conversation-stopper. Buzzy could size up a crowd immediately and cut out of the herd the one candidate who was always vulnerable to his act.

At the same Howard Johnson's, that same summer, Buzzy wheeled onto the porch one night at eleven, having consumed most of a case of Haffenreffer beer. He had a female companion from Huntsville, Alabama, a counselor from a local camp that prided itself on attracting blonde employees from the South. "Ah'm hungry, Buz," she kept insisting. So Buz escorted her onto the porch and up to a screened order window. "A hot dog okay?" he asked. The Alabama beauty, full of Haffenreffer, nodded her approval.

As always the porch was jammed with counselors, male and female, sniffing around each other. It was like a cocktail party with the guests in shorts and tee shirts, toasting each other with chocolate milk shakes.

Buzzy took the hot dog and walked with Miss Alabama to the table in the middle of the porch. The table was laden with mustard, ketchup, and relish dispensers. "Still hungry?" he asked his date.

"Starved," she reiterated.

Buzzy proceeded to strip the hot dog from its roll, stuff it in his mouth, and devour it in two bites. Then he once again unzipped his fly, inserted his organ into the hot dog roll, and covered it quickly with mustard and relish. Looking at his date with a mad look in his eyes he said, "You want it to go, or you wanna eat it here?"

These are examples of how crude Buzzy Graham could be. But he is no dummy. "People are fascinated by the outrageous," he has told me. "That is why freak shows at circuses and horror movies have a strange appeal. And let me tell you, women who are used to being treated as ladies will react unbelievably to treatment of the crudest kind, on the lowest sexual level. Certain people despise me, of course. But men suck around me for stories of things *they* don't dare do. And I must have had over fifteen hundred women, some easy, some the hard way."

"What's the hard way?"

"The hard way is something I call the 'Stop-I-Love-It-Rape.' That's where you have to fight for it, even though you know it'll be good for everybody, and where you know she is secretly dying to be bad. Sometimes my routines have gotten me into trouble. But it always turns out that I was a good judge of character, penalized for my accurate readouts."

Roughriders give people something they do not like large doses of. Reality. And socially, reality can be terribly disrupting.

My wife and I were at a birthday party within the last year. Buzzy Graham was there also, with his third wife, a woman seven years older than he is, who owned a hundred thousand shares of Weyerhaeuser, among other odds and ends, like IBM, Exxon, and a shopping mall in Houston. The party was given by a bachelor in honor of the end of Lent.

"I'm having close friends who are all married," the host told me before the party. "But I'm also having Buzzy Graham, who I hear is an old buddy of yours. I do a lot of business with his wife's family, and he's always supervising. But I'll tell you, I'm honestly worried. If there's anything wrong with relationships in a gathering where Buzzy is, his presence is sure to aggravate the problems."

There were fourteen people at the party, and cocktails went on much too long. When dinner was served, Buzzy was seated next to a woman from St. Louis who thought she was happily married and whose husband spent money on vacations the way you do on groceries. She had always been proud of her large breasts. But she was not ready for Buzzy's first remarks. "I'd like to play windshield wiper with those tits of yours," he said. "I'd like to gobble them like this crabmeat cocktail," he said, proceeding to give an imitation on the crabmeat of what he would do to her, if given the chance.

She made the mistake of not shutting him off immediately. She only said, "Oh, Buzzy, hush up," in a way that instantly made him step up the pace.

Much wine was poured and much loose talk colored the conversations around the table.

Buzzy had his standard procedure going for what he calls "unexpected women who want it." The procedure always ends with his trying the punch line "Show me a husband who won't go down on his wife, and I'll show you a woman I can steal."

Naturally, Buzzy's dinner partner confided to him that oral sex was something in which her husband had no interest.

"You're getting moist just thinking about it, right?" he said to her. Everyone else at the table noticed what was going on. Buzzy's wife became loud and unhappy. The woman's husband played the gentleman and pointedly ignored what was happening at the other end of the table. After dinner, when the host put on his old Fred Astaire records, Buzzy led the woman out of the dining room, through the kitchen, and into the laundry room. There he proceeded to pull down her pantyhose and, as he said later, "tried to put her away against the dryer, with her standing on Tide and Dash boxes to give me leverage." One of the other male guests, drunk enough to be outraged for the cuckolded husband, barged into the laundry room thinking to protect the woman's honor and to preserve the good name of his host. The rest of the guests followed like the people of the village storming after Frankenstein's monster.

Buzzy looked at the intruder. "If you don't get out of here, you've got two choices. I can kill you or I can screw you. Which do you want?"

"Let her go," the brave guest yelled.

"Get lost, inconsiderate fuck," said Buzzy, who had long since crossed over the line.

The guest would go only so far for honor. Not far enough to pull Buzzy away from the dryer.

The party ended in chaos with Buzzy's wife defending his actions. "That woman led him on the whole night," she said. "Don't think I couldn't hear from across the table."

The host had a memorable party. Four divorces resulted from the evening, the laundry-room incident bringing shocks of recognition, accusations, denials, and admissions from other guests who never recovered.

Buzzy and I had lunch some time later. He was not sorry for his actions. Only bitter.

"I closed my wife's account with the host," Buzzy said. "He's bad-mouthing me all through the city. Those other people? I told you, I'm a great judge of character. *I* didn't give them all bad marriages. I just held a mirror up to how phony they all were. What's more natural than getting laid? I want it; I do it with the people who want to do it with me."

"You're ahead of your time, Buz."

"Well, you may be right. But this caused such a flap I'm re-forming."

"Reforming? No more extramarital sex?"

"Not with other people's wives anyway," he said. "It's a much better game to get a whore to fall in love with you. Listen, it's two-thirty. Come on with me to the Leopard Lounge. Waitresses there double as hookers. They got half Wheaton graduates working the place. There's no crap, no games, no chase involved. You go, you pay, you get your rocks off. The only real play is getting one to fall in love with you. It'll happen, you work on it enough."

I talked with Red Henry about Buzzy. "What about the lessons from someone like that? You don't really want that person as your best friend. What is the attraction?"

Red Henry didn't hesitate. "Most of us draw on the adventures of others to enrich our lives. Everyone loves stories about sex, and the more salacious the better. We *like* to be titillated. Too often, unfortunately, we don't get titillated enough ourselves. We *need* the Buzzys of the world to feed our cowardice. They remind us of the black side of the personality. In a way we wish *we* dared to go up to strange women and tell them we'd love to play windshield wiper. Also, it's a hell of a lot safer to revel in *stories* about lust than to act them out."

"Let me revel in one of your stories about lust," I said.

"Did I ever tell you my cabinet-member story?" Red Henry asked — and plunged right on, not waiting for my response.

"It illustrates how important a Buzzy can be as one of your Roughriders," he began. "A friend of mine who is Canadian was a big shot when he was an undergraduate at McGill. He was an athlete and very involved in student politics. During his last year, the student union invited a professor from Columbia who later became a cabinet member to speak. My friend was in charge of greeting the guest and squiring him around. The lecture took place at night and was a huge success. But the future secretary was sleeping over until the next morning, and my friend was faced with entertaining him.

"'Sir, any ideas of what you'd like to do?' my friend asked him.

"The professor smiled almost conspiratorially. 'Well,' he said, 'you took a colleague of mine to see some night spots when he was in Montreal. I would enjoy that,' he went on, adding softly, 'if it's not too conservative.' My friend paraded the man to one dive after another, from topless joints to bottomless bars, and finally to a spot that offered the lewdest form of entertainment short of penetration on the dance floor. The future secretary was so obviously enthralled, as my friend tells it, that he forgot himself for a moment, losing himself in the spectacle around him. Then it was as if he suddenly realized his position, recognizing that he was not supposed to be reveling in the lewd show. Retreating to a highly indignant, academic posture, he feigned disgust, saying, 'I'm curious about the kinds of people who would go to places like this. What kinds of people would come here on a regular basis?'

"My friend took a long pull from his bottle of Molson's ale, looked at his guest, and said, 'Only Columbia professors, sir. Only Columbia professors.'"

Henry the Red laughed. "You can always put sex in the right perspective by remembering that presidents do it, senators, prime ministers, dictators. Almost everyone is a Buzzy under the skin."

To have a friend of the opposite sex is to open up an endless source of discovery. To understand sex you have to have Smart People on your team who are honest with you. All people long to tell their story. If you are lucky enough to have someone of the opposite sex tell you his or hers . . . listen. The experience can only help you.

My sexual Maven is a client. She was referred to me by her divorce lawyer who promised, "She may not be worth much money, but she's got ten million dollars' worth of adventures."

"I'm too busy these days for adventures," I told him.

"You won't be too busy for these."

Natasha came to see me that afternoon. It was winter. She swept into my office wearing a fur hat, fur coat, high-heeled boots, and a long black wool skirt.

"Can I take your coat?" I offered.

"Not until I find out if you're the guy who's going to watch my money. First of all," she said, "did you ever screw anyone in the afternoon?"

"Figuratively or literally?" I asked.

She ignored the quibble. "Did you ever sleep with a woman in the afternoon?"

"Guilty," I said to Natasha with one breath. "Hold all calls," I said to my secretary with the next.

Natasha wanted to sell only several thousand dollars' worth of Texaco, part of the settlement from her husband. "He made two mistakes," she told me. "He didn't believe in oral sex, which is like not believing in the tooth fairy. *And,* he was a plastic surgeon who thought that his years in medical school made him the world's leading authority on human relations. I surprised him on both counts, when he arrived home after bobbing three noses and doing a hair transplant to find me going down on the man who was there installing the alarm system. I mean it sounds like some sort of skin flick, but it was real enough for my husband to take away everything in court except for Texaco."

Natasha is small with skin the color of Pocahontas's and hair dark as Worcestershire in a steak house. She works with disturbed children in public school systems on weekdays, and she experiments with sexuality at night, on weekends, on her vacations.

"I dressed up for you when we met," she said, "because women's money needs attention. If you paid attention to *me,* you would make sure, if you wanted to see me again, that my money was well tended."

"I'm a professional," I told her. "I would pay attention under any circumstances."

Natasha smiled. "I was just cutting down the odds."

Natasha's theme is cutting down the odds, getting the edge. "I use sexuality to get attention," she says. "Not sexuality in a teasing sense but in the sense of new freedom. I'm interested; I'm frank. And if I want you, I'm not going to play games. I have a tremendous advantage over any man. If you come up to me and grab me by the breast, I can call a cop. If I come up to *you* and grab you by the joint, you'll wonder why it's your lucky day."

It's *your* lucky day if a woman offers you insights into sexuality. By appreciating the diversity of sexual experience you can only feel comfortable about how healthy your experiences are. Remember: These are only samplings to show you various approaches. Your Smart People will be equally various, equally diverse.

Natasha is forty. Until the age of twenty-seven she had been to bed with only one person: her husband. Now she admits to affairs with eighty-eight men, ranging in age from seventeen to fifty-three. "I'll tell you the nice thing about older men," Natasha says, echoing the old saw about older women. "They don't tell, they don't yell, they don't swell. And they're grateful as hell." And she goes on, paraphrasing Robert Frost, "But if I had to go down twice, I think eighteen is awfully nice, and would suffice."

"Actually," she says, "eighteen is the classic age for a man in many ways. At eighteen a man is at his ultimate in hopefulness, and also, by the way, probably at his ultimate in terms of enjoying an older woman."

You cannot find out from a Mr. Goodbar woman what the sexual revolution has meant to society. You need to have communication with the generation of women that grew up believing in virginity before marriage, the generation that lived in mortal terror of getting pregnant. Natasha is old enough to remember the telltale circle in boys' wallets and young enough to react to a system that treats women as second-class citizens. But my sexual Maven gives her lessons better than I can.

"Anyone who has optimism, who has hope," she says, "should read my favorite book, *The Once and Future King*, by T. E. White. I have a lot of dreams now, not a lot of illusions. Understanding the difference has been a key to my life. But the book is crucial to my living patterns. *The Once and Future King* is about King Arthur. It's about magic and the adventures of growing and learning. That's how I see myself now, able to grow for the first time in my life, because I'm allowed the freedom of choice. Other women choose involvement in politics, or career, or going back to school. My career is sex and adventures with people that I could never have had in the past.

"One problem I find is that sexual freedom is helping increase the sense of anarchy in our society. For instance, I am selectively amoral. It doesn't bother me in the least that I seduce another woman's husband. One night last fall I was at a party, not a big party, dinner for a dozen. Near the end of cocktails one of my friends reminded her husband that he had to go on a quick run to the train station to pick up a daughter coming home from school. I needed cigarettes so I offered to go along for the ride. Innocent. No plot in mind. When we got to the station we found the train was late. So we sat out on the platform on a long ribbed bench, smoking cigarettes, talking and waiting. He was sweet and didn't go on about his marriage. He told me about buying and raising parrots and that parrots are the most desirable items for theft in housebreaks after silverware and television sets. I felt moved enough by his sweetness to get up in the dim light of the train platform, take off my pants, unzip his fly and straddle him right there with people standing on the other side of the tracks. That experience changed his life. He couldn't get excited by his wife anymore. And he lost all interest in the parrots. But I wouldn't see him again. My excitement was for the moment, strictly selfish. Christ, at last women can be sexually selfish."

"You didn't have any guilt about ruining his marriage?" I asked.

"I told you, I'm selectively amoral. Besides, I believe what Zsa Zsa Gabor says: 'A man is incomplete until he's married. And then he's finished.'"

"Does this make you any happier than you used to be?"

"I'll tell you something about happiness. I was raised in a scholastically competitive atmosphere. I was taught that if I was not brilliant, I was not acceptable. How could I be happy if I weren't brilliant? The big lesson for me of the last ten years, to me who was a virgin at marriage, is that my freedom teaches me that I don't have to be happy. My God, what a revelation when I realized that."

Not everyone needs a sexual Maven. Natasha feels that true friendship with a man is possible only after they have become lovers. I tell her that the tension is everything, and that the possibility of becoming lovers is far more interesting than consummation. I also tell her that the worst possible person to become involved with is your stockbroker. "Don't get anything confused with making money when you're seeing the money man," I tell her.

She has accepted this relationship and has helped me immeasurably toward understanding the problems facing the modern woman. She has nothing to lose or gain by not being completely honest, and she holds nothing back. Getting at truth helps us all. Getting close to how a woman copes with the sexual freedom available to her helps me handle my wife's desires and makes me more sympathetic to her needs. Also to the needs of women friends and women clients.

Natasha tells me that I'm full of crap. "You just want to get off on other people's stories," she accuses. Perhaps that's part of it. But there are lessons in what she tells me.

"I'm liberated, right? I use my sexuality to get me things. I've had more than eighty lovers, and not too long ago I'd have had to be in films or in the oldest profession to have that much experience. I don't think I could ever be faithful to one man. As a matter of fact, I think monogamy is an unnatural act, invented by people who never tried it in the first place. Like priests. I have found in discussing promiscuity with many women that variety of experience is the most wonderful by-product of the nuclear age. *But* also that women still desire, more than anything else, touching on many levels. Thoughtfulness. And gentleness. Regardless of how many people they get it from. Now gentleness is what you should strive for in lovemaking. But the key to sexual conquest is contrast. I can dress like a lady and act like a whore and it knocks them out. I flash my white teeth and think my black thoughts. That's how I see myself. I flash my white teeth and think my black thoughts."

Not only do I have a friend of the opposite sex who will tell me her stories, I have a Smart Person who serves a special role. Natasha the sexual Maven will answer *any* question, *any* time. It is like having a sexual "Information Please" at the end of your hot line, any time you choose. Imagine the lift your mornings might have if you can dial Natasha about eleven, just as the pre-lunch letdown sets in, and say, "Tell me something, since you claim to be bisexual. Are women better kissers than men?" You'd be amazed how Natasha's answers can last you until the lunch waiter's question, "Will there be cocktails before you order?"

I'm not telling any of you to act like my sexual Smart People. I am only telling you that most of sex is in your attitudes and your mental approach. Accumulate Smart People who reassure you about the diversity of sexual activity. And be reassured about the endlessness of sex. One story can end this chapter and illustrate this endlessness. *If* your mind remains open, your body will follow and respond.

The big unspoken fear for all of us, aside from worries about health and prosperity as we grow older, is, What happens to sex in our later years? We all rejoice over stories of couples who continue to cohabit into their eighties, of men who sire children in their seventies, of women like Marlene Dietrich and Mae West who retain their sexuality indefinitely. I feel confident about myself when I recall my grandfather coming back from his second honeymoon several years after the death of my grandmother. He married a woman devoted to him, a bookkeeper from his factory. Grandpa was seventy at the time, his wife eighteen years younger. They went to Mexico on their honeymoon. The family was all gathered at my grandfather's house to welcome them back. At dinner, attended by sons, daughters, grandchildren, and friends, during an infrequent lull in the conversation, a daughter-in-law asked my step-grandmother how she liked their hotel room in Mexico City. My grandfather stopped a forkful of noodle pudding in midair and boomed, "How the hell would she know about the room? All she saw of it was the ceiling." Grandpa always prided himself on the truth.

See what you have to look forward to?

# 5 MY SMART WOMEN

Why a separate chapter about women? Mather Stevens has handled over three thousand divorce cases and feels that he is only beginning to comprehend how wonderful it is to be female. He has told me that the greatest achievement of knowledge is "to know the opposite sex." This is why I have a chapter on my Smart Women. If I were a woman, there would be a separate chapter on my Smart Men. In expanding your life to find others to help you, you must not neglect using Smart People Principles to recruit the opposite sex. My Smart Women have taught me the importance of understanding one another. They have taught me about winning through submission, about the exertion of power through feminine techniques. We are *not* all the same. Exploring the differences between us can lead to greater understanding of ourselves. The lessons I have learned from my Smart Women have enriched my life, materially and emotionally. Women, seek out your Smart Men and use *them* to change your life. Men, seek out your Smart Women as I have sought mine.

If you are female, the same principles can be applied to understanding the male. All of the techniques in this book can be reversed to deal with people of the other gender.

There is too much space today devoted to unisex, to sameness. We should revel in our differences and wonder at our understanding of these differences. To have a friend of the opposite sex is astonishing. I can never understand completely what it is like to be a woman. A female's understanding of man is equally impossible. But achieving expansiveness in your life, developing the true richness of your personality and experience demand that you try to understand.

You need Smart People of the opposite sex the way you need Smart People who are lawyers, doctors, bankers, or plumbers. To enrich yourself is the point of any education. And good education is not pursued by most people. With Smart People techniques you never stop learning. They offer the most painless education of all, an education that expands your experience and the meaning of your life.

This chapter is really about learning to listen, which is essential to building your network of Smart People. Philosopher-King Henry the Red, who has opinions about everything, has an opinion about listening. "First of all," he says, "I've got to tell you that I'm the best manufacturer of maternity clothes in America. You know why? Because I understand women. And I never underestimate them. My opening line for years, when I'd meet a new woman was, 'Admit you're better looking now than at any other time in your life.' This line immediately throws open the entire relationship."

The key to getting women to respond to you involves two essential elements: being a good listener and asking unusual questions. Ask a good question. It always works. "Are you more attractive now than at any other time in your life?" Of course, I stole this from Henry the Red. "Take it," Henry says. "That's how Milton Berle has made a living all his life." But no woman I have ever used this on has failed to remember me. Most consider the question an extraordinary compliment and will immediately begin an in-depth discussion of possible lasting value to both of you. The secret to understanding women, Henry the Red says, "is the realization that they are capable of anything. Very seldom am I wrong, I'll tell you. But I'm always prepared."

## THE "I UNDERSTAND YOU" METHOD

My Smart Women have led me to the technique I call the "I Understand You" Method. This method incorporates two parts: one, the unusual question and, two, the ability to listen. Never ask a man what he does. Ask him, "Did you play a sport in high school?"

Never ask a woman, "Do you have children?" Ask her, "What did you always want to be when you grew up?" I can guarantee you results. Not only will you get an animated reaction, but that person is not going to forget you. Probe for the secret desire, then stand back and bind that person to you for good. But only if you really want that person. Do not use the I Understand You Method at ordinary meetings or dinner parties. You have to be selective in choosing your Smart People, and there must be a certain amount of cold-blooded picking and choosing to prevent your becoming a living clinic. When all is said and done you must select Smart People who can operate for *you.*

Secret Summas have to be treated as special objects. They give the impression that you must rush your time with them lest they become impatient. Or worse, bored and preoccupied. The Summa Smart People ration the moments they spend on relaxation. Most of the time they are center stage, performing, executing their specialty, radiating confidence and calm.

Rather than scatter my Smart Women throughout this book, I want to present them en masse. This is as much for me to view them next to one another as for the reader to absorb feminine advice in a uniform package, without having to sift through chapters searching for the goodies. This chapter is also about how power is exerted, how women get their way. The various power techniques take different shapes. Watch them work.

Once again I have recruited my Smart People in three basic ways. First, through the old-school method of staying in touch with people from my past. Second, through having something to trade off for the services of others. And third, through making myself enough of a character to force people's positive response.

My secret woman Summa sticks out in a crowd like an emerald in a dirt circle full of marbles. She is seventy-five years old and she is beautiful. I call her "the countess," although she would be most annoyed if she felt that I thought of her in those terms. One of the countess's sons was a classmate of mine in college. He once invited me to stay at his mother's apartment, which was at the very end of East Sixty-ninth Street in New York. It was where the city meets the East River, and the noises of boats at night made you feel in your dreams that you were at sea. The countess's apartment always made me think of Never-Never Land. A place for boys who refused to grow up.

The first time I stayed in the countess's apartment I awoke on a Saturday morning with the kind of hangover that has you saying silent prayers to God. Prayers about how you will never do certain things again in your life if only the headache and the upset stomach will disappear. I lay in a twin bed in her son's room. It was ten-thirty in the morning, and he hadn't even made it home from the night before. We were to graduate from college in the spring, and we thought there wasn't *anyone* who deserved good times more than we. The countess burst into the bedroom carrying a tray laden with scrambled eggs, English muffins with Keiller's Dundee marmalade, orange juice, and black coffee.

"You know," she said, "you are really good fellows. Why do you make such dreadful asses of yourselves?"

That was the last thing I wanted to hear that morning. But the first thing I *did* want was what lay on that breakfast tray. I sat up eagerly, arranging the covers so that the tray might fit comfortably over my lap. The countess sat down in a chair at the foot of my bed. She deliberately picked up the glass of orange juice and drank it down. Then, as I watched, she attacked the eggs and English muffins. "It's about time you started planning for graduation," she said between bites. "From now on, never expect that the world owes you a living. Chester Bowles told me years ago about success in life. 'Success is not the result of good looks or brains or even money,' he said. 'Success is the result of perseverance.' I always remember that."

She finished her coffee. The eggs and muffins were gone. She got up and left her tray on the chair. "You can take a shower now," she said, leaving the room. "And you may take my dishes to the kitchen and wash them."

Now this, I thought, was a lady of leisure. She was rich and sophisticated and beautiful. But what she had just done let me know, at a crucial time in my life, that the world did *not* owe me a living, that there would come a time when I was going to have to fend for myself.

After that incident, the countess became as much a friend of mine as her son was. She was one of the first to teach me the value of perseverance, and another major lesson as well — the secret of quitting as a winner, of not outstaying success.

The countess has filled her years with achievement and service. She grew up in Philadelphia where her parents were artists and musicians, both players in the Philadelphia Symphony. The countess was a child prodigy on the violin, playing concerts all over Europe, several times on the same program with Paderewski, who called her Sunshine.

"He would play the piano, practicing until his fingers bled," she told me. "And that was when he was the finest pianist in the world. That was a lesson to me. But I stopped playing the violin seriously after World War I, when Poland was destroyed by the Germans. My parents were Polish, and I think my inherent seriousness about helping others comes from their efforts in behalf of the homeland. I was brought up in a patriotic tradition, a tradition that assumed you helped people less fortunate. I suppose I've been a true liberal all my life, at least until that term began to imply fuzzy thinking. It was love of people that made me become an actress. I did a lot of club shows in Philadelphia, and I guess people noticed me. Winthrop Ames, one of the biggest producers of the day, sent a limousine to pick me up when I was eighteen. He was a friend of my parents and, I suppose, trying to gently discourage me. He took me to the Winter Garden Theater, just off Broadway, and took me onto the empty stage. Very dramatic.

" 'You have been delicately nurtured, my dear,' Ames said. 'Only tough peasant flowers can thrive in the theater.'

"That was a challenge," she said. "And for the next seven years I was on the stage, finishing in New York opposite Freddie March who was a friend until he died. During that period I was also in six films, including several with Mary Astor, Augie Perkins, and Glen Hunter." She laughed. "I was very big in *The Life of Anne Hutchinson*, shot on the old sound stages in Astoria, New York."

The countess was one of the famous beauties of her era. She went to parties on the Lido in Venice with Elsa Maxwell. She was a guest at Gerald and Sara Murphy's in Cap Ferrat when Scott Fitzgerald threatened to leap naked off the cliffs into the sea. She flew upside down in a biplane piloted by Harry Crosby over the Harvard-Yale boat race in New London, and she sang after hours in bistros with Josephine Baker in the Paris of the Lost Generation.

"I participated," she told me, "yet I was always the observer. Most of the notorious people of that time were like children, sweet, innocent, self-destructive children. Harry Crosby sent me violets every day for a year. Fitzgerald would pinch me and see if anyone was looking. I think that, because my parents took me to destroyed Poland each year while I was a little girl, I grew up knowing that one had to give life a purpose, that the most important pursuit in life was in preserving an innate seriousness that said, 'Give of yourself.' "

She left the theater at a time when directors called daily and scripts flowed to her apartment at the rate of thirty a week. "There became too much self-absorption in the acting profession," she told me. "Laurette Taylor was the greatest actress I ever saw. She could fill a stage with panic. But the drinking . . . so self-destructive. I seem to know instinctively when I've had enough of anything, even though with the theater I'm like a war-horse smelling gunpowder. The discipline it has taught has allowed me to survive loneliness, disappointment, unhappiness. And discipline in the theater is the most important element, discipline that rivals that of West Point."

Most of my meetings with the countess now are on the beach where we both spend our summers. She rallies on the tennis courts with her son for half an hour early in the morning. Then she reads and writes letters. I see her on the beach where she brings her lunch and holds a salon under a striped umbrella. Over the years, her themes have remained the same: optimism about the human condition and the sense that self can overcome obstacles.

"I had a feeling years ago," she told me, "that Ernest Hemingway was a desperate man and would destroy himself. So much talent I've seen in this century turned to alcohol and eventual suicide. Dorothy Parker, I remember, tried to kill herself unsuccessfully. Bob Benchley wrote her a note saying, 'Stop it. You'll ruin your health.' "

When the countess's husband was killed in the Second World War she became instrumental in organizing UNICEF at the United Nations. "After everything that happened in the war, I felt that saving children was the key to the future. But not just saving lives, not just catering to people's stomachs. I felt our job was bigger than that. How to motivate people so they can build better lives."

Part of what makes a Summa Smart Person is the degree to which they fight one of America's biggest diseases: loneliness. "Loneliness is particularly hard for women today," says the countess. "Women who are widows, divorced, and single have been cheated by the liberation movement. The lie that the movement perpetuates," the countess continues, "is that there are wonderful jobs and wonderful men waiting, if only women will fulfill the promise of their early education. So a woman dumps the boring husband and retains custody of the children. Then she finds out that the marvelous jobs waiting are all either secretarial (and she never learned to type) or volunteer. And then the parade of men begins, all wanting to jump into her bed. And her children become polarized and she discovers that her ex-husband dates only girls under the age of twenty-two and he's deliriously happy.

"Women are milling today. I feel sorry for most of them. There is no long-range thinking. Young women ask me all the time how I do it, how I cope with loneliness. And why I never remarried. I cope with loneliness in several ways. I read books. I go to the theater. I stay close to friends I have known for years. I pay attention to detail, which is everything in being successful. The big picture is made up of many small details. Above all, and this is more important than any element in building a life that makes sense, *I listen to what people say*. Most of us don't ever listen to others; our egos get in the way. We don't want to get involved. When I am interested enough to hear someone out, I get results. Eugene O'Neill thought I was a wonderful woman. I acted in Provincetown in 1923 and he brought fresh eggs to the theater to make me omelettes after the performance. 'Fresh eggs for the throat and the physique,' he would tell me. He'd never share the omelette, though; he always had a bottle of whiskey for himself. I'd eat some of the omelette and listen to him talk until it was time to go home. Luckily, I've always known when it was time to go home."

The countess can still listen. Her lesson to me is what draws people to her. They cannot believe a beautiful grande dame will bother listening to *their* story. She still lives in New York, in the same apartment where the boats go by in the night. When I saw her on the beach last summer I asked if she were finally ready to give up on New York with its problems and expenses.

"Are you serious?" she asked me. "With more excitement than any city in the world? They've been talking about problems in London and Paris. God, London and Paris have been breathing their last for *centuries*." I started to have lunch with her on the beach. She drank iced tea and ate small cucumber sandwiches, with slices of cantaloupe covered with fresh lime juice for dessert. Several people joined us. The countess always has attracted an entourage. People love to be seen with her. Perhaps the special places, the memories will rub off on *us*. An assistant curator at a Texas museum comes by, a senior editor of *The Reader's Digest*, an heir apparent at Citibank all come to sit at her feet. I often worry about the country, where we're going, what the future will bring. I want to be reassured. We all ask the countess questions.

"The problem with America," she says, "is that we haven't suffered enough. In 1958 I came back from touring Asia for UNICEF. I felt I was coming back to the Roman Empire. We had so *much*. We do not learn from history. H. L. Mencken called us 'Boobus Americanus,' and I often think that that's so accurate. Are we bound for perdition?" Taking a bite of cantaloupe, the countess continued, "We've gotten so far away from religion. So much of 'I, I, I' is all we hear. The shibboleths of our culture are no longer supported by science. We've licked the natural forces, and we can't believe in mystery any more. Science and technology have become the opiate of the people. Much to their sadness, I'm sure. If you could strip away the glee over impending Disc-o-Vision and a better detergent, we'd all be better off. We have to search for new identity to overcome the spiritual blankness. But whatever the search will produce, they'd better hurry." She stood up and adjusted her wide-brimmed hat so that the sun would not dare violate her cheeks. "I'm going home to write letters," she announced, "while you children can 'fleet the time carelessly as they did in the Golden World.'" She drops lines like these as if she were born to make entrances and exits written by Shakespeare expressly for her. Rosalind, in *As You Like It*, had been her favorite role.

She handed me her used paper plate. Nothing was left on it but crumbs and lime juice. "Dump this for me, please," she asked, reminding me of that time years ago when I was hung over and did her breakfast dishes. "You have to be reminded, no matter how old you get — never coast on your charm."

She walked across the sand to her car, a 1962 Bentley that had a hundred and forty thousand miles on the odometer and that she always drove herself.

My female Lamplighter grew up in Beverly Hills in a house built by a silent-film star. My Lamplighter was a skinny little thing as a child, nervous around other children. She always thought she was ugly, and being shy as well, retreated early into books and solitary games that involved her fantasies of playing opposite imaginary Douglas Fairbankses and John Gilberts. She developed a style over the years that has her featured endlessly as Lillian Gish, the child/woman who always gets her way.

"I am Holly the Heroine," she told me when we were introduced. Smart People often instinctively give themselves nicknames. They are making sure they are remembered. Holly the Heroine dazzles with her routines. Then she brings you to earth with the surprise of her intelligence. This knowledge spills out so quickly that, by the time you understand it was there, you're beaten. She remains a Lamplighter, an inspiration, because nothing is going to overcome her determination to succeed.

I met Holly in New York, during a dinner given at Lutèce by a corporation whose pension fund I advise. It was a dinner for thirty people, and I had not been introduced to Holly. She sat at the other end of the table, too far away for me to see her, other than as a blond blur. But after dinner, when most of the guests had left, I lingered with the president of the company while he told me what the meal had cost. Then I noticed Holly. She was tall and thin and dressed in a long Albert Nipon gown that was green enough to match her big green eyes. She was moving from one empty place to another, drinking the dregs from departed guests' wineglasses. I escaped the president and confronted her.

"I can't believe you're drinking dregs from other people's glasses," I said to her.

"Don't be foolish," Holly said to me, as if I were nuts. "I look at it simply as a wonderful opportunity."

Holly asked me to get her a cab, explaining as we left Lutèce that she was an attorney who had assisted the corporation with some labor negotiations. As I helped her with her coat, I commented on a gold ID bracelet with a medical-alert symbol affixed to the links. She smiled. "It tells anyone who finds me dead that Harvard Medical School can have my body for research. Everything except my eyes."

"Why not your eyes?" I asked.

"Because I wouldn't want to live in hell without my eyes." She slammed the door of the cab and was gone.

She has become one of the most successful labor negotiators in the East. Why? "Because," she has told me, "although I grew up in Beverly Hills and had dreams, my father died when I was very young. My mother was left without relatives and without money. We moved up the coast to a small town, and I went to a high school where the women did not go on to college. Wanting to escape the facts that I was ugly and poor, I read books and magazines. One *New York Times* Sunday magazine article was about the Seven Sisters, the great women's colleges in the East, and I thought, 'How great to go to a place where everyone is smarter than you.' So I lay in bed for two weeks and memorized three thousand words to prepare for the college boards. When I got to Wellesley and saw the wealth there, I couldn't believe it, like a dog seeing steak for the first time after eating nothing but kibble. Some moments were embarrassing. In my small town at home, I had been sent to a Catholic school. Every time I was asked a question in class at Wellesley, I jumped to my feet like the nuns had taught me. But what came out of that was that everyone knew me, and they all wanted to lend me their cashmere sweaters."

Holly's success with people is based upon her experience in life, her exposure to all levels of society while she was growing up. She is a truly Smart Person, smart for herself, as well as for others. Because of the range, because of the different places in her life.

"Eskimos have many words for snow," she has told me, "because they know so much about it — in all its forms. And I've had enough experience to place things in perspective. There comes a breakthrough in life when you realize that you have to get along with society, that it is not going to adjust to you. The beauty of being an artist is that an artist sees the world in different ways. This is my talent as well, because of the scope of my past: East/West, rich/poor, woman in a man's profession. I can't tell you the advantages I have over my associates who grew up with only the best of everything.

"Once I was locked in a hotel suite negotiating a truck lease. The lawyers on the other side (all men) were being as difficult as they could be, including staring at my tits and making it very obvious that I was of no consequence. At one point, my client said something that had the other lawyers pounding on the table. When the yelling subsided, I looked at them all and said, 'The only thing I don't like about men lawyers is that they're so emotional.' Silence. Then everyone broke up. The tone of the negotiations changed and my client ended up making the deal he wanted."

Holly the Heroine is a perfect example of the kind of attorney you should use. Someone who appears vulnerable, gets you to relax, and then shows extraordinary preparation and toughmindedness. Again, as with so many Smart People, contrast is the key. Holly the Heroine has shared several lessons with me over the years. Here are samples of her particular Lamplighting advice:

1. "When I was escaping from poverty years ago," she told me,

"my great retreat was into books. My favorite book ever since has been James Thurber's *Many Moons*. A line from it has been my motto, the magic phrase that keeps me on track. I particularly suggest it for women worried about their role. In *Many Moons*, a counselor to the king has provided him with the cloak of invisibility. The king keeps tripping over tables and complains to the counselor, who tells him, 'Your majesty, the cloak of invisibility is supposed to make you invisible, not to keep you from bumping into things.'"

2. "This is how to choose a lawyer if you're a woman: call a reform group. Almost every state has a governor's commission on the status of women. These are true reformers. *Do not* call a special-interest group, such as anti- or pro-abortion types. But rather, call a community organization. This is the best way to get the best person."

3. "Next to oxygen, a sense of humor is the most important thing for a woman."

4. "In a French restaurant, you are guaranteed good treatment if you say to your waiter, first thing, 'Fait le plein.' It means 'fill 'er up' and should also be used in gas stations. Your waiter will invariably be amused and take good care of you."

5. "For almost any problem you have, use a lawyer from a big-city firm. Big-city lawyers are the most talented people we have in America. I'm talking about attorneys in the large firms. They have better self-control and, most important, a more open-minded attitude than people in other professions or other locations. The odds are that, if you choose a big-firm, big-city attorney, you will discover one great person and a life-long counselor.

6. "The truly interesting person has nothing at home that suggests where that person works."

7. "Being too tall as a child and during adolescence changed my life and made my career possible. If I *weren't* tall, someone would have fallen in love with me."

There is a real lesson in this last piece of advice.

Smart People turn disasters into victory the way Holly the

Heroine thinks of her childhood problems with her height. There are advantages to every condition in life, because you can get people to respond to every condition. If you start to think in Smart People terms, you will begin to react automatically to situations you would have formerly dreaded.

More from Holly:

8. "Sex for me is like fancy people's vacation houses."

9. "The big lesson in the law: you don't get anywhere by denigrating anyone."

10. "Nice guys don't finish last if they're twice as smart as you."

Holly's ability to be effective is based upon constant surprise. Several months ago I wanted to steer some business her way. The client, a corporation that needed a smart litigator, was reluctant to hire a woman lawyer.

"I need someone special," the client insisted, "someone who is unusual, creative."

But I kept after him until he agreed to bring his senior people to dinner with Holly and me. By coffee and brandy, she had them three-quarters convinced that she and her firm were just what the corporation needed.

"But I want to make it clear," the corporation president said, "That I want an attorney who can deliver the surprise, the knock-out punch."

Holly took us back to her apartment for a nightcap. She lives in a duplex on a converted wharf where clipper ships from the China trade used to unload their Marco Polo cargoes. Holly seated her guests in the living room overlooking the dark harbor. She got us drinks. Then, leaving us alone to talk about quiet things, she disappeared for five minutes. Our late-night reflections were shattered suddenly by the sounds of a marching band playing the Notre Dame fight song. Speakers hidden in the apartment covered us with brass and cymbals and drums as Holly the Heroine burst from her bedroom wearing a complete drum majorette outfit, twirling a baton as if she were a finalist in a Miss

Oklahoma contest. The corporation president bit the end off his Antony y Cleopatra. Holly's law firm got the account, which last year provided billings in excess of four hundred thousand dollars.

Holly's concept of the constant surprise works for her and it can work for you. It will always keep people interested and help to make you unique.

Every Smart Person needs *the* East Side New York woman on their team. The Smart East Side New York woman can be your Maven of Mavens. Mine is Zan Furnace, whose name sounds like an Industrial Revolution invention, but who is actually someone so chic and effective that she makes Jackie Kennedy Onassis seem bewildered.

"First of all," Zan says, "my name is Sandra. But you cannot be effective in New York unless you have a name that is unusual. A title is good. But nobody really believes titles anymore. So you say "Zan" and tell everyone it's what your baby brother called you when he couldn't pronounce Sandra."

My wife recruited Zan Furnace. She plays tennis with her in the summer at the place where we escape.

Others will recruit for you. Smart People, remember, is an organic concept. Once others are aware of what Smart People can do for them, they will be increasingly conscious of trade-offs. "You help me; I'll help you." New friends are certainly one of the best places to start your recruiting.

Zan needed the same escape that we did from the intensity of her social New York winters and the exhaustion of spring weekends in the Hamptons. Zan adopted us, giving parties for us in New York and constantly bird-dogging clients for me, using a strong-arm approach that I wouldn't dare employ, but which I am thrilled that Zan can do.

She is tall, about five ten. She has short, honey-colored hair and the athletic, leggy look that makes her seem like someone who swam with the Santa Clara swim team and Don Schollander in the 1964 Olympics. She was born in Milwaukee, met her husband, an investment banker, at Michigan, where they both were graduate students. They moved to New York when he joined Goldman Sachs. Her story is a lesson in never making the same mistake twice, and in constantly paying attention.

"Do you believe," says Zan, "that when we first came to the city I used to miss my subway stop all the time. I'd wait for people to get off first and be carried fifteen blocks past where I'd want off. It took me two years to get emotionally and physically aggressive and still be a lady. Your instinct is to fling an elbow or a verb. The true secret is to be polite yet *firm*. I was a princess from the Midwest. Things were done for me; I didn't have to think about coping. No woman in my mother's generation worked. It was unladylike. And those women were not discontented."

"Being unhappy in New York for the first six months," she went on, "I suddenly realized that Johnny, my husband, was having a marvelous time. I thought, 'Jesus, if Johnny leaves me, I'm not going to have any food.' You get kind of crazy when you first move to New York. My father taught me a phrase when I was a kid, something to think about whenever I was troubled. The phrase was 'Nothing but easy and nary a hitch.' It didn't help me a damn bit in New York City. One day Johnny came home from work and asked me if I had had a good day. He was full of that high that money and sniffs of power produce even without martinis, and I said to him blankly, 'Look at my whites, they're whiter than white. Look at my brights, they're brighter than bright.'

" 'Should I call a doctor?' Johnny asked.

"That's the minute I decided to get my ass in gear. The next day I dropped Sandra, became Zan Furnace, and began my attack on New York through antiques. The big revelation I got, early in my New York career, was shopping in an antique store on Twenty-third Street. I was about to pay for an old gilt mirror when the owner, an old-timer, was called to the phone. I saw a slip of paper lying on my mirror, and it had three prices written on it. When the man came back to take my money, I asked him, 'Are these three prices for the *same* item?'

"He peered at me over his Ben Franklins and made a nasty face. 'Where have you been all your life, sweetie?'

"Of course, one price was retail, another wholesale, and a third for dealers. I determined never again to be taken, nor to set foot in a store in New York without knowing the territory. Of course, I was grounded in old people. The best lesson I ever got was when a dull old uncle of mine was at my parents' house telling stories about World War II and I was being rude and bored stiff, a perfect bitch. My nine-year-old sister, on the other hand, climbed all over his lap, kissed his nose, ears, and neck. How was anyone to know that she'd become seminympho, in the best sense of the word? But, when my uncle died, I kid you not, he left her ten thousand dollars and me a special mention in his will, a codicil, that said, 'Indulge the past of older people. You can never tell.' Can you believe it?

"So every morning in New York I haunted the elderly dealers, the philosophers of Madison and Third avenues. I asked the old men questions. 'Is that Louis Seize?' I'd be enthusiastic while they'd go into the glories of carved Chippendale feet. I'd bring them chopped-liver sandwiches or apples, and they opened up to me as if I were a daughter. One of the dealers came to see my apartment and said, 'There's not a *thing* here I would keep.' After I stopped crying the next day, I asked an orphanage to come pick up all of the furniture.

"The Weeperoo number worked also. Old men who can teach you are fools for tears. The next month the same dealer — and he was one of the biggies, heart of stone — took Johnny and me to Ireland (England is *much* too picked over) and helped us buy enough to make Billy Baldwin drool into his vermouth cassis. Of course, if you collect *anything*, it's worth being serious about. So for ages I would haunt the dealers, then go to the Metropolitan to check out what I had seen. I went to auctions at Parke-Bernet, and, when they had lectures at noon, I was there. I figured out I had the best shot at bargains during Friday auctions in late spring when the heavies went away for weekends. And the *best* day of the year is the Friday after Thanksgiving. *No* one is in New York. They all rediscover that they have mothers or fathers in Memphis or Pittsburgh, and they go *there* for turkey.

"When I finally got a Massachusetts bonnet-top chest-on-chest with corkscrew finials, a Louis Quinze red lacquer writing table, and a Fitzhugh Lane (from a junk store in the Village), I decided that school was over and it was time to consolidate the role.

"With two little boys in school," Zan continued, "and Johnny to consider, I really didn't want a full-time job. And, not being a floppy dolly, I did not want to work *for* anyone else.

"I was waiting to see a new gynecologist in his reception room, thumbing through *Scientific American* (which assured me that he was in the swim), when I heard the doctor's voice on the intercom to his receptionist, telling her to order flowers sent to a patient.

" 'Did he screw up?' I asked the receptionist, who chilled me with a glance. I listened to her call three florists before she found one who would deliver *what* the doctor wanted *where* the doctor wanted them. As I was called in for my appointment I thought to myself, 'Flowers, flowers,' to keep from thinking about a fresh set of strange fingers about to explore me. 'Hello, Dr. Langford,' I said, holding out my hand.

" 'Hello, Sandra,' he said to me, making his first and last mistake.

"I withdrew my hand and said, 'Dr. Langford, we've never met. And I'm no Crusader Rabbit. This first-name game sets the whole scene of your infallibility. I am *Mrs. Furnace* to you until we break bread. I dislike doctors and anyone else who patronizes me. Thanks for a peek at *Scientific American.*' I walked out, annoyed at doctors who call you by your first name, but pleased that the experience had given me my business . . . flowers."

I watched Zan smoke a cigarette and cross her legs. She does everything as if she loves it, something that always seems to reflect the quality of New York's Smart Women.

"Now a good idea alone is *worthless*," she says. "It has to be pursued and carried out. Persistence is my strong suit. The next day I was at the flower market at five in the morning, bothering people. After a week's search for the most grandfatherly wholesalers, I was in business. Everything costs a fortune today. But people can still buy flowers. The markup on flowers in stores is about three hundred percent. I work on about thirty percent. I wrap fresh flowers in newspaper (cheaper) and do weddings, offices, parties. I use delivery help from halfway houses where they're under the thumb of several shrinks who are my friends. I work two days a week and rely on word of mouth and free publicity that I've gotten in the *Times*, *McCall's*, and *Cosmo*. They call me 'the flower lady.' People ring me and leave an order on an answering tape for delivery the next day. Last year, working two days a week, I grossed a hundred and fifteen thousand dollars and made people happy at the same time."

There are Smart People everywhere. Women in New York are not necessarily smarter than you and I are. But it appears to the stranger that New York may be tougher to crack than most towns. Here are some of Zan Furnace's secrets, themes that recur in her verbal wanderings.

1. "If you're a working woman, do errands at lunchtime. It's productive and it uses up calories."

2. "I *never* buy anything at retail. In New York, I got a resale number from City Hall, which establishes me as a retailer and allows me to get into any decorator's, manufacturer's, or antique-dealer's showroom. To get the number I just called City Hall and said, 'I'm a consultant and I'd like a resale number.' No problem."

3. "A lot of husbands travel. Have men pick things up for you abroad. Use them as your agents. One man brought me a dozen turquoise rings from Florence. I give them as presents. Another

brought me gold jewelry from South Africa. Don't hold back; it's amazing what people will do for you if they're asked."

4. "You get domestic help mostly through leads. But a good idea is to advertise in the *Irish Echo* and *El Diario*, the Spanish-language newspaper. Speak to other people's maids or cleaning help for leads. There is an underground for such things, Jamaican, Chinese, Irish. Dig for it."

5. "Your *look* in New York is important. I can always get into any disco, any club, even though they don't know me, if I wear a long black dress off the shoulder. New York loves show biz. So always act as if you absolutely belong."

6. "If you're going out for a special dinner and you want to make sure the maitre d' doesn't plant you in Siberia, go into the restaurant about three o'clock on the afternoon of the dinner, when the restaurant is emptied of lunchers. See the maitre d' or, better yet, the owner. Tell him it's your father's seventieth birthday. Or your tenth anniversary, and please special attention and no Siberia. You will invariably get royal treatment that night when you return. Because you have been there alone, when it's empty. When *you* can make an impression."

7. "This ploy involves some subterfuge. But you know it's a jungle out there, and it's subterfuge in a good cause. Yours. Whenever you read an article and it quotes an expert in something that you want to know about, pick up a *Who's Who*, a *Reader's Digest*, and a phone. *Who's Who* will give you the expert's addresses, both office and home, and Directory Assistance can get you at least the office number. The *Reader's Digest*, like most magazines, has the names of researchers and editorial assistants on the masthead. These people are mostly pieces of fluff who leave regularly to get married back in Cleveland. Take one of their names, call the expert, and say, 'Dr. Margaret Mead?' (or whoever you want), 'I'm Sandy Von Rusher with the *Reader's Digest*. I need a quick expert answer, something fast; I won't waste your time. Which Pacific island had the best sense of birth control in the 1930s?' When she solves your problem, it's 'Thank

you very much' and good-bye. Flatter people on these calls. They love to be recognized, and they often will give you more than you bargained for."

8. "When you are bored stiff at a dinner party and are seated next to impossible people with whom you couldn't possibly communicate and are stuck for a subject (this often happens in New York), do this: Think of something beginning with the letter A (architecture is good). 'What do you think of your office building?'

"Then go on to B. 'Does anyone play the bongos anymore?' Then to C, D, E, and so on. And I guarantee the game can get you through any dinner successfully."

"What happens when the game sours?" I asked Zan Furnace, the flower lady. "How do you cope with that?"

Zan laughed. "There are days," she said, "when every step you take in New York is into dog doo-doo, when every cab is occupied, when the wind and the rain threaten to blow out Bergdorf's windows, and every third-world underprivileged face looks as if its owner wants to grab your handbag and slash you. Then I remember one thing and feel better."

"What's that?"

"I'll think about it tomorrow at Tara." Zan twisted her lapis ring, set in gold and brought back for her from Istanbul by her best friend's husband.

My woman Roughrider is a marvel. In an age of going with the flow and conforming more than ever to a herd instinct, be it for jogging or for Mercedes Benzes or for macrobiotics, my female Roughrider is unusual because she is not afraid to *cross the line*. She is my model for what is possible in life if you carry things too far. All of us need friends who secretly thrill us, thrill us because of the danger they face or the excitement they seek — friends who do things we would not venture to do. My Roughrider who is not afraid to cross the line is Daring Dora. Dora believes in pushing events to their extreme.

Dora is the assistant to a prominent and respected obstetrical and gynecological team. She tells a story about a woman who grew hysterical at the thought of going on the pill. An IUD was the only answer. Daring Dora was assisting her boss in the insertion of the device, and the patient was, again, verging on hysteria. As the doctor conducted the preliminary examination, he held out his hand for the speculum, the examining instrument that he expected Dora to slap into his palm. From behind her back Dora produced a pair of antique ice tongs, those wicked pincers used to carry fifty-pound blocks in the days when ice was delivered from horse-drawn wagons. Slapping the tongs into the doctor's hand forced his eyes to the strange-feeling instrument. His sudden belt of laughter jerked the woman in the stirrups up as if she had touched a third rail. They all collapsed in glee, the IUD was inserted without incident, and the patient bird-dogged many new patients for the gynecologist.

Daring Dora was a neighbor when we first met. She kept English sheepdogs and a racoon named Dillinger, and we all, including Dora's husband, became friends immediately. The husband was named William.

Daring Dora is divorced now, with one son, and there are several good reasons why she is divorced. Essentially they involve something her Philadelphia mother often told her: "Methinks, darling, you've o'erstepped the boundaries of good taste."

When Dora was married, there was a cat in her home in the suburbs. The cat was the favorite pet of Dora's husband, who came to Dora as "Billy" but whom she called "William" almost from the moment she married him.

"Why do you call Billy William?" Billy's mother asked Dora.

"I calls 'em the way I sees 'em," said Dora, silencing her mother-in-law and making her retreat to do what she always did when she was forced to be silent: picking wool balls off of afghans.

William loved his cat, and for a time Dora tolerated it and constantly cleaned up after the endless deposits left by the unhousebroken creature. "I'll go along with any habits, hobbies, or interests," Dora would tell William, expecting him to hear, "but I'm *not* going to keep on cleaning up after your cat."

"Uhmmm," William would say, paying no attention as he read another book about Stonewall Jackson. Stonewall Jackson was William's hero. He and Dora spent their honeymoon touring the sites of Stonewall's battles. (It was after they had tramped for a day at Chancellorsville that she began calling her husband "William.")

Later in their marriage, one night the cat fouled the end of their bed. The bed, which had a canopy over it, had been bought by William from a maker in Clarksburg, West Virginia, birthplace of Stonewall Jackson.

"Your cat shat," said Dora to her husband.

"Uhmmm," said William, reading Bruce Catton's *A Stillness at Appomattox*.

"Are you going to clean it up?"

"Uhmmm," said William, who was lying down in the bed with only his pajama bottoms on.

Dora picked up the cat's mess with a shirt cardboard and dropped it on William's naked belly. "Here's a present from Ulysses S. Grant," she said, taking her pillow to the guest room.

"One of the problems in relationships," Dora tells me, "is The Nickname Game." She explains it:

"Unfortunately, the only way we learn in life is by bitter experience. You don't go through life in America as a *true* human being if you're called Robert or William or Richard or Thomas. There is something *strange* about any Robert or William who is never called Bob or Bill. Think about it. Any woman who calls her husband by his formal name, through either her insistence or his, has a marriage that is in big trouble. (Of course, I do not include the South in this discussion. Certainly Buford or Leroy need no nicknames.) My advice to women who want to straighten out their relationships would be to look at their men in disgust and say, 'Don't be such a Robert.' Even if their name is Clyde, if they have a brain, they'll get the message."

Another time, William and Daring Dora had been entertained at the home of a major client of William's. (William was a CPA, a partner of a Big Eight accounting firm.) The client was a banker who, with his wife, was very proud of their newly redone cellar playroom with its combination poker and Ping-Pong table. They served dinner in the cellar playroom, with a paper tablecloth covering the poker table. "It really saves the furniture upstairs," the banker's wife confided to Dora. "We use the dining room for Christmas, Thanksgiving. You know, the *majors*."

Being relegated to the minors never pleased Dora, but William urged her for months afterward to reciprocate, to invite the clients to *their* house. "I'm not having them here," said Dora. "I am not being served dinner on a Ping-Pong table in a *cellar* and asking anyone back here. They wouldn't understand anyway. I mean we'd have to be on *ground* level at our house. How would they breathe?"

But the invitation was finally given, and Dora made sure that on the big night she spilled three ounces of Christian Dior's Diorissimo all over the suit William was to wear. While he was choosing a new ensemble from his closet, the banker and his wife arrived. Dora greeted them enthusiastically at the door and got their drinks. "Where's Billy?" asked the banker.

"Oh, William's upstairs," said Dora, "putting a final buff on his suit. Why don't you both just go down in the cellar to the playroom. Make yourselves comfortable while I fix some hors d'oeuvres." She led them to the cellar stairs and watched them walk down, being careful not to spill their drinks. Dora's cellar was a dank hole full of furnace, coal from years past, cobwebs, garden hose, rusting lawn furniture, and dripping pipes that would catch you in the throat if you could stand up straight. Which you couldn't.

The banker and his wife wandered around in a crouch, searching for the finished family room, looking for the paneled bar with the framed French lithographs of poodles peeing against walls or playing poker. But they saw, on their bent-over tour, only spiders and broken croquet mallets.

"I thought I heard the Martins come in," said William to Daring Dora, bouncing into the kitchen in his second suit choice of the evening.

"You did," said Dora, sprinkling paprika onto some stuffed eggs.

"They're not in the living room," said William.

"No," said Dora slowly, "they're down in the cellar." William ran from the room to retrieve the client and his wife. Dora popped a stuffed egg into her mouth.

Daring Dora is constantly ready to risk everything. You meet very few people in your life you can say that about. She is a practical joker with a strong sense of the absurd. She is a clown whose heart can break while the smile is painted on her face, because she hunts for an audience of one. Someone who can laugh at absurdities with her and love her when the laughter is gone. "We all fight lonely battles," Daring Dora says. "When I act out fantasies it seems to release tension in others. They're almost grateful for it."

"Look," continues Dora, "as adults we're constantly subject to stress. Our parents die; children have to be raised amidst repeated traumas; the divorce rate is staggering. Yet most people are *not* at all good at being alone. I see the world as a Fellini movie. When I'm trapped in my kitchen, when I want a man, when I need a friend, I have a trick that saves me. It's my Peehole in the Snow trick. Whatever is bothering me, I force myself to realize that it's really just a peehole in the snow compared with my life in general, everyone else's life, history. My problem? It's nothing. Then I think of the people less fortunate. I concentrate on disaster victims, paraplegics, starving children. Immediately I feel better about myself. My sense of humor returns and I throw off self-pity. How can you feel sorry for yourself when you take a moment to consider the other poor bastards in your life."

Use the Peehole in the Snow concept. It works better than transcendental meditation, because after the first blush of the TM fad wears off, you find that forty minutes a day for meditation is unrealistic to grab for in our society. After you admit that thoughts of reality *constantly* intrude upon your blank quiet, then you'll find that comparing yourself to those "other poor bastards" can relieve a great deal of depression. Once again I say, walk on any street in America at any lunchtime. Look around. Instantly you'll see people older, uglier, even sorrier than you. Your problems? Peeholes in the snow.

Daring Dora also believes in an eye for an eye. Especially if the insult is aimed at or the hurt is done to others who happen to be friends. A neighbor of Dora's, a shy woman who does everything carefully, visited her gynecologist, a spare-time admiral in the Navy Reserve who always wished he had been Supreme Allied Commander in the Pacific. Now we must all believe that we are someone special. This concept is central to Smart People Principles that tell us how to develop that special feeling so that others will respond to us, how to rise above anonymity in an anonymous environment. This timid neighbor of Dora's, Nancy Ross, felt that her doctor-admiral, who had delivered her two children, was almost the closest person to her in the world. She knew that he had been more intimate with her than anyone else except her husband would ever be. She felt close to him, safe with him. As she lay on the examining table, with her legs spread, waiting, draped with a sheet, the doctor moved to her, beginning the procedure. Nancy was relaxed with him, confident in his expertise and his caring. "Nurse," he suddenly said to his attendant in his quiet, professional voice, "when are we expecting Nancy Ross?"

Nancy clammed up like a Mafioso button man, quickly got

dressed, and, in tears, ran from the doctor's office, humiliated and alone. Daring Dora was outraged for her friend. She brought Nancy to her own sympathetic physician and gave the doctor-admiral with the Bull Halsey complex her own brand of urban revenge.

"Flat tires are a nuisance," Dora reported to me. "Everyone is irritated and annoyed by flat tires. Moreover, I had discovered that if you insert a standard hypodermic needle into a syringe, stick that syringe into any steel-belted radial, and then break off the needle, the resulting flat will be achieved in exactly twenty-seven minutes. It will be obvious to the tire owner, when he gets the flat repaired, that it was no accident. This infuses him with anxiety. Will it happen again? Who's after me? It chips away at his ego. Perhaps it will even make him think more sympathetically of others."

And so, on her way out to lunch one day, Daring Dora pushed *four* hypodermic needles into the *four* tires on the doctor-admiral's new Cadillac Seville. "When I returned from lunch, a toasted tuna and iced tea with artificial sweetener, I was pleased to see the Seville riding low in the water. In fact, sunk. Flatter than my chest, freshman year in high school."

This story teaches *me* two lessons. First, don't screw around with Daring Dora. And second, *stand up for your friends.*

There is no hot ticket like a hot-ticket woman. Very few men would push situations to the limit the way Daring Dora does. She exerts her power by the willingness to always be surprising. Do people respond to this technique? You bet they do. Last week I drove fifty miles out of my way to get homemade pistachio ice cream for Dora who was sick at home with the flu. Anyone who attacks life the way she does at least deserves pistachio ice cream when they're sick.

# 6 LET ME HELP YOU— SMART SERVICE

People take advantage of us continually because society forces others to look at us as numbers, anonymous beings at the mercy of the system. We must get the recognition of others to have a chance at survival in this anonymous society. As in every other field where we need help, service people differ. How do we find the experts who will respond to us as human beings? Here's how.

"Getting people to care is a problem. Every time I think about getting people to do things for me," Henry the Red says, "I remember my friend with the mule. 'I've got the gentlest, most obedient mule,' my friend would tell me. 'Come over to the house some weekend. You've never seen a more obedient creature.'

"I went to visit my friend, and he showed me his wonderful mule. The beast stood in the road in front of my friend's house, hooked up to a carriage that could pull my friend's family. My friend loaded his brood into the carriage and looked at me. 'Now, Henry,' he said, 'this mule always follows orders and instructions perfectly. You barely have to whisper commands to him, it's remarkable.' Then my friend took a Louisville Slugger baseball bat and, with all his might, slammed the mule right between the eyes. The mule almost dropped from the blow, staggered, but stood. I was shocked.

" 'How could you do such a thing?' I asked my friend. 'I thought the mule always responds to your command.'

"My friend stared at me, then got into the carriage with his family. 'He obeys. But first I have to get his attention.' "

Thus far I have spoken only of Smart People *giving* smart information. But all of us are dumb sometimes; all of us do dumb things. How do we extricate ourselves from stupid situations using Smart People techniques? I'm going to tell you a story about an afternoon in my life, a dumb afternoon where I needed help in a hurry.

I shared a summer house years ago with a brother-in-law who knows food and wine the way we know to turn left on a left arrow. He was on a week's vacation while I was back at work, scheduled to come down on Friday night for the weekend. We were to give a dinner party featuring special five-alarm chili. My brother-in-law called me. "We're having five-alarm chili at the party," he said. "We need some good Mexican beer. I can't get it down here. Why don't you scout around for Carta Blanca? We'll need two cases."

I'll do almost anything for my brother-in-law, who knows more about having a good time than Xaviera Hollander. Hunting for Mexican beer before facing weekend August beach traffic calls for a large dose of love. But the thought of forcing him to serve a domestic beer with his special chili forced me to hunt for the requested brew in a neighboring town noted for its Pop Warner football and its discount liquor stores.

I parked on Main Street and, as I got out of my three-year-old Mercedes, I noticed a policeman across the street. He was eye-balling me as if I were about to tunnel under the savings bank. The reason was simple: all the people walking by me on their way home from work were wearing overalls or jeans or modest doubleknits. I was wearing a pink seersucker three-piece suit and plain silk bowtie with a white shirt. In the eyes of the policeman, I was either a pimp or a gay decorator, two varieties of people unfamiliar to the town since its incorporation in 1827. But, knowing I was clean, I proceeded to the first of six liquor stores in that block. The first two stores produced no Mexican beer. The third had only Coors as their most exotic feature. But nothing from south of St. Louis. After each of my empty-handed exits, the officer on the beat put up his antenna as if I were more prominent in his post office than Dillinger. Naturally, still knowing I was clean, and still being annoyed at my fool's errand, I decided to amuse myself with the policeman. I embarked on a Routine.

If I was on a dumb errand, the foolishness of it could be relieved by doing *Routines*.

Doing Routines can relieve boredom even better than books. And the retelling of Routines at parties leads to the further recruitment of your team. Making the decision to do a Routine turned the beer-buying into a game.

While crossing the street to the next liquor store, I purposely fell into step with two workers from the electronics plant, carrying lunchpails. They hid me from the policeman's view. This maneuver whipped the cop into a frenzy. He moved down the block and waited outside another store as I made my fourth attempt to find two cases of Carta Blanca. Striking out again, I hid myself behind two Italian women leaving the store after buying Chianti in straw-covered bottles. Knowing the inspector was waiting, I bent my knees and slithered alongside of them out the automatic doors and into the neon August of Main Street. The policeman caught a glimpse of my pink seersucker legs behind the Italian women's shopping bags and loosened the handcuffs from his Sam Browne belt. I could see his thought balloons:

"That sucker is either setting up the liquor stores to knock 'em off, or he's giving the squeeze to put in pinballs or numbers or phones."

Still hiding behind pedestrians I moved to my car, figuring that the Routine was over and my brother-in-law would have to make do with Budweiser. Feeling smug, I turned on the ignition, just in time to see the patrolman coming across the street toward me.

"Knock, knock," on my windshield. Very polite. "Could I see your license and registration please?"

Smiling, I produced.

"Out of the car, please," he said. "This automobile is being impounded. Your registration expired two months ago. You're on the road illegally, you silly-looking son of a bitch."

The Routine was dead. My insurance man had neglected to send out renewal forms on time, and the last thing anyone ever notices are expiration dates on licenses or registrations. But Smart People don't panic, even when the Routine collapses. Immediately I retreated into the Chameleon Phase, a defensive posture that emphasizes things people like to hear. (1) I am the innocent victim of non-professional oversight (my insurance man) and isn't it a shame how no one cares about doing a good job anymore? (2) How can an American get into trouble buying *beer?* (All good working men drink beer.) (3) Can you believe this suit? My wife bought it for me as a surprise. (All us working guys have wives, and, since the suit is a wife's fault I obviously wasn't either gay or a pimp.) (4) And in addition to the beer, which I was getting to take on my vacation, I had to pick up a sponge for my kid's catcher's mitt. He's a Little League All-Star. (Policemen love sports and kids.)

Suddenly the policeman says, "You know, it's too bad. The fine can be a hundred dollars, and you have to go to court plus pay storage charges for the car." We both waited. "Of course," he said, "if you knew a gas station that had repair plates, they could put them on and you could drive the car until you got your registration renewed. I'm going to call a tow truck. It will take him a half-hour to arrive. If you can get repair plates before then, we'll call it sayonara and you go on vacation with the sponge for the kid's mitt. I used to be a chucker. A hard thrower. A hard thrower can hurt you, you catch it in the right place."

Kevin, my garage man, was there in twenty minutes with his truck and a set of repair plates. He responded so quickly because I give him champagne at Christmas. Not Scotch or Canadian or bourbon. No one else ever gave him champagne, and, because of it, I always had gasoline during the embargo, I always had my back and side windows cleaned, I was always driven home when my car was being tuned. The small touches ensure that the service team remains in place. And on St. Patrick's day, a case of beer is delivered to the station for everyone.

Could you get a garage man there in twenty minutes? Champagne for Christmas works wonders.

For most people, stress and anxiety are long-term problems. But if we had to pick specific moments when our need for Smart People is the greatest, we would have to say "in an emergency." Most of us panic when faced with immediate trouble or danger. What do you do (*a*) if, walking down a dark city street after the theater, you and your spouse are confronted by muggers? (*b*) if a friend with whom you are dining suddenly chokes on a chicken bone? (*c*) if your child goes into convulsions in the night? or (*d*) if police in a small Southern town pull you in for speeding and discover a social supply of marijuana in your glove compartment?

Most of us do not function well in these situations. Our adrenalin pumps overtime. Our heartbeat and blood pressure shift into high. We often lose the ability to function at all at the very moment when we need to function most effectively.

We need different people for different emergencies. There were several ways I could have dealt with the situation with the small-town cop, if things had gone sour. They all involve the use of Smart People. The first method would be to use my political lawyer, the one who knows all the judges. That would have sprung me, but not before a trip to the station house. The second method would have been to track down the smart insurance agent who got me into the situation in the first place. My insurance man may have forgotten to send out auto registration forms on time. But he has it where it counts. And this should be the major factor you pay attention to in picking an insurance agent.

Can he get you the money when you have a claim? Everything else is peripheral and can be done by any clerk.

I will bet that among the most fast-talking and glib of your high school or grammar school classmates is an insurance agent. I use an agent who, as a boy, used to break squad-car windows with snowballs and, as a result, knew every cop in town. Today he insures most of the town's municipal workers, including fire-fighters and police. He has both a CB *and* a phone in his car, and he knows more Polish and Italian jokes than anyone would want to know. Use your childhood network to find an insurance agent. Look at class directories or alumni notes to find out who has become an insurance agent. Identify the class clown or the big-gest wise guy who has gone into insurance. They're the ones who probably will have access to the most diverse people. Even if you have moved across the country, call your old classmate. Ask him to recommend someone where *you* live. Insurance people always know names of other agents everywhere in America, because insurance agents, good ones, go to more conventions and sales contest trips than people in any other profession.

I could have called my agent and he could have reached the right people. But again, it would have taken time—and a trip to police headquarters.

There is another, instant method that involves one of my Mavens in the service area. I could have called Sam Hennick, with his pearl-handled revolver in his belt. Sam is a sergeant in our local police department, and I know he's in my pocket the way I know that Thanksgiving is always the fourth Thursday in November. Sam Hennick is my service Maven. You don't *need* a police officer on your Smart People team. But we live in a world where law enforcement is a major industry and where crime is equally pervasive. Especially the crimes we fear the most: per-sonal attacks, civil disorder, housebreaking, arson, theft. Sam Hennick is a jolly man who has four children, a receding hairline, and a graduate degree in social work that took him five years of night school to obtain. He plans to put in twenty years on the force, retire with his pension, and do social service work at a hospital that has already promised to hire him. A police officer Maven can help you in two big ways. He can give you the true gossip of the town or city where you live. And he can pull you out of trouble, whether it's a traffic ticket or something more serious. I recruited Sergeant Sam Hennick while he was coaching one of my children in the town's Little League. I suppose you could say my son recruited him. The kid was a pretty fair left-handed pitcher with good speed and something that most youngsters do not possess, especially lefties. He had control. After the season we took the boys and the coach to a major-league game. We sat in a third-base box, ate hotdogs, and kept score in the programs. Sam Hennick and I drank beer, and he told me about the cop they just caught in town selling VH cards. A VH card is a vacant-house record, a file that lists the town occupants who are away on vacation trips or on business or for the summer. The VH cards were sold for two hundred dollars apiece, and the bad cop who stole them was taken into the woods in back of the station house and given a lesson he would never forget. Until the inmates in the house of correction where he was sent found out he was a policeman. Then there were a few more lessons.

Sam and I became friends at the ballpark, and he proved it by teaching me about the Daisy Diner Syndrome.


## THE DAISY DINER SYNDROME

There is a Daisy Diner, or its equivalent, in your hometown. And big cities are no different from small towns. Any city has its neighborhood restaurant or cafe where the tradespeople stop for breakfast, lunch, a drink. It is usually a small restaurant or deli or diner that opens early in the morning and is frequented by most of the police, firemen, and tradespeople. It is their club. Newcomers have to prove themselves. They are never automatically welcomed, whether it is in South Dakota, New York City, Georgia, or Alaska. You have to earn your way into the Daisy Diner.

The week after the big-league game Sam Hennick took me to the diner for breakfast at six-thirty. The town's carpenter was there, the leading electrician and plumber, the man with the biggest fuel business, the hardware-store owner — and the clique of police officers who call themselves "the choirboys," after Joe Wambaugh's novel. They ran the police department the way everyone else there ran the town. I told them two stories over french toast and coffee. I told them about the research I had done about the biggest city in the state during Prohibition and how I was writing a book about a police patrolman who ran vice and liquor in that city between 1928 and 1932. The patrolman never made more than forty dollars a week on the job. But he managed to stuff his safe deposit box full of four hundred and seventy thousand dollars in old bills before he was indicted. The patrolman had tremendous power. He owned several dairies south of the city, and every speakeasy was forced to buy its milk from the cop. At fifty dollars a quart. Everybody on a fixed income appreciates the entrepreneur.

Then I told them about my cousin, the auxiliary police officer in Milwaukee, whom everyone in the family calls "Blow 'em Away Jimmy." He works for an aerospace manufacturing company and is the only engineer I ever heard of who carries three weapons to work, a Mauser under his arm, a small throwaway taped to his calf, and a switchblade made in Genoa, Italy.

"He's got a family full of nuts," Officer Sam Hennick assured them.

And I was officially welcomed into the Daisy Diner inner circle.

Often, Sam Hennick will stop by our house for a beer or some Celestial Seasonings tea, which he loves. Sam Hennick is waiting for immortality. He wants to be a hero in the first television series about the suburban policeman. He tells me the gossip.

"This town," he told me recently," has too much money and not

enough sense of what to do with it. We got a call from a baby-
sitter in one of the new areas of town, a development where
every house is in the six figures. The baby-sitter has a curfew of
midnight and it's two A.M. and the owners of the house not back
yet. She says they went to a party in town but no one answered
when she rang there. So I go out with my partner, Sully, and we
get to the party house. We ring the bell. Nothing. We look in the
windows and there's a man lying on the couch in the living room,
not moving. Sully and me think he's dead and we jimmy the
window. The guy's alive, but passed out drunk. We shook him
awake. 'Where is everyone?' we asked him.

" 'Over at the Hunts'. Playing The Game. I didn't feel like
playing The Game so I went to sleep.'

"We went to the Hunts', around the corner. There were thirteen of the so-called finest of the town: engineers, a doctor, several lawyers, one of the school committee, female. All of them is
bollicky, bare-ass naked, as drunk as the guy on the couch. Well,
the school-committee woman ordered us out, and the doctor told
us to take off our uniforms. We hurried the couple home who had
the baby-sitter, and we learned about The Game. This couple
was eight sheets to the wind and the wife had fallen asleep, but
the husband tells us, 'Look, officers. It looks foolish, but a man's
home is his castle, right? The Game is harmless. We get in a
living room or a playroom and we turn all the lights off. Then we
get all undressed and throw the clothes in a pile. We've got
two minutes to put on anything we can grab before the lights go
back on. It's harmless, officer, and you can forget you saw it,
yes?' "

Sam Hennick, my service Maven, watches our house like a
stakeout when we're away. His network in other police departments around the state provides material for books, ideas, and
information about what really goes on in politics, even in the
economy.

"*You're* in the network, Johnny boy," Sam Hennick tells me.
Then a shadow crosses his face because, when all is said and

done, I'm on the other side. "Tell me something, Johnny," he says.
"You and your wife. You don't play The Game, do you?"

If you can recruit a policeman for your team, it's a bonus. With
Sam Hennick, it's a trade-off. He knows I'm entertained by his
stories, and he also knows I can help him with free financial
advice. Whenever you move to a new location, call your local
police station. They all have a community-affairs specialist. Talk
to him. Ask him if there is a pet community program with police
support that you can help out with, either with time or contributions. Once you meet this officer he will always alert his fellow
police to give you special treatment.


## THE POLITE SOCIETY

One major revolution has occurred in the middle class in the last
decade. In an egalitarian society, people would rather *not* work
than be involved in work they consider demeaning. Potential
cooks open catering businesses, potential chauffeurs drive cabs,
cleaning people join industrial-maintenance companies, parlor
maids and butlers appear only in sweet memory. The truth is that
no one will do the work in households on other than an hourly
basis with full Social Security and insurance benefits. This is the
Polite Society of sanitation engineers and summer baby-sitters.
The nanny is dead, long live television. This Polite Society, paying lip service to the myth that we are all created equal, has
destroyed the ability of most of us to get anyone to give a damn
about tending our special needs. What does a Smart Person do
when Brigitte won't get into the uniform? When, indeed, she
wants to sell records in Discomania at the mall near the turnpike?

The truly Smart Person penetrates the secret need of today's
society. The need for human companionship, the hope that others
will care.

If you can make the breakthrough, anything is possible. Particularly service. My service Lamplighter is my wife, Susan. Because of her interest in medicine, we are as fully staffed by unobtrusive part-time help as the Bellamys in Eaton Place were staffed by dependent full-timers. Medicine intrigues her. But her true genius is in obtaining help.

My father-in-law died some years ago. He was a surgeon and a professor of anatomy at a major eastern medical school. We have a picture of him performing an autopsy on an elephant. My wife was a child in times that did not encourage women to pursue professional careers. But she used to be taken by her father to observe operations, standing in gown and mask to watch appendectomies, childbirths, gall-bladder removals. Then he would take her to his club on Commonwealth Avenue, near his office in the Back Bay, and buy her lunches of a Shirley Temple, a club sandwich, and a butterscotch parfait.

"What if I get a job?" my wife asked several years ago, when all the children were spending their days in school.

"Terrific," I responded. Meaning it, because I'm compulsive about everyone in my house being happy.

She didn't get a job, but she did go down to our town's police station and asked about emergency medical training programs. "They're only given for police and fire personnel, lady," she was told by the desk sergeant. She leaned over the counter and looked straight into his face. "They're also going to be given for *me*," she said. People don't know how to react when you emphatically include yourself. They're not used to it. You become a problem.

"I think you get more accomplished being a persistent *lady* than as a Bella Abzug," my wife says. "Go to the police station in an Albert Nipon suit and Andrew Geller shoes, smelling slightly of Audace, and they'll bend every regulation in police procedures to let you into the course. Don't kid yourself. If a businessman's fantasy is to make love to the nurse or the stewardess, the fantasy of the suburban or city police and firemen is to bed the civilian housewife. I was the only person in our town outside of official personnel to take the approved CPR course. One secret about operating with the town or city people. Don't tell your friends. Guard your sources as if you were a CIA operative."

My wife passed the course and now instructs at hospitals and adult-education centers. But the key to our service problems is that she recruited for our team virtually every member of the local police and fire departments.

Where does the average person deal with service more than any other place? In a restaurant. Convincing owners and maitre d's that we are the best people and deserve the best tables is difficult for most of us. Getting the ultimate from waiters and waitresses can be impossible. I have a short story about how an expert once dealt with this situation, demonstrating a brilliant solution to one of life's problems.

While my wife, Susan, and I were dating, we were invited to a wedding at St. Patrick's Cathedral with a reception later at the Pierre. I forget what we argued about, something silly. We left the reception slightly high and not talking to one another. "Mexican food" was all Susan would say to me as we walked together, but miles apart, away from the Pierre. We headed down the Avenue of the Americas to La Fonda del Sol, a shining restaurant at the bottom of the Time-Life Building. It was seven-thirty in the evening, amateur night, when everyone who stays at home all week goes out for a toot. The line waiting to get into La Fonda extended all the way from the doors to the edge of the fountains set in the Time-Life plaza. "I'm not going to stand in that line to eat quasi-Mexican food and pay two-fifty for a margarita," I told her. She said nothing, but walked right by the line, into the building, through the lobby, through the cocktail lounge. I followed her closely, murmering "Excuse me, excuse me" to all the waiting people we were pushing by. Susan led us right to the front of the line. As the maitre d' looked us over, she didn't hesitate for an instant. "Reservations for two at eight o'clock, please," Susan said. "Mr. Stevenson's party." She announced this with such authority that the maitre d' stared at us for a moment, ran his finger down the reservation list, glancing downward. Then he snapped his fingers and said, "Certainly, Mrs. Stevenson. This way, please." I heard a mutter from behind us. Someone said, "It's Adlai's son and daughter-in-law." But I was already following Susan and the boss to a choice table for two. "Thanks," I said to the maitre d'. "We appreciate it."

"My pleasure, Mr. Stevenson," he said. "I remember the good old days."

"Who doesn't," I said. "Thanks." He left us and I jumped up to hug Susan, both of us dissolved in laughter. "How did you have any idea?" I asked her.

"I didn't," she said. "But John Fell Stevenson looks vaguely like you when you get that young-lawyer expression. It was worth a try."

When we moved from an apartment to a house in the country, we did it anticipating numerous service problems. We bought a Revolutionary War–vintage house with a plaque on the side indicating that General Burgoyne's troops had used the site for a comfort station on their march to Concord. "It's my job, I suppose," Susan said at the time, "to juggle carpenters, masons, plumbers, painters. Right?"

"Well," I said, "I'm at work during the day . . ."

"Say no more," she replied. And, being in a totally new community, she began hunting for people in the Yellow Pages. One day, several months after we moved, I arrived home to find a sheet cut into the shape of a banner hanging across the driveway, connected from the house to a tree. "I don't need this," read the foot-high painted letters. Susan was sitting in the kitchen juggling three different dinners for our three children who had various midwinter illnesses.

"We're doing this wrong," she said. "After today we're going into Phase Two. If we're shoveling money into this antique of a house, we're going to channel it to people who love it and love us."

"What triggered this?" I asked.

"The electrician."

"That little old man?"

"That little old man, I think, would have an affair with a snake if he could hold it down. I don't want him around anymore. I don't want any Yellow Pages creep coming into this house overcharging and underperforming." It seemed that Morris, our electrician, a bent-over strange little man who prided himself on telling us that he was "pushing seventy," came into the kitchen. He asked my wife if she could hold a wrench on a plug while he went into the cellar to adjust some wires. "Don't be afraid, Missus," he said; "nothing happened to anyone doing this since that woman up the center."

"What happened to the woman up the center?" my wife asked.

"Well," said Morris, "this woman comes into the kitchen where I'm working and she's wearing one of them see-through peignoir sets, you know? Well, I try not to look at her, and she says she's gonna make breakfast and I go into the cellar to the fuse box. I'm down there two minutes and I hear a scream '*Morris*' like she's being killed. I run upstairs and into the kitchen. The woman is holding onto a fork stuck into a toaster and the room is ablaze with sparks. I could see her two nipples through the peignoir set. They're lighting up red and green. Like stoplights."

Morris stared at my wife, waiting for a reaction. She just dropped the wrench and retired to a neutral part of the house. The incident changed our lives. It was the next week that Susan talked herself into the police department's course in advanced emergency first aid and cardiopulmonary resuscitation.

Susan became the class pet immediately. The first night, everyone in the class was asked to stand, state their name, occupation, and previous experience. Men stood and gave responses like, "Tony Rosco. Police sergeant. I pulled a man from the surf once. He wanted to be saved."

My wife, Susan, the only woman, got up and said, "I'm Susan Spooner. I've had three babies. I'm a lady of leisure." The men all cheered. When they stopped cheering, they were in her pocket.

Since that day we have recruited the following people, all of whom have become friends, all of whom serve special roles for us: the driver of Engine No. 1 cleans our house once a week. The local dog warden cleans our windows and gutters every fall. One of the sergeants is our carpenter. He has put all new windows on our third floor, built a tree house for our children, and fashioned a bridge over a stream that runs through our property. All for a small fraction of the cost estimated by local professional people. Of course, these men are moonlighting and they are paid in cash. But they are efficient, do quality work, and, being an integral part of the community, care about their reputations because of future referrals within the town. When we're away, our house is more closely watched than our neighbors'. We know all the goodies of the town before the papers know.

We have a large boulder wall bordering our property, lining the street. Over the years many of the giant stones were pushed down an embankment into our woods, giving the impression of a rude battlement that had been breached by too many enemy attacks. I obtained quotes on repairing the wall that ranged from a thousand to seventeen hundred dollars. "Day and a half with a backhoe, Mac. Plus we gotta reroute traffic. Them stones is a bitch." My wife went to CPR class one night and mentioned the problem to her buddies during coffee break.

"You need Tony Geruzzi at the highway department," she was told. When she called Tony she mentioned the people who had recommended him. "The town plows in the winter caused most of the damage," she had been told to say, while adding, "The boys think perhaps you could take a look." The next week the town highway crew repaired the wall for the right price. Nothing!

Because Susan used her Smart People, we got results. The local service people in the network always take care of each other. *And* their friends.

This is not the kind of story you can tell your neighbors. They, believing in democracy, would be wild. But Smart People technique involves taking care of *your* needs in a society that does not care. We have our service team in place, and my wife can treat abrasions, incisions, lacerations, punctures, and avulsions. She can prevent bleeding, detect shock, administer fluids, do cardio-pulmonary resuscitation, remove foreign bodies from the throat, get you out of a smashed automobile and apply traction, splint a fracture of the femur. Let me tell you, I can sleep secure.

My service Summa is an institution. He makes and sells men's clothing in his specialty shop, which he has never allowed to grow beyond intimate size. He runs the shop as if it were a salon. He treats the patrons as if they were entering a club, but a club where only he approves the membership, and where the member-ship is constantly subject to review. The store has an ordinary name. But everyone calls it Fancy David's because of the man who owns it. More than anyone else in the city, Fancy David is an arbiter of taste and style, and, because he never compromises, his reputation among clothing merchants is nationwide. "Every-thing good in life," Fancy David says, "builds toward people rec-ognizing you, caring about you."

Picture a small shop built on three levels connected by circular stairs. Polished brass railings line each stairway. Fancy David himself patrols the upper level where he is able to observe the entire structure of his playhouse. It is difficult to imagine David naked. Skin would seem an anticlimax because he looks so well in his clothes. He is of medium height, slim, a perfect forty regular, with close-cropped gray hair and a seductive sparkle in his eyes that appears almost conspiratorial, as if he were always motion-ing you closer to hear the real goods about a mutual friend.

David is the ultimate service Summa because, although he provides goods and services for others, he makes his customers feel as if it is the other way around, as if they serve *him*. And he makes them love it. I would like to recommend a book that perfectly illustrates the theme of a servant being totally in control of master. The book is a little gem of the macabre: *The Cook,* by Harry Kressing. It is a diabolical story, told in fairy-tale fashion and set in a mythical kingdom. It tells of the complete takeover of the kingdom by a man who makes himself indispensable through his cooking abilities. Power is transferred to the cook because no one can get enough of his *spécialités*. People will give the cook anything. Fancy David has this same power. But he is not diabolical. He binds people to him in order to have an audience for his judgments on the passing scene.

I had always bought ties and sweaters from David when I was in college. I could afford to buy ties and sweaters. Suits were bought elsewhere, from manufacturers, at maker's cost. When I started to work and had received my first few paychecks I went to see Fancy David. I really wanted to show him that I had graduated from sweaters and ties.

It was early May, and students on David's street sat in windows and on steps of dormitories with aluminum reflectors tucked under their chins. I went to see Fancy David and told him to make me a three-piece white linen suit.

"Not bad," David said, "but you cannot wear this suit more than once without having it pressed. Linen wrinkles. White linen turns yellow. The two best dressers I ever saw, Averell Harriman and a guy named Choo-Choo Roberts who was a drunk, wore linen suits after they turned yellow. But the suits were always pressed, even after Choo-Choo Roberts's liver began to look like a crabapple and his arms were so withered that his custom broadcloth shirts from Turnbull and Asser surrounded him like a shroud."

"Whom do you give service to?" I asked David long ago, noticing that he ignored several people fingering merchandise until they walked out of the store.

"I break my tail for two kinds of people," David said. "Characters. And kids who look like they may make it someday. I've got a whole network of ex-students who have scattered all over the world but still treat me like a father. They use my shop as a message center whenever they're in town. These kids order some clothes, tell me about what's happening. It's like having your own CIA."

"You feel that there's not only satisfaction in your work, there's also power?"

"Let me tell you how you build a reputation and a big volume in any service business — carpentry, plumbing, auto repair, whatever. Two things: One, let them know in your own quiet way that you're not their equal . . . you're *superior*. Two, let everyone think that there's a quota on the business you do and that you do not do business with just anyone. You pick and choose your clientele. I'll illustrate:

"One day several years ago, a representative of a Middle Eastern prince came into the shop. The prince was on a diplomatic mission and was in town to catch his breath and sample the fish. He was en route to visit Jack Kennedy at Palm Beach. 'His majesty, the prince, needs appropriate uniforms,' the representative said. The representative was American, right out of Skull and Bones at Yale," David told me. "The kind of guy who could have been captain of Spring track and participated in the fabled naked wrestling at Bones, while everyone else drank gin until they were sure they would be sick in their beds."

" 'His majesty has a desire,' said the Yale boy. 'He wishes you to design and make him uniforms.'

" 'I'll need a day to consider,' I said, and, although he didn't want delay for an answer, I ushered him into the street where the motor was running in the biggest Lincoln limo you ever saw. The next day I accepted the assignment because of curiosity, a sense of challenge, and the fact that I told Mr. Yale that my fee for three uniforms in five days (their time frame) would be twenty-five thousand dollars. I got the instant acceptance that makes you feel you've been taken to the cleaners and you should have asked fifty thousand. But, everything for art, I told myself.

"I was the first person in the main city library the next morning, ahead of the winos and the woman who has been researching

the life of Elizabeth Barrett Browning for twenty-six years and
keeps her notes tucked into a mink muff. In a *Book of Knowledge*
edition of 1933 I found a page of uniform designs from the court
of Napoleon the Second. I took an epaulet here, a sash there, a
double-breasted cherry-picker touch here, a gold-braided waist-
coat there, and I whipped up three incredible uniforms in less
time than it would take you to say 'Louis Vuitton.' By the way,"
Fancy David said, "you know how I feel about designers and
about men who wear designer clothes. Anyone who wears clothes
with someone else's initials is a turd of turds. Designers are to
clothing what hookers are to sex.

"Anyway," David went on, "I go back to the shop, hire extra
tailors, and start work. We work nineteen hours a day for two
days, and I haven't heard a word from the prince. I stop the
tailors and take a cab into the hotel where the prince and his
entourage, including nineteen women, are staying. Getting out of
the cab I stop to talk with Sam, the doorman, who is an old pro
and has been at this hotel since the jazz of Benny Goodman
poured out of the lounge.

" 'You see many of the Arabs around here, Sam?' I asked him.

" 'Are you kidding?' Sam said. 'Every hour Sears, Zayre's, Jordan's trucks pull up, and they carry in washing machines, dryers,
sewing machines, TVs you wouldn't believe. These characters in
sheets are signing for hundreds of thousands of dollars worth of
merchandise. State Department boys are following them okaying
the signatures with the stores.'

" 'The prince paying all the bills?' I asked.

" 'Christ, no,' Sam said. 'The oil company is paying the bills.'

"Feeling comforted by that, but still somewhat anxious, having
spent thirty-seven hundred dollars for gold braid and other special materials for the uniforms, I took an elevator to the prince's
floor. The corridor had a special odor that reminded me of the
year my wife stocked the refrigerator with nothing but yogurt. I
was stopped immediately by someone who looked like a junior

Bowie Kuhn, glasses, pinstripe, tight rear end. Before he opened his mouth I said, 'You can get away with striped tie on a striped shirt. You can get away with it.' Momentarily flustered, he softened. 'Can I help you?'

"'Yes,' says I. 'I'm Fancy David who is halfway through His Majesty's uniforms, and I respectfully would like to know who's going to pay me, and when.'

"As I'm standing there, men in burnooses are pushing by me, carrying Sony TV's, Radarranges, shopping bags from Bonwit's and Saks. They all looked as if they were bearing gifts for some 1970s Christ-child born in a discount store."

"'That's it,' junior Bowie yelled, stamping his feet. 'No more charges, no more refrigerators. We're not paying for one more thing,' he blared at me. 'Uniforms for His Majesty? His Majesty is a simple man. Never ostentatious. Enough people are stealing from us. Out! Uniforms? We never gave such an order. Out! Sell them to a museum, the marines.'

"Unfortunately, in life," David told me, "you can only learn by your mistakes. I went back to the shop feeling like a fool, but partially glad that I had seen such a show. I dismissed the extra tailors, hung the unfinished uniforms on a rack where I could look at them, put fiddle music on the stereo system, took a small glass of wine and did my Rumpelstiltskin dance. That's the dance I do when the ridiculousness of life pours over me.

"The next morning at nine-thirty the Lincoln limo skidded to a halt outside the shop. Bowie Kuhn, Jr., came running in, looking as crushed as if he had been told he would not play against Yale. 'I apologize,' he said. 'God, do I apologize, Mr. David. I had no idea that the prince . . .'

"'Forget it,' I told him. 'The Salvation Army is picking them up this afternoon.'

"Making people like Bowie, Jr., beg is one of the most satisfying of life's pursuits," David went on. "He didn't balk when I raised the price for the three uniforms to thirty thousand, finally saying, 'The company makes billions in the Middle East. What the hell is thirty thou? Right? We want our puppets standing tall, looking good.'

"I called the extra tailors back, and we worked day and night for three days finishing the uniforms. Six people including Bowie, Jr., picked them up, flew them by helicopter to Hyannis airport where Air Force Two took the prince to Palm Beach to see Jack Kennedy. I heard later that the prince and his boys sweated like bastards because it was a hundred and two in Palm Beach and the uniforms were all winter issue, flannel, or cashmere lined in silk. Made for parades in Leningrad in February. You see, even in the days of the Emperor's New Clothes, the smart tailor is always in control."

Fancy David's theory of the quota is essential in getting people to respond to you. "If people think that you may not do business with them," he says, "they'll beat down your door waving dollars. One man years ago brought his son into the shop to buy him some jackets and slacks. The man smoked a big cigar, had a diamond pinkie ring, patent leather Guccis, cashmere double-breasted overcoat, size forty-eight short. He starts fingering materials, bolts of cloth, looking at the displays. He's suddenly wanting to be Averell Harriman, not Lee J. Cobb in *On the Waterfront.*"

" 'How about you make me a couple of suits?' the man said, being careful to knock his ashes in the ashtray. The more I told him he wouldn't be happy in our clothes, the more he insisted. I wouldn't even sell him a tie. But I did it with great courtesy and left him with the feeling that if he could measure up to the Fancy David look, it would be everything."

David's quota system is nothing more than supply and demand with some sleight of hand: the-grass-is-always-greener routine.

"You can work this on people forever," says David, "because of the miserable nature of most folk. The average poor bastard gets up in the morning and goes in for breakfast which his wife has

said David, "is the lining. The lining is in
d blue silk, small tattersall checks like you
n weekends in the country."
e the lining," I said.
y David. "No one *has* to see the lining. But
ere. Style, not fashion. Remember that," he
on."

right. But in the office I often take off my
und in the vest which shows off the special
ve to talk about it. But it never hurts to let
lo not buy your clothes off the rack. I told
t this weakness on my part and he smiled.
s secure as Averell Harriman," he said, "but

hy over the years has taught me many lessons.
s of life and style, I shall attempt to pass on:
uld be a statement; your clothes alone should
ond. I knew a woman, Mrs. Kudish, who loved
Everything she wore had a purple accent. Her
her automobile was purple. They called her
ou don't think she got attention?"
e best. Low price should be no temptation to
salesman showed me some ties last year. They

d, marveling at how well they were made.
e salesman, 'acrylic. Aren't they great? I knew

n't want them,' I said. 'I won't buy acrylic that

p for bargains in stereo, you can get a discount on
you should never look for a discount tailor. Good
combination of things: taste, workmanship, and
land has only materials now. It's very sad."
should not be everything. I always allow myself
e of nonspenders in a shop, if they interest me. This

prepare
softens
him bec
part of w

On the
quota the
at a partic
that perioc
shares of P
in a golf-clu
television an
"I've got an
about five th
give you the b

"Well, I ap
handle it. My
efficient I'm for
thousand dollars

"Doing that w

He called me
thousand somewl
son-in-law with tl
bum gets another
used to doing bus
fifty, we'll all go ou
him."

You would be am
last few dollars to n
know that not everyo
can have you at a dis
can do turnaway busin

David made me a gr
gray flannel suit of cons
buttonholes on the sleev

difference in this suit,
smart checks of red a
see on a Viyella shirt

"But nobody will se

"Ahhhh," said Fan
you will know it's th
said. "Style, not fashi

I know David is
jacket and walk aro
lining. You don't ha
people know you
Fancy David abou
"You'll never be a
you're learning."

David's philosop
Several, about way

1. "Dressing sh
get people to resp
the color purple.
house was purple
'Purple Kudish.' Y

2. "Pay for th
compromise. A
looked terrific.

" 'Wool?' I sai

" 'No,' said t
you'd love them

" "Then I do
looks like wool.

"You can sh
Cuisinarts. Bu
clothing is a
materials. Eng

3. "Busines
the indulgenc

way I can give my customers a kicker. And the kicker is gossip. Knowing gossip is very important, because people realize they can come to the shop not only for clothing, but for tidbits."

4. "Survival in life is uppermost. I mean survival as a business-man, as a person. The 1960s were a killer for tailors and fine-clothing people, as you might imagine. Not for jeans and tee shirts, but for proper adult attire. Drinking and jazz pulled me through the 1960s. And another thing to remember: survivors have the ability to put everything on the backburner. America totally forgot something no civilization should ever forget: people seventeen to twenty-two years old should not be taken seriously."

5. "Judge your heroes only in their arenas. Sinatra, Miles Davis, Babe Ruth should be seen only in the context of their specialties. They're much better out there than behind closed doors lifting a cocktail with you."

6. "You've got to be invited to everything important. But you should almost never go."

7. "One secret of life is to work your ass off and give the impression that you don't. Remember, Bing Crosby finished in the low seventies."

Scooter Walsh is a dealer in things — "In any things," as he says. Scooter Walsh's creed is "Limo City," which means that his approach to living is having the ability to go first-class all the way, whether you can afford it or not. Scooter Walsh is my Roughrider in the area of service and represents, in many ways, the essential type of Smart Person you must recruit to make your life easier. There is almost nothing Scooter cannot get — free for his friends, at a heavy price for his customers.

I was closing down an office several years ago after a merger. There was a sign in my window: "For Rent, Furniture for Sale." The second day, in walked a man about forty-four years old, wearing a knitted Montreal Canadiens' cap, a double knit blazer over yellow wide-wale corduroy trousers. If I were casting a re-make of *The Quiet Man* I could never have picked a better country lad. His hair hung down below the cap in back, hair red as Santa's mittens. He took off his cap with a flourish and handed me a soiled calling card. It read "Scooter Walsh—Sundries and You Name It."

There are people you meet in life who you know are stringing you along. But you cannot help but enjoy their company. Walsh is a charming con man. He can deliver, but there is always something in it for him. He screwed me slightly on the office furniture. For his pride's sake. But I knew that I would have reason to use his services again. There are business people who need a small dishonest edge to make themselves feel good. But they feel guilty about it. Next time they'll give you a break. Because I let him get away with a few hundred dollars, I knew he owed me one.

Planning an office party some months later, I called Scooter and asked him if he could get the right price on cases of beer and liquor.

"Hey," Walsh said, "is the Virgin Mary pure as the driven snow? What do you need?"

"I'd like five cases of Michelob. It's ten a case at my dealer's."

"*If* I got it — and I ain't saying I do, now, you understand — *if* I got it, it'll cost you five-fifty a case."

"Are you serious?" I said.

"I'm always serious. But it depends what fell off the truck."

I was to park my car next to a downtown bar, identify myself to the bartender, pay him in cash, and carry the cases of beer away.

I walked into the bar. It was dark as a cave, illuminated only by the light shining from plugged-in Budweiser signs. It was a workingmen's place, a place for hard hats to arm wrestle, play pinball, and watch sports on the TV. I stood at the bar, waiting for the bartender to come over. A kid stood next to me, watching a football game and drinking Miller's from the bottle. He had a dragon tattooed on his left forearm. Above it was tattooed the name Amy. I didn't ask him if the dragon was called Amy. "Any score?" I asked instead.

He looked at me. And he was drunk. I was wearing a turtle-neck, rust-colored hacking jacket, and gray flannel slacks. He knew I was about to pass out buttons for gay liberation, that I was in there on my search for rough trade.

"You an iron worker?" he asked with much suspicion. "You know the iron worker is King Tut in this town. King fucking Tut."

The bartender arrived, and I stated my business. He motioned me toward a storeroom in the back. "The cases are against the wall with a red blanket over them," he said. "I'd help you carry them, but I'm all alone. And for that price, *you* can carry the beer." In the storeroom were boxes of whiskey, cartons of ciga-rettes stacked to the ceiling, tape recorders, television sets in their cartons. And a red blanket thrown over six cases of Michelob. On top of the red blanket were two Thompson submachine guns, the kind you think of as being shoved through back windows of 1928 Fords. I moved them to the top of a pile of gift boxes of Fanny Farmer chocolates.

The drunk hard hat, seeing I knew the management, helped me carry the cases to the car. He could think only in terms of his buildings, his jobs. "I was up the Federal Reserve today in the rain," he told me. "Topping off in the rain."

I made the mistake of asking him if it is true that the Indians walk the high steel because they have no fear of heights. It drove him into a frenzy. He banged his fists on top of a convenient car hood. "I never saw an Indian on one of them buildings in my life. We're white men, bozo. White men." The last case was loaded, and I was sliding into my exit lines.

"You know what a white man is?" he continued, poking a finger into my chest.

"The iron worker is King Tut," I said to him. "King fucking Tut."

While he thought about that I jumped in the car, locked it, started the engine, and roared off. Sometimes, in finding a bargain and getting certain services, you have to be prepared for the unexpected.

## GETTING THE MARKERS OUT

Scooter Walsh likes to do favors for me. He likes to tell me stories of his exploits because he thinks I'm shocked by them. "I like to have the markers out," he says. "I build up a mountain of good-will, and I do favors for people because it's nice to be nice. I do it because I want to, not because I have to. Then, somewhere down the line, when I need it, I call in the markers, and they remember me."

"You don't like to talk about people, Scooter," I said. "Most people love to talk about others."

"My grandmother told me," he said, "a tongue has no bones. But many it will break."

"Who do you perform tricks for, Scooter? What kind of people do you work for?"

"There are two kinds of people I work for," he answered. "I work for the heavy dough. I'll arrange anything, I'll deliver anything. For big money. When I do the small stuff, cases of beer, take a bet, a gram of cocaine, I've got to do it for people who understand. For people who appreciate me, and who appreciate the truth of life. And the truth is that anyone who thinks there's equality is either an asshole or he inherited money. For instance," he said, "my cousin is a state trooper. He drives the lieutenant governor around, the lieutenant governor of the state, right? One day the lieutenant gov. is complaining he can't get tickets to *A Chorus Line*. The show is all sold out. My cousin makes one call, doesn't say anything to his boss, gets two in the third row on the aisle, gives them to his boss, tucked in the middle of the sports pages. The lieutenant governor is knocked out. He can't get tick-

ets, *but his driver can*. You've got to know how to operate. You've
got to stay wired to the people who can *produce*."

The secret to having Scooter continue to come through for you
is to treat him as if you believe he could do anything. With
service Roughriders you ask for the big story first.

"Scooter, if I have a guy owes me five thousand dollars and he
refuses to pay and I've used a lawyer but it doesn't work, what
recourse do I have?"

"I know at least three boys," Scooter says, "who for twenty
dollars each will break any leg in America."

He knows you are thrilled by this, so you push him. "And what
if I want something more than broken legs?"

"Whacking people out right is a complicated business," Walsh
tells me, his eyes alight with the possibility of sticking it to the
straight world. "I had a serious problem a few years ago," he said.
"A man had hurt the family very badly. I remember cashing a
check for ten thousand dollars and having the cashier give it to
me in old bills, fives and tens. I drove to a resort town on the sea,
and I met a man who owned a guest house with his mother. Very
clean rooms and a john in every hall with a tile shower. The man
was famous at tying acid bottles to people's accelerator linkage so
they continued to drive until they hit something. He was very
inventive that way. I gave him the ten thousand and he said,
'Let's go in the parlor and have a chat.' We had a chat, and he
gave me back the ten thou. 'You don't want the responsibility of
this,' the man said. 'You've got a heart.'

"He was right," Scooter said. "Can you believe he talked me
out of it? He was a helluva guy, and his mother brought me an
Irish whiskey before I drove back. My enemy? I hadda be satisfied about a year later with screwing his wife. You gotta die a
little anyway, that happens to you."

After the big question to the Roughrider, the small favor is a
breeze. *Now* you hit him with the ridiculously simple. "What can
you do for my father-in-law on a new El Dorado?"

Walsh scoffed, but one phone call later he said, "The list is eighteen thou. He can pick his color and options, cost him sixty-five hundred delivered. Only hitch is, it's delivered in Springfield, Illinois. You can pick it up, drive it back. Or pay another three hundred, I get a driver for you, door to door."

You start with a big question, a contract hit, then you ask for an automobile. It's a relief for Scooter. And he gets a bigger commission for an El Dorado than for a broken leg.

Scooter Walsh files an IRS Form 1040, the same as millions of other Americans. He reports gross income of approximately thirteen thousand dollars and lists as dependents his wife, three children, and his mother who lives with him in a triple-decker house and remembers every time her husband broke her jaw when the whiskey was on him. Cash is the item of preference in Walsh's world. He usually carries a thousand in fifties and twenties with a heavy-duty elastic around it. When he flashes the money he laughs. "This is my Kansas City bankroll," he says. "Five ones wrapped around a cucumber." The cash Walsh took in last year from his various enterprises amounted to forty-seven thousand four hundred ninety dollars and eleven cents. Tax free and unreported.

There is only one way to recruit Roughriders: have something to trade. Only by offering them some service or specialty of your own will you hold their interest long enough to have them be of use. The method of gaining their confidence initially is to show them how impressed you are with the uses of street smarts. "God," you say, "I could never have the guts for that." Or, "Everything in my education was all wrong. Where could I have gone to have ever learned *that?*" When Roughriders feel you are impressed, they'll continue to perform for you to earn more praise.

What do I trade Walsh for his services? As much as I love his stories of gambling and drugs and gangland vengeance, he loves stories of the rich and famous, of skiing in Gstaad, summers in

Southampton, cruising the Greek islands, and golf in Augusta. Scooter Walsh's weakness is that he is an incurable snob.

One sure method of getting response from service people is this: when you give them presents, give them gifts that are monogrammed. A pewter mug bought for eleven dollars inscribed "Scooter" and given to him for Christmas has ensured Scooter's responding to me not only by his services, but also by answers to my questions about anything that is illicit. Any monogrammed gift to an employee or anyone who serves you will be more remembered than almost anything else. It lets your service people know they are special. Give them their initials on a gift belt buckle or mug or shirt or blouse. It lets them know that you care. And they will work a little harder in your behalf.

My service Roughrider reflects the wisdom and knowledge of the street. Here are several of Scooter Walsh's Scooterisms.

1. "My motto has always been 'What goes around, comes around.' The difference between winners and losers is knowing when your chance comes around."

2. "I had a bad problem with cocaine a year ago. I was dealing a little, but I got so I did it all the time myself. You know that powder is mostly twenty-two hundred dollars an ounce in the East. Maybe eighteen hundred if you know someone. There are twenty-seven grams in an ounce, and one gram gives you about forty lines on little mirrors. Doing it right, you should take about two or three lines every forty minutes. I like snorting through a hundred-dollar bill. You know why? Hundred dollar bills are less handled than any other kind. Not so many germs up your nose. An expensive habit. But let me tell you, sex on a coke high is the greatest sex of all. When you screw on cocaine the women put you in the Hall of Fame. 'Oh, my God,' they say. And I keep telling them my name is Scooter."

3. "I'm a big believer in the cycles of life. In high school I wanted to be a great athlete. What I really wanted was a cheerleader girl friend, anything in a uniform. Then I went to my tenth

high school reunion, in a white limo, and I discovered that the football heroes had all peaked out at age seventeen. And the cheerleaders were still cheerleaders; they had never progressed from there. Speaking of women, I want to tell you that I'm happily married. I love my kids. But everybody has got to be broken in, you know what I mean? Two things I did with my wife. She was complaining that she heard I was still seeing an old girlfriend. I told her, 'Hey, if you want to listen to other people, we'll never be happy.' Then, the first week of our marriage, I stayed in a hotel one night. I didn't call; I didn't come home. She was frantic, but I told her that I didn't want to set a precedent. I'll tell you, I *wanted* to come home; I didn't *want* to stay at the hotel; I was lonely. But I didn't want to set a precedent that she could expect me every night. Sometimes you gotta suffer for what you believe."

4. "New morality? Are you serious? Human nature doesn't change. The captain of the city police still gets five thousand at Christmas to leave the bookies alone. Watergate helped us to play ball, to have business as usual. Because everyone watched Watergate and left us alone. Every system is there to be beat. Only when people can no longer use the system do they expose it."

I have a drink once a month with Walsh, just to find out what is happening in the city, if the restaurants are doing business, if the stores are selling merchandise. Scooter knows all about restaurants because many of his friends are in the business. "You can steal so much money in a restaurant," he says. "The cash. That's the attraction."

Every time we leave each other, it's a ritual. I think he worries about my being too straight. We walk in opposite directions, and he stops to call to me. "Remember," he yells, "nobody ever bats a thousand." Then Scooter Walsh moves off to another adventure.

"You know why life is impossible today?" said Mather Stevens. "You are owned by anyone who does something for you. A friend of mine was just named a judge in the Superior Court, a brilliant man who takes power for granted. The day he was appointed he was too busy to celebrate at lunch so, working through, he asked his secretary to go out and get him a Coke and a corned-beef sandwich from a deli across the street. Big deal, right? She came back and gives him the corned-beef sandwich on white bread with butter. Something snapped and he hit the roof. "Corned beef on *white bread?*" he screamed. "With *butter?*" When he calmed down he asked her to exchange it for rye bread with mustard. She refused. "I just became a judge," he said.

She still refused, quit on the spot, and sued the judge. On top of that, a women's organization marched outside his office with picket signs saying "Judge not, lest ye be judged." Stevens went on, "It's not the ability to pay that counts anymore. People won't do certain kinds of work for any price."

"I grew up," he told me, "with a full-time cook in our house. We had a maid, a laundress, and a chauffeur. Now, all the wives in America serve most of these roles. With most of the husbands helping out. There's no rest; that's a big strain. When our children were little we certainly thought we could preserve some of the old customs, a nanny, a mother's helper, an au pair. Some of the people we had in the house were unbelievable. One girl was from France. Her father owned a restaurant near Marseille, and she came recommended by a British client of mine. Yvonne was her name, and every month for three days she would take to bed. 'Oooh,' she would be in tears. 'Ze cycle is upon me,' she would say. My wife would take meals to her room, make special broth for her, from Yvonne's father's recipe, for God's sake.

" 'What's he call it, Cycle Soup?' I'd ask. We almost got divorced over Yvonne.

"The next two girls we had were Finnish, both from the same town. It was like having delinquents in the house. They lived to sneak out to town and pick up men in the bars frequented by the city's au pair girls. But they picked *any* men. They'd come home at all hours of the morning, if they came home at all. One of them was named Anali. She'd call from the trolley station at three in the morning. I'd answer the phone, half dead. She'd say, 'Here is Anali.'

" 'Where is Anali?' I'd moan. And she'd start to cry because she never really knew where she was.

"The finale was when we decided to try another tack. I alerted my gynecologist friends to find us an unwed mother. Someone who might like a nice home while she came to term. I told my wife, 'It's ideal. Give her a place to hide. We'll be grateful; she'll be grateful. She probably won't ever want to go out, and I'll never be awakened at three in the morning worrying about who's coming into the house.'

"Joanie was a terrific person, trained as an engineer. She loved the children and they loved her. She never spoke about the father of the child and we didn't pry. Along into her sixth month, she asked one evening, 'Is it all right if the father pays me a visit?'

" 'Sure,' I said, thinking some young bastard lawyer would be coming over, a man who wouldn't make her an honest woman.

"That Saturday, with the father due that evening, Joanie cleaned the house and put flowers around on all the tables. It was obvious she was in love. My wife and I stayed around to supervise, and, about six-thirty, the peace of the neighborhood was shattered as twelve Hell's Angels or the equivalent roared into our driveway looking as filthy, scruffy, and mean as if they had just driven from Watsonville, California, into East Los Angeles without stopping for a beer. Their warlord, if you can believe it, was the father of Joanie's child.

"Well, our whole experience with help has been like scenes from a Fellini movie. The people you are presumably paying to serve you end up as part of the family and running your lives. The final straw was our Canadian girl, Ronnie, who had the most obnoxious boyfriend — Ralph, the computer expert. Ralph considered our home to be his own. When he'd arrive to take Ronnie out for the evening, he'd pull up a chair at the dining-room table while we were eating and engage us in conversation. And he always talked down to us, as if he were doing us a favor, sharing his views on politics, technology, and human behavior. He worked for a public company listed on the Big Board. The company made minicomputers, and Ralph was allowed to wear sweat shirts to the office, name his own hours, accept stock options, and use the company Ford Fairlane whenever it was free. One night while he chewed on a lamb chop at my dinner table I suddenly called a halt. I grabbed the lamb chop from his hand," Stevens told me, "and ordered him from the house. I also ordered Ronnie from the house, took a bath, and came down to the living room wearing a towel. 'This is the way life should be,' I said to my family. 'I haven't been able to walk around naked in my own house for years. From now on, we are back in control. No more working permits, no more visa extensions, no more Hell's Angels, no more Finnish advice to the lovelorn. We have recaptured our house.' The next day I went to the office, called my broker, and sold short Ralph's computer company. The stock soon collapsed, after *Barron's* pointed out their shoddy management practices, and I made seventeen thousand dollars' profit, almost enough to compensate for the annoyance over the years, for all the girls we waited on, hand and foot."

The best Smart People method for recruiting help, other than referrals from friends, is writing Smart Advertisements. Look at the classified section in your newspaper. The vast majority of ads for help are prosaic, uninteresting, boring. Always make yourself sound interesting or unusual when advertising for help. For instance, this is an ad we have used for summer help: "Happy family with unusual hobbies seeks mother's helper for August in vacation paradise."

Having the "happy family" noted should relieve anxiety about the "unusual hobbies." But the hobbies and mention of "paradise" bring in triple the usual response for a summer sitter. Once you interview the applicants you'll have enough of the curious to have your pick. The same sort of ads should be written for whatever your domestic needs. Smart People cannot depend upon ordinary methods to recruit service.

And if Smart Ads don't work, post requests for help in these places: your local fire or police department bulletin boards and nurses' dormitories in local hospitals. Nurses in training are often looking to pick up extra money doing baby-sitting or weekend house-sitting. Children of fire and police personnel will never quit on you midway through a summer. They have almost universally been raised by their parents to fulfill their obligations.

"There is no way, in our society, to avoid being owned by your help, if they are full-time. My godfather was a magnificent drunk," Mather Stevens told me. "He used to say, 'You are never a hero to your wife or your valet. A good reason to change them both every few years. Have a brandy. A brandy is never a bad solution.' "

# 7 MEDICAL SMARTS

Make a friend of your doctor. This is the single most important piece of medical advice you can get. I shall repeat the message throughout this chapter. *Make a friend of your doctor.*

A large part of this book is devoted to health. The less you have to be irritated by petty, daily annoyances, the better you should feel. Jonathan Swift said, "The best doctors in the world are Doctor Diet, Doctor Quiet, and Doctor Merryman." Every philosopher, statesman, and public personality through history sooner or later makes statements about good health and its preservation. No country in the history of civilization has spent more time, energy, thought, and money on ways of improving and extending health services, as well as trying to extend long, and beautiful, life. I say beautiful, because America is obsessed not only with being healthy, but also with looking good while we're doing it. We are a nation that follows the current fad, whatever it may be. Whatever we're told will make us feel good we embrace, be it winter swimming in Vermont, standing on our heads, becoming macrobiotic or vegetarian, or hot soaking in wooden tubs. Sir William Osler, one of medicine's greatest philosophers and practitioners, said, "No person is really happy or safe without a hobby. And it makes precious little difference what the outside interest may be. Botany, beetles, or butterflies, roses, tulips, or irises; fishing, mountaineering, or antiquities. Anything will do so long as he straddles a hobby and rides it hard."

I have a method for recruiting Smart People at the same time I ensure my physical and mental well-being. It is simple, not over-expensive, and available in one form or another to everyone who reads this book. A Smart Person joins a sporting club, a tennis or squash or handball center, or an exercise program in any place about which people can say, "I'll meet you at the club." *Belonging* to something is very definitely a part of the Smart People approach to life. But this belonging must involve physical exercise, showering, and relaxing *at the point where the sport is played*. Belonging to something is essential to my Smart People health plan. It is crucial to sit around with other people who are also relieving the pressures of the day. I have learned more of the gossip of the city, picked up more information about how to beat the odds of daily life, and recruited more Smart People for my team in my club's steam room than in any other place where I spend time. Including my office. People relax after exercise. They are in the mood for conversation, for swapping stories and ideas. They are receptive to other people's problems, be they business problems or physical, emotional, or personal ones. There is no pressure. People are at ease. You know your club is a place where you feel better when you leave than when you arrived. This is obviously not a new idea. The ruins of the baths of Caracalla still stand. Romans would spend hours there, discussing the state of the empire, swapping stories and gossip. Relaxing.

And this belonging is a good health technique for everyone.

The big change in club life in the last five years is the entry of women into the social sporting world. Women always had friend-ships. But they never had *buddies*. They never played team sports on the scale they do today. My squash club, formerly all male, now is coed. At any hour at least a third of the courts are occupied by women. But the phenomenon is extended: most of the women *hang around* after playing to rehash the contest and to tell one another stories. This is the real revolution of women

joining clubs: they are understanding what men had all to themselves for so many years — the physical activity followed by the
release, the unbending. There is no one I know who participates
in sports at a Y or club who doesn't say, "This is the best part of
my day." And because of economics, a club is open to virtually
everyone in America. If not a club, then a YMCA, YWCA, or
YMHA, where regulars always congregate. Any small group of
people who see one another constantly can be a club. Make time
for club life. It can be the most important element of each day.
And you will find doctors, lawyers, bankers, judges, newspaper
people, brokers, and other professional people who can help you,
or refer you to help, in any area of society.

I met my medical Summa in the steam room of my club. He
was introduced to me by two people, the owner of the largest
secretarial school in the city and the man who was president of
America's third largest hotel chain. In the steam room, all people
are truly equal.

The Rockefeller Foundation occupies five floors at Fifty-first
Street above the Avenue of the Americas. Funded with over eight
hundred million dollars, it is the third largest private charitable
trust in the United States. The foundation, quite simply, exists to
do good works. It exists to fund programs that improve the quality of life all over the planet. These programs assist in medical
research, environmental controls, population limitation, educational and cultural improvement in underdeveloped and underprivileged areas. When I saw it, the office of the president of the
Rockefeller Foundation was large, unpretentious, personal. One
wall was lined with books. Pictures of family and friends dominated the decorating scheme. People and learning were the elements that surrounded the life of the man who was then president
of the foundation, Dr. John Hilton Knowles. Dr. Knowles died
of cancer in March 1979. At his memorial service, someone
quoted his motto: "A sense of humor is a prelude to faith, and
laughter is the beginning of prayer."

"You're goddamn right, I'm a smart person," he told me. "I step up to the plate is part of the reason; and I orchestrate the whole goddamn picture. And you know what? It's mostly getting others to respond to your leadership. *That's* my smarts, if you want to know. There was an old vaudeville act, back in the days when taking off your clothes to music was erotic. Out comes Professor Fazooli in a frock coat, and he's playing the xylophone. He's stage right, down front. And of course he's terrible. As he's playing, out comes a broad in back of him, bumps and grinds and takes off a long glove. She exits and the crowd breaks into applause. Professor Fazooli bows, thinking the applause is for the goddamn xylophone. Well, that's me: Professor Fazooli. It's not so much what I'm doing; it's what the people behind me are doing." He paused for a long moment and threw me a smile. "Of course, *I'm* picking all the people behind me," he said. "*That's* the secret."

Dr. John Knowles was my public Summa in matters of health and medicine. Very seldom in life will you meet people who really think they *know*. Daily, people say to me, "*They* are putting the market up; *they* are lowering interest rates; *they* are going to increase taxes."

*They* are an invisible hand. But if, indeed, there is a *they* behind the cloak of invisibility, Dr. John Knowles had to be one of them. I met him at my squash club. Again, a club is a place for improving your health *and* for recruiting Smart People. I watched Dr. Knowles playing doubles in a group in which all the men were over fifty years old. I noticed two qualities about him after observing him in groups: he dominated the people around him, and he always appeared to be in motion. Both of these qualities are amply demonstrated by all of my Summa types, both public and private. "I have energy to burn," Knowles told me. "If I have a secret, it is that I was born with energy to burn."

You must see a man in several places to truly judge him. One place is in repose, among friends, where barriers are down. Another place is at his office, to see how he functions at his life's work.

John Knowles and I were sitting at a large round table, informal, personal. Even though he knew me from social surroundings he was then in a business atmosphere. His attitude said one thing: "I do not suffer fools gladly; don't waste my time."

I launched into my Smart People questionnaire, which is designed to make people think about questions no one else ever asks them. It makes people want to respond interestingly. It makes people want to appear smart, even if they already know that they are.

"I'll give you a scenario for life," he told me. "You start off knowing that everybody is different, some pretty, some ugly, some smart, most dumb as shit. Don't kid yourself about the prerogatives of power. I have to go halfway around the globe to meet Robert McNamara of the World Bank, then figure out how to feed millions of starving people. And the plane I'm supposed to go on is full. You better believe I'm gonna bump someone off that plane. You better believe they better find someone I'm more important than. If you're smart, then you go for the best. You go for the top. But you help people less fortunate all the way along, because that is the key to a successful life. Four elements: hard work, energy, use of the intellect, and humor. Jesus, if you can't laugh at yourself and the other poor bastards, you might as well dry up and blow away."

Let's examine some of a Summa's attributes, particularly ones that we may copy. You've noticed the doctor's salty language? It was his most effective tool in dealing with others.

## THE ONE OF THE BOYS SYNDROME

Dr. John Knowles, my medical Summa, got people to respond to him through what I call the One of the Boys Syndrome. His language was colorful, colloquial. It was the language of the emergency room, not the boardroom. But it was effective. Auto

mechanics, traffic cops, plumbers, I'm sure, could believe that
John Knowles was such a good guy, could believe that he used
strong language. Knowles was like a company commander in
World War II for whom men would put their hands in the fire.
He inspired fierce loyalty, because he would go through the flames
himself to take care of his boys. And they knew it. People responded to his methods, to his sense of humor and his tireless
mind.

"You bet your ass details make the big picture," he said.
"Money is important. And I believe you've got to spend it to
make it. But when all is said and done, you know, you can't eat
the *Wall Street Journal.*"

His language and offhand manner got people to pay attention.
Then he zeroed in on what was important, and you inevitably
found yourself listening hard. He used the technique of *contrast*,
the same technique used so widely by other Smart People.
Knowles was one of the boys. "Because he jokes with you," one of
his colleagues told me, "you want to bust your butt for him." The
One of the Boys Syndrome worked for my medical Summa. It can
work for you.

When I knew him Dr. John Knowles was whippet-thin and
younger-looking than his fifty years. He appeared boyish. It was
because of his energy, his restlessness, and the feeling that he was
always ready to laugh, to see the ridiculous side of life. He knew
life too well not to appreciate Jonathan Swift. His view of the
world was realistic, ironic. "You have to gather information from
many sources," he told me. "And you must never limit yourself to
narrow vistas. I read constantly. Norman Mailer's *A Prisoner of
Sex*, Barzun's *House of Intellect*, every week the *New York Times*
literary supplement to find out what is being produced that
makes us *think*. And I'll tell you something about information.
You better be a goddamn good listener. People love to talk. I
listen to cabdrivers, doormen. They're the ones who let me know
that there was a revolution going on in the middle class, that the
man in the street wants the American Dream. He doesn't want it

handed to him on a government platter. And while you're making it, several things: make your work your play. Enjoy it until you don't any more, then never be afraid of change. Exercise. Blow the cobwebs out of your mind periodically. Clear out the rust. I play squash, I play golf, I play the piano. If you accumulate money, if you arrive economically, the hell with it: go first-class all the way. Don't feel guilty; you've earned it."

John Knowles exuded confidence and good sense. He had been controversial in his career, essentially because institutions of any sort cannot stand too much honesty. Balloons of bureaucracy — government, the AMA, hospitals, pretentious politicians — cannot stand being pricked. Dr. Knowles got your attention by being opinionated, by being humorous, by not suffering fools gladly. Then he zeroed in on what he was deadly serious about: health care and the responsibility of the individual. His views are continually articulated. "Over ninety-nine percent of us," he wrote, "are born healthy and made sick as a result of personal misbehavior and environmental conditions." He went on to say, "Most individuals do not worry about their health until they lose it. Uncertain attempts at healthy living may be thwarted by the temptations of a culture whose economy depends upon high production and high consumption." Knowles insisted that our society has eroded the sense of individual responsibility, while at the same time insisting on maintaining individual rights. I would suggest that all people seriously interested in their own health obtain a copy of the book that he edited, *Doing Better and Feeling Worse: Health in the United States.*

Dr. Knowles quoted a study of almost seven thousand adults over a five-and-a-half-year period, relating health and longevity to the following regime:

1. three meals a day at regular times and no snacking
2. breakfast every day
3. moderate exercise two or three times a week
4. adequate sleep (seven or eight hours a night)

5. no smoking
6. maintaining moderate weight
7. no alcohol or only in moderation

The day I saw him in his office, John Knowles looked down on the Avenue of the Americas. "Christ," he said, "life is to be enjoyed. Laughter, sex. God, the odor of sex overlays everything. But sex shouldn't be anxiety-laden. It isn't quantity in sex, it's quality that counts. If you feel like hooking yourself up to the goddamn vacuum cleaner and it doesn't hurt anyone else, go to it. But have some discipline in your life. Have yearly checkups, don't abuse your body with pills, drugs, tobacco."

Then he joked about my rainbow heart lapel pin, and we laughed about style and talked about change and taking chances in life. "You have to step up to the plate," Dr. John Knowles said to me. "You have to do something with your life. Never forget," he added, "faint heart never slept with the cook."

Kid Manning is the kind of old-timer you feel good about. His eyes are lively. He appreciates the women. He can remember both the Czar and Teddy Roosevelt. Kid Manning is ninety-three, and he knows Boston at the turn of the century the way you and I know that the big Sunday family dinner in current America is going to be either takeout Chinese food or pizza. He came to this country in 1893 and he told me, "The biggest difference between Europe and America, and it amazed me when it first happened, is that in America, when you got in a fight, the other guy always let you up."

Kid Manning is my good-health Lamplighter. Although he is now old and tired, he has achieved long life with generally excellent health. His attitude about health and longevity has always been an inspiration to me. He is physically a small man, the kind that is always called "wiry." His hundred and twenty-five pounds make him only five pounds lighter than when he was a professional fighter under the name I am calling him here. Kid

weight champion. He would do a routine, punch a bag,
rope, demonstrate his famous solar plexus punch.

st about that time a most wonderful thing happened. It was
1904. They built a gym a few blocks from our house. It
nged the life of the gang on the corner, because it meant we
d a place to play inside, all winter. And it was also a place to
athe. We all lived in apartment houses. My home was a four-
oom flat. My mother, my father, and I lived with my three
brothers and sisters. There was one bathroom, and we all washed
ourselves in the sink. We had a bathtub, but that was where we
stored the coal for our stove."

It is marvelously therapeutic to listen to the stories of older
people. It is one of the secrets to a satisfying life because it gives
you a sense of history that does not come from a book. Another
lesson: The method of getting older people to respond to you is
to ask them questions about their past. Not only will they think
you are a wonderful person for asking, but they will immediately
feel better about themselves, knowing that someone cares. There
was a janitor in my building some years ago, a bitter, crotchety
old man who greeted everyone with sour looks and muttered
responses. Coming up on the elevator with him once, I saw him
toss a Coca-Cola can into a barrel. "Pretty good," I said. "You
used to be a ballplayer, right?" Well, it turned out that he used to
barnstorm with the old Negro traveling teams of the 1920s and
1930s. He had stories about an America very few people ever
knew. His face would light up like opening night whenever he
told me about those days.

For years I have listened to Kid Manning searching for secrets
to long life and good health that may go beyond inheritance from
the gene pool.

"For my money," he has told me, "there are two things that can
ensure a long life with good health. You've got to feel good about
yourself. And this means you have to have places of your very
own to escape into. I was lucky," he said. "I had two places,

Manning is Jewish, but his faith in h.
strong as his faith in Judaism. Kid N
often about his early days in America.
said, "full of wonder, I understood fast tha.
your rights. You couldn't let yourself be p
why my father left Europe. He was a bu.
nothing against the soldiers who would come i.
burn houses, stick swords into our beds, into our
for money, jewelry, anything of value. In America
of fights. You had to fight because everything was c.
corner where you'd hang out with your friends. Go.
grandchildren watch television. They have everything
complain to me sometimes about having nothing to do.
and self-pity are the two elements that will kill you fas.
any disease. You'll be dead between the ears."

Kid Manning spent most of his childhood on the stree.
competition, playing games. He and his friends rolled hoops
the Boston Common, spun tops on the sidewalks, swam in t.
Charles River, now so loaded with bacteria and foreign object.
that I had to have a typhoid shot after falling out of a boat into
the water in 1960.

"All of our entertainment was outside the home," Kid Manning
has told me. "Fruit and vegetable men would peddle their produce from carts outside our window. We would steal ice from the
milk cart, and the milkman would chase us through alleys, over
fences. He didn't care whether the milk soured or not; the chase
after naughty boys was everything. Our year was spent in contests: jumping, running, baseball, swimming, sneaking into
burlesque shows. The shows cost ten cents for the gallery. A
dozen of us would come in and individually march by the ticket
taker, telling him the next guy would pay for all. The last kid
would pay a dime, but by then we would be all over the theater,
the show would be starting, and most of us they'd never catch. At
the burlesque it wasn't just stripping. It was variety shows,
vaudeville. There I saw Gentlemen Jim Corbett, who was the

sports and music. Sports were easy. We all played everything there was to play. I was a catcher, the leader. Our team was the Hemlocks, from the West End, and we played every town or regional team around Boston. I boxed professionally also, at a hundred and thirty pounds, on barges in the Charles River and in clubs in Cambridge, Boston, and Providence, Rhode Island. That's what the gym taught me. For fifteen dollars a fight I'd go up against all the tough little guys who grew up just like me, whether they were Jewish, Italian, or Irish.

"And you've got to remember," Kid Manning told me, "this was always in our spare time, when we weren't working. All the kids worked. I was a delivery boy for the butcher, a paper boy, I carried ice, I was an usher. Six days a week, after school and on Saturdays. Did we bitch and moan about it? It was *life;* everybody in the same boat. When I was getting married my wife made me stop fighting. It was marriage or boxing. I got married. But I never gave up the love of sports. Two years after our wedding, in 1912 it was, I was going to the store to buy some milk and bread on a Sunday morning. I was wearing a suit and tie and hat like all the other Sunday strollers. At the corner there were all sorts of people gathered. As it happened, that was the starting line for a fifteen-mile race, a walking race. Walking was a big event then, the shuffling, fast heel-and-toe event you see in the Olympics. Several of my friends were in the race, in running clothes, including Slobodkin, the harmonica player whom I could beat with one leg. I couldn't help it. I had told my wife I would be right back. But I left my bundle in the bakery, left my hat and tie and jacket also, and entered the race. It was fifteen miles up Commonwealth Avenue and back to the starting point. In my street shoes, out of seventy participants, I finished third. I did show up at home with the milk at seven at night. And I still have the cup—pewter, with my name on it.

"The music went along with this," Kid Manning said, "ever since I stood in line for Caruso in 1913 in *The Girl of the Golden*

*West* at the old Boston Theater on Washington Street. I squeezed into standing room in the orchestra. Caruso brought down the house; they wouldn't let him off the stage. He sang an encore, 'The Last Rose of Summer,' and the way people reacted would make the Beatles look like four pishers. That's when I began taking singing lessons and performing in minstrel shows at the West End House, the famous neighborhood settlement house. I always sang a solo, and it was always 'My Little Gray Home in the West.'"

"You've told me about your secret places," I said to Kid Manning. "What's the other factor that has contributed to your long life?"

Manning smiled. "People nowadays may think it's strange," he said, "but I had a hero from the time I was fourteen. I modeled my life after that hero, tried to emulate him in every respect. The hero was Frank Merriwell, from the dime-novel series. Frank Merriwell played every sport, saved every game. He went from school success to a brilliant career at Yale in about fifty books. Some people who reach old age say they always smoked, others that they chased women or took the occasional cocktail. Frank Merriwell never smoked or drank," said Kid Manning. "And he invariably triumphed in every sport and in life. I followed his life then, I follow him now. I went to every Harvard-Yale game from 1905 through 1970 and yelled like hell for Yale. My oldest boy went to Yale, my other sons to Penn where they played baseball and ran the hurdles. I'll be ninety-four years old in a few weeks, but I've never found any reason to have a better hero than Frank Merriwell."

Kid Manning used to play catch with me until he was in his late eighties. He had a battered catcher's mitt from the 1920s that he would take every spring to the Boston Braves Florida training camp, where he'd pester the players to throw to him. After the Braves left for Milwaukee, he would take his glove and follow the Red Sox to Sarasota. He always threw a heavy ball and always aimed to hit me in the chest with his throw. The last time we played he could still throw a bigger curve than I could ever manage in my life. And I was a leftie, where the curve should have been natural.

I visited Kid Manning recently in the hospital. He is finally winding down, his frame shrunken, his body fighting more problems than a dress manufacturer in bankruptcy. He is worn out, but is still glad to see me. His handshake is dry and firm. His hands are large for the rest of him, the hands of a catcher, of a fighter. He feels as if his lessons have to be reemphasized while he has time.

"Exercise your body," he tells me. "Break away from where you spend your days. And always have a place of the soul to escape to. Listen to people if you want them to care about you. Have a hero. It sometimes allows you to believe in yourself more, and to keep up the fight." Kid Manning lies back on his pillow. He is exhausted, and it is time for me to leave. As I head for the door he calls to me and holds up his right hand. He flashes one finger at me, then two.

"What's that?" I ask him.

"Remember," he says to me, "one finger for a fast ball, two for a curve."

Kid Manning is my grandfather.


I'm lucky. My medical Roughrider is a psychiatrist. We are a nation blessed with enough leisure time not to know what to do with ourselves, we are hooked with obsessions about mental health. There seem to be two prevailing attitudes about psychiatrists in America. One is, "All psychiatrists are crazy." The other is, "I've (you've) got to go into analysis."

I met this Roughrider in my Army Reserve unit. I was in the six-month military, being of that generation too young for World War II and Korea, just too old for Vietnam. When I came out of college, the world was at peace. But there was a draft and no good reason I could see for a two- or three-year hitch in the service playing Robert E. Lee Prewitt. The reserves meant six

months of active duty and four and a half years of local weekly
meetings, with two weeks at camp each summer. I enlisted in the
medical corps because it was the program that would take me
farthest from home and closest to a foreign country. The base was
Fort Sam Houston, Texas, just a few hours from Nuevo Laredo
on the Mexican border. But it was at summer training camp that
I met my medical Roughrider. My unit was to operate a field
hospital on a base used strictly for training reserves and the National Guard.

When I arrived at camp, I was told to report to a field lecture
on mental health. In front of a hospital tent a captain in fatigues
was lecturing a group of summer soldiers. The captain had taken
off his jacket and tee shirt, and his plastic helmet liner was filled
with water. He began soaping his armpits as I walked up. "It is
important to have the pits feeling clean before you begin any
enterprise," he was saying. "Clean fresh-smelling pits allow you to
approach any job with certainty." He was rinsing his armpits
from the water in his helmet. He was a small, dark, wild-looking
man, with a receding hairline and a Vincent Price goatee. He
wanted you to laugh.

"I am going to lecture you today," he went on, "on preserving
mental health in the field, a subject I am eminently unprepared to
teach you about since it is tough enough to preserve it in the
home. I am a psychiatrist. You know a psychiatrist is a doctor
who knows nothing and does nothing. But, of course, an internist
knows everything and does nothing. A surgeon knows nothing
and does everything. And a pathologist knows everything and
does everything. But too late! You people are all civilians, as am
I, caught up in the madness of escaping the draft. Bear with me
for two weeks, and we'll all have clean armpits. It could be worse.
It's the beginning of summer and you could be in the hospital at
home. That's when the new interns come to begin training, right
from medical school. A lot of people die in hospitals in the sum-
mertime. It's like getting a Buick built on a Monday, after a

weekend." He put the helmet, half filled with water, on his head.

That was my introduction to Dr. Lionel Vail, an unreconstructed original. He's a psychiatrist who you'd swear was an act preparing for the old Ed Sullivan show, to follow the dog who could fart the "Star-Spangled Banner." But Lionel Vail has one quality that shines out of him like the exit sign in a movie theater. He cares about people. He understands them and, as a psychiatrist, he cures them. He once told me about a patient, a grande dame who would come to therapy sessions wearing pearls that had belonged to the Empress Josephine. "I have some trouble, doctor," she admitted to him in the first session, "coping with the fact of your Jewishness."

"Madame," said Dr. Vail, "all of our boys are Jewish. Freud, Jung, Adler. Do you want your appendix out? I'll find you a nice Episcopal surgeon with great hands and a three handicap. You want your mind straightened out, you go to the people who understand people. Show me a gentile psychiatrist, I'll show you a lost gentile longing for a bar mitzvah."

Lionel Vail is the kind of person who is made for the practice of psychiatry. His life is full of appearances and reality, the essence of Shakespeare. Indeed, the sonnets are his favorite reading. And his favorite book is *The Catcher in the Rye*. The appearance of Lionel Vail is that he plays the fool. He admits to having done magic tricks at high school parties to get attention. He played the half-time mascot at football games in a bear suit to get attention. He was the funny little boy who couldn't get a girlfriend, so he would be a girl's best friend, the confidant, the go-between. "Marion likes you; she'll be at Howard Johnson's at the circle Saturday afternoon." All this time he was getting C's and interrupting class with wise-guy pranks, while he had an IQ that was off the charts and was composing symphonies at home, orchestrating all of the instruments. He was, and is, like Prince Hal, the wastrel in *King Henry the Fourth*.

"The more outrageous I act," says Dr. Lionel, "the more effective I am as a serious doctor helping to cure people. Life is not one-dimensional, and the people who try to make it so lead disastrous lives."

I have seen Lionel Vail save lives. I saw him jump over two tables in a restaurant to do an emergency tracheotomy on a man choking on fried chicken. I saw him work for forty minutes giving CPR to a man at a football stadium until an ambulance arrived. Several other doctors, including a surgeon and an internist, had backed into the crowd, avoiding the crisis, worried about lawsuits that could spoil football Saturdays. But not Dr. Lionel Vail. I have seen him diagnose medical problems that had been missed by specialists: diabetes in a four-year-old boy, deafness in a baby girl everyone thought brain-damaged. He came to our house in a blizzard once at three in the morning to hold our daughter next to a steaming shower until an attack of croup had passed. This is a friend, a Roughrider because he refused to play by the rules of his profession. He is a product of an Eastern establishment medical school. But he acts like a combination Jewish cowboy in jeans and Jaguar and Laurence Olivier in *The Entertainer*.

Dealing with a woman who seemed hopelessly psychotic and depressed, Dr. Vail discovered that she was an idiot savant, incredible on detail.

"I'd ask her, 'What day of the week was July 12, 1959?' 'It was a Sunday,' she'd say, 'partly cloudy and a little rain.' A check of old newspapers and, amazingly, she was dead on. She could give you any day back to the year one. Remarkable.

"I had to get to this girl. I do something very few psychiatrists do, even with their most difficult cases. I interview the family. Sure enough, her mother was an opera buff. I played the girl Verdi, Wagner, on my recorder. She went wild, remembered that, years before, her crib was next to her mother's piano and she used to bang her head in tempo to the playing. She couldn't clean up after herself, mind you, as an adult. But I could give her my recorder, call out a key, and she could go into it. Music saved her life. It brought her out of her black pit and into the world. Christ, she could sit down at the piano, make her right hand play like Stravinsky, her left hand like Mozart. Now she works in a diet kitchen, in the real world, measuring carbohydrates.

"These things can happen. That's why for years I've stayed active at state hospitals to save lives on the back wards. The back wards are where the sun doesn't filter in because even the sun is afraid it will be trapped there."

Dr. Lionel often drops in on us of a Saturday afternoon, when he knows I'm tired of writing. "How about a stroll in the woods?" he'll say, and we'll cross our small stream by the footbridge I've had built by a moonlighting fireman and walk through Audubon Society property adjoining my land. The woods are unspoiled except for conservation-commission markings of trails that wander through a hundred acres of ponds, birch forests, and an aqueduct. "You should charge me for this, you know," Lionel tells me. "You're my analyst."

He has told me a lot about himself on these walks and a lot about the practice of psychiatry. "You've got to like yourself to give therapy," he has told me. "So much of the profession is full of crap. I know analysts who build high fences around their property so that no one can see that their children play. These people don't have the guts to reveal themselves. One of the problems today is money. There's a limit to how much we can charge people per hour. Thirty patients a week is about what constitutes a full practice, giving a doctor $75,000 a year. This case load allows recovery time between patients, which a doctor must have because of the mental concentration demanded. Forty-five dollars per session seems reasonable, but you'd be amazed at the therapists I talk with who are going broke, no referrals, people not able to pay the rates. This leads to what I think borders on the irresponsible and, in many cases, on fraud. That's electroshock therapy, fifty bucks a buzz. Zap, a little juice, not time-dependent. You can hit twenty people in a morning at fifty bucks a crack."

I asked him how his approach to therapy differed from that of most practitioners he had observed. "Several ways," Dr. Lionel told me. "I nurture the good. That's my motto, if anything is. That's how I do therapy. I fall back on the best in my patients and concentrate on bringing those elements to the fore. Also I don't merely rely upon *talk*. I'm big on smells, sounds, sight. I use the entire sensory apparatus. 'What did your grandmother's kitchen smell like?' You'd be amazed how that works every time."

"What about people being in analysis or therapy for years?"

"Nonsense, mostly. I believe in short-term intensive therapy with the doctor *involved*, in there with both feet. God damn it," he says, "we exist as a profession because Americans don't have other people who will listen to them. Everyone is too busy, too concerned to care. So Americans pay to have someone listen. For nine-tenths of the patients in therapy and analysis, it's a carnival game. That high a percentage don't belong in psychiatrists' offices. They go to us like sailors go to whores, seeking love, temporary solace. Christ, ninety percent of the doctors who are psychiatrists have no business counseling patients. You have to know people. No degree will give you that, no internship. Medium-term therapy is about six months. Long-term, one to two years. I'm doing intensive short-term therapy in one-and-a-half-hour sessions. Let's uncover your biggest problem and why you can't solve it. Let's find out why you can't get what you need so you don't have to be upset, sick, worried, or nervous."

On our walks we usually arrive at a large spring-fed pond. If it is any season but winter Dr. Lionel will strip off his clothes. Once I said to him, "You know, you do a lot of talking to me. I really know *who* I am. What I have trouble with is knowing what to do about it." He ran full tilt into the water. Then he floated on his back, spewing water up into the air from his mouth. "You don't have problems," he said happily. "What you have is *life*."

Dr. Lionel Vail, as a true Roughrider, is spending lots of time chasing private dreams when he should be practicing his profession. This makes him a Roughrider. He gets sidetracked. His eye is not on the ball, but rather somewhere up in the stands. Lately his dreams include psychic readings. "I've also been in touch with the vibrations of others," Dr. Lionel tells me. "I can read energy levels that speak to me of the jagged shape of life. I'm clairvoyant, too. I walked into a clothing store last week and went up to the most attractive clerk.

" 'Good morning, Elaine,' I said. 'You are about to hear from your long lost love.'

" 'Who are you, weird person?' she said to me, just as the manager came over and called her to the phone. Later she came back and told me it was Stephen, whom she hadn't heard from in four years. She was ready to follow me into battle, I swear to God.

"I'm going up the coast today with a family who are sure there's a fortune buried in their grandmother's house. They know about my other consciousness. If a fortune's in that house, I'll feel it.

"Did I tell you I cured a nun last week, an obsessive, compulsive neurotic? She couldn't get through the Mass. She'd start, stop, have to go back to the beginning endlessly. I laid hands on her; she was shivering. After minutes I said, 'Who put the tape over your mouth in church when you were a child?' She had blocked her father doing that to her. The psychic healing did the trick. Recalling the image broke his hold on her. Now she's through her prayers faster than any nun in the convent."

But clairvoyance brings the doctor problems. He was in a hotel bar several weeks ago, with his wife and some friends, two couples. It is his habit to engage strangers in conversation. He believes everyone should have the benefit of his knowledge, wit, and charm. The bar was crowded. There was an hour's wait for dinner, even with reservations. It was a drinking crowd, jovial, Saturday night. Dr. Vail said to a young woman standing next to him, "You've been thinking about your high school days. You were a cheerleader, and you dated a player . . . a lineman. He had a nickname, Moose perhaps. No. No. Not Moose. House. That's it, *House*. You are about to be pregnant."

She gushed for a few minutes, then turned back to her own group, as did Dr. Vail to his. Several seconds later, someone had grabbed the doctor by what was left of his hair and was beating his head very sharply against the solid mahogany bar.

"Try to clamp it on my wife, you little bastard," a man was yelling. It was House, the lineman, now the husband of the lady, and he was trying to force the doctor's clairvoyance out through his ears. This happens in life sometimes when your good intentions are misconstrued. The beating became a general fight. Dr. Lionel's noncombatant friends were forced willy-nilly into the combat they abhorred. The wives shrieked, a plate-glass window was broken, death was threatened. In the ambulance that took Dr. Lionel and his friends to an emergency room for X rays he kept raving, "People don't want the truth. But I must speak it. She'll be pregnant, and the father will be a pastry chef."

When his eye is on the apple, Dr. Lionel's insights into the practice of psychiatry make sense, both for people involved in therapy and for those thinking about entering it. Here are some of his impressions of the proper approach to psychiatry:

1. "Drugs given on prescription by psychiatrists can be a cop-out. They often are an expression of the fact that the doctor can't do his job. All tranquilizers just dull the moment and make it easier to handle. But *you* have to handle it eventually, and without pills. And the side effects from drugs can be worse than what we're trying to cure. The less poison you put into your body, the better off you'll be."

2. "If you do not relate to your psychiatrist, shop around. Be honest. You're paying good money for help; don't accept the first person you see just because he's a doctor. I think the best therapists reveal themselves, have the guts to jump into the fray. The more honest you, the patient, are up front, the more responsive the doctor, and the less time and money you will waste."

3. "For the patient: Be truthful in everything. Don't deny reality. Don't pretend. And don't make excuses for your failures; they're human. Difficulties in life arise when your defenses are

raised to protect you from pain. If you're anxious, what can you lose by expressing it? When you're hurt, express it. When you're angry, express it. Saying what hurts prevents guilt and depression."

4. "Always have as your goal becoming your best self. And enter therapy with definite goals in mind, e.g., 'I shall cure my insomnia.' Don't invite anything that blocks the realization of that goal."

5. "Try for a relationship with someone else where you can grow as a person. This is an essential for those times when you are low."

On one of our periodic walks, I asked Dr. Lionel if he had lessons for people who wanted to avoid therapy and analysis. "What would you concentrate on to stay well, mentally and physically?"

We were approaching the swimming pond in the woods. "It's simple," he said. "Be happy in your work. Do something, auto repair or heart repair, that allows you to express whatever your natural talent is. Anything else is a mistake, and you'll end up on a couch or worse. When Mozart wrote *Don Giovanni,* he also wrote *Ein Kleine Nachtmusik, A Little Night Music,* songs to amuse himself. Cultivate a second dimension."

He paused by the edge of the pond. Two young men and two young women were swimming in the middle of the pond, skinny-dipping. "If you have those two things in life," Dr. Lionel said, "then you value your life, and you won't do anything bad. Why would you? My job is the simple act of making people aware of themselves, aware of the world, and encouraging them to give it all they can." He stared at the unclothed kids in the pond, then began stripping off his clothes. Naked and free, he dived in, stroking immediately and yelling at the kids, "Wait for me. Wait for me. . . ."

Henry the Red is an amateur physician. World War II forced him out of medical school in his second year and into the navy.

After Hiroshima and his return to civilian life, family pressures turned him into the maternity business and away from the maternity ward. But Henry the Red has practiced medicine without a license since 1944. Dozens of friends literally call him first with symptoms, before they call their real physicians. This is because my Philosopher-King always gives the impression that he knows the answer and that you must be an idiot to go anywhere else for an opinion. "The practice of medicine is an art," he says, "not a science."

Henry the Red will talk about medicine anywhere. Today I am in his bedroom where he holds court every evening in his pajamas for whoever wanders over for a visit or a diagnosis. I complained to him about a pain on the right side of my abdomen. "Never worry about involvement on the right side. Nothing serious ever happens on that side." Bookshelves line the wall of Henry's bedroom. Opposite his night table, where he can reach over and pluck a volume from the shelf, is his medical library. There is Cecil and Loeb's *A Textbook of Medicine,* Grulee and Eley's *The Child in Health and Disease,* Van Nostrand's *Scientific Encyclopedia,* Morris's *Human Anatomy,* and the book Henry says should be on the desk of every writer, *Stedman's Medical Dictionary.*

"The tragedy of medicine," he says to me, lying in the midst of several pillows on his bed and eating chopped liver on rye, "is that most people never see doctors who know them personally. Suppose that the skin on your calves is extremely sore. Well, this can mean circulatory problems, or that you're a very old person. The public is forced to go to a specialist today, perhaps a dermatologist. I'd go to my internist, someone who *knows* me. This internist is the most important factor in your ultimate survival. What is a good internist? He knows whether you're sick or well by looking at you. Outside of your wife, he should be your best friend. He is the only one who knows you medically (including mentally) and can help you make the important physical decisions of your life."

Henry the Red holds forth from his bed which he uses like a throne. He is talking to me while he is reading the *Christian Science Monitor*. The television set at the foot of the bed is sending "The Gong Show" out at us. Red Henry is speaking between bites of chopped liver chased with small stuffed olives.

"Personality means nothing in a doctor," he tells me. "And another fact: the bottom quarter of every medical school class becomes surgeons. The average poor slob doesn't stand a chance today. All real medicine is being practiced by professors; no general physician feels he can make a diagnosis. The guy *you* see won't move without consulting someone else. If nothing special shows up in your annual physical, and all the blood workups (done by independent laboratories) are negative, all your doctor feels safe saying to you is, 'There's no harm if you lose five to ten pounds.'"

Red Henry goes on, now wound up in his monologue, "So you can't win unless you find an internist who gets your history, and your family's history. Only if you get TB is there a partial victory. Because TB is an aphrodisiac. Read Thomas Mann's *The Magic Mountain*. People screw all day long. But the costs of TB today are out of sight; no one can afford a lengthy illness. No one wants to be a nurse today; doctors want to play God. You ever sit in on surgery? If you see enough bodies, you realize everyone's got organs and bones in the wrong places. You watch an operation, a human stomach opened up on a table, mass confusion, doctors yelling, 'Where the Christ is the appendix?'"

Red Henry lays aside the *Christian Science Monitor* and picks up the *New York Times*. He switches channels to watch Julia Child work on a soufflé.

A young man walks into the bedroom. "How are you, Mr. Henry?" the young man says. He has dropped in for a visit before he goes back to college. He is a fan.

"A lot you care," says Red Henry, pleased to have friends drop into the throne room. After the young man leaves, full of my Philosopher-King's philosophy, Henry says to me, "The kid was rotten. Used to diddle himself something wicked. I set him straight. Now he's fabulous. Wants to go to med school. You know why his name is Henry also? I delivered the sucker. Nineteen years ago on his parents' living-room couch. They called me before they called the ambulance, and the father's only concern was that I not look at the mother's snatch. But they named him Henry after me." He ate the last of the chopped liver and switched channels to "Mork and Mindy."

Developing true medical smarts depends upon one thing. And this is the most important single point to remember in relation to your health and the health of your family. *Make a friend of your doctor.* Do what Red Henry says: develop a close relationship with your internist. This may sound easy. But it is crucial. You develop an acute pain in your abdomen that doubles you up and does not abate. Your daughter's school calls with the information that she has a deep gash on her head from a fall; your spouse is suffering from severe chest pain with shortness of breath. There is only one truly practical thing to know in these situations, or in any medical emergency. You must know that *one* person who is responsive to you, who knows the right specialist, who can get the right room in the right hospital with the proper treatment. Leverage means everything in medicine; your bargaining power is crucial.

Why should this one person be an internist? Because an internist can act as the general, the person who can identify all the specialists you need. Americans bemoan the loss of the old hand-holding relationship with their physicians. *You can still establish this relationship.*

In conversations and interviews I have had with over fifty doctors, every single one of them said that the primary medical responsibility of the modern American family is to identify this personal internist who can act as an advocate for the family. You think you're healthy. But you never know when a problem will arise. The first thing you must do in any new community is to

ne hospitals. He told
ine is being compul-
boat, and he played
tment with him im-
my physician, confi-
world authority in his
come so large there is
y the Red has advice
n't get in to see Dr.
e the attitude 'Pull up

once a month. His in-
that he beats me with
the winner always buys
y question him about the
whether every business at
ilar pressures.
d-looking he is. His seri-
ion make him unconscious
if his wife is happy with
Sitting down and having a
asses by and asks Peter a
ople who ask your opinion
something they feel is seri-
e have been thinking about
appointment with a doctor.
ave four hundred thousand
a hundred and eighty-one
cost of medicine is through
oblem that concerns me: so
hings that have nothing to do
ns, observing government bu-
rvice is being choked to death

for a week in the securities

---

identify and recruit your physician. Then cement that relationship. Make it personal. Because you must have this person always available when you need him. Smart People need this message above all others.

How many times have you said, "If only this went away. If only I felt better. I'd do anything if I could get rid of this." Prior to our Age of Indifference, people had family physicians, doctors who were more than doctors. They were counselors and friends. They knew everyone in your family; they knew their history. What made everything seem comfortable and safe is that they *cared*. They remembered that you were allergic to cats; they knew you reacted to penicillin; they mourned for your father; they hid the secret of the abortion; they made house calls. My medical Maven makes house calls. He knows everyone in my family. He is a friend to whom I would tell anything, and he is certainly one of the prime components of any Smart People team.

I found my medical Maven in an unusual way, a way I would suggest for all Smart People or aspiring Smart People. Until the age of twenty-five I had no internist. I would always use the family pediatrician as my personal doctor, the same physician I had had as a child and as an adolescent. Henry the Red, knowing my pediatrician, finally made me break the cord. "I know your doctor," he said. "He's terrific giving you tetanus shots and handing out lollipops if you've been a good little boy. But he won't stick his finger up your tail. He's never been able to bring himself to do that. Rule One: Never retain a personal physician who refuses to stick his finger up your tail. It's the most important act of a doctor."

That week I called a leading medical school and asked for the names of the heads of two departments: gastroenterology and cardiology. I reached those two doctor/professors and asked each of them the same questions: "I'm new to this town and I have a successful career. I'm interested in people and in the improvement of the quality of living for all people. Whom do you con-

sider to be your finest pupils in the last ten yea~ ⸻
in town are practicing internal medicine ⸻
— gastroenterology or cardiology — "as ⸻
expertise?" Each department head gave me ⸻
all in my city. You should use this procedure ⸻
as well:

I went to a local library with a good referenc ⸻
checked the *Directory of Medical Specialists*, pu ⸻
quis Publications, the people who compile *Who'* ⸻
rectory lists the specialists certified by the boards ⸻
American Board of Medical Specialties. Why use a ⸻
anything unless he has taken the time to gain the ap ⸻
peers and become board-certified in his specialty? Cei ⸻
*not* a guarantee of quality. But it does shift the odd ⸻
favor. The information supplied gives you the purpose a ⸻
tion of each of the twenty-two specialty boards. The ⸻
ments for certification are also listed. Then, in alphabetical ⸻
the doctors' biographical sketches appear, noting each do ⸻
educational background, career history, and professional n ⸻
berships. In general, it is a good, brief study of the person ⸻
whose hands your life may be. I looked up all of the physicia ⸻
recommended to me, used my prejudices about places of birth ⸻
education, age, and family, and made appointments with three of
them. What I was looking for was someone who understood
human nature and who would be young, with a possibly brilliant
future ahead of him. Also, someone likely to remain in the area.
Why did I choose experts in the stomach and the heart? Those
are the primary spots for trouble in adults, and certainly the areas
I am most prone to worry about. I also wanted a doctor with
strong hospital affiliations, someone who could get me and my
family the best accommodations, the best treatment and service
in a first-rate hospital, if the occasion for hospitalization ever
arose.

There is another proven method to identify the right doctor for

troenterology. He was associated with two f⸻
me that day, "The secret of success in medi⸻
sive." He believed in exercise. He sailed a⸻
squash and tennis. I made my first appoi⸻
mediately, and since that day he has beer⸻
dant, and friend. He also has become a⸻
specialty and a man whose practice has b⸻
almost no room for new patients. (Hen⸻
about feeling bad about people who c⸻
George. "Hey," he says, "you've got to ta⸻
the gangplank; I'm aboard.'")

I play squash with Dr. Peter George⸻
tensity about everything he does is suc⸻
regularity. But the matches are close, an⸻
the drinks. During these sessions I usual⸻
practice of medicine. I'm curious about⸻
the bottom line has similar problems, si⸻
Dr. George has no sense of how go⸻
ousness and intensity about his profess⸻
of appearances. I sometimes wonder⸻
him. But I know that his patients are⸻
beer in the locker room, someone p⸻
question about a queasy stomach. "P⸻
in a locker room are worried about⸻
ous," he tells me later. "Those peopl⸻
their problem a lot, afraid to make a⸻
I'll tell you," the doctor says, "we⸻
doctors in America, and we spend⸻
*billion* dollars a year on health. Th⸻
the roof, and there is one huge p⸻
much of my time is taken up with⸻
with saving lives — filling out for⸻
reaucratic rules and regulations. S⸻
by paper."

"I know," I told him. "If I'm

business and I don't write one order in that time, I come back to work to find my desk piled high with nonsense, paperwork. It has nothing to do with being productive or making a living."

"That's right," the doctor said, "except that the nonsense *you* put up with doesn't interfere with saving lives. Medicine is an inexact art. It is not an exact science. For instance, a diagnosis of diphtheria used to be done by smell. Diphtheria actually smells like a mouse. The problem is that, on the one hand, people want the kindly old general practitioner. But they also want all the latest technology. The people demand science *plus* art; they want the old one-on-one relationship. Often they won't pay for it, though. We're forced to eat an incredible number of bad bills, and we pay three to five percent for billing services. I diagnosed throat cancer in a man whom specialists had told that his huskiness was caused by psychosomatic reaction. I saved his life. When the bills I sent kept being unpaid I called him myself. 'Dr. Peter George calling,' I said, 'the man who diagnosed your malignancy?'

" 'Dr. Who?' he said. 'I don't recall any Dr. George. You've got the wrong sucker.' "

Dr. George laughed. "There are economic problems in every business. Bill collecting comes with the territory."

We finished our beers. "But it's interesting about cures," he said. "Christ, until thirty-five years ago doctors really couldn't do anything for anyone. Franklin Roosevelt died essentially of high blood pressure. He could have been saved by something available to anyone today for thirty-seven cents. Dierel would have saved him. Calvin Coolidge's son died of a heel blister." He paused a moment. "You know I'm on to your game," he said.

"What do you mean?" I asked him.

"You want reassurance that everything will be all right. You want me slaying dragons, Spooner. You really want me imposed between you and your fate."

I couldn't say anything in rebuttal. Of course, he was right.

Dr. Peter George has maintained a balance of good sense and

good medicine in treating me and my family. Without the artificial prop of fads and passing medical fancies, here is some of Dr. George's good-health advice to his patients.

1. "Simply, the individual must retain responsibility for his or her own health habits. This should include a once-a-year general physical examination that covers blood pressure, rectal prostate exam, chest X ray, hematocrit, stool test for blood, blood sugar and cholesterol tests, height and weight, EKG. For women, add the breast and pelvic examinations. The history part of the exam is essential. In many ways it's more important than the physical. Hippocrates said, 'Listen to the patient. He'll tell you what's wrong.'"

2. "Surgery is the ideal retreat in our society today for the authoritarian mind."

3. "The antibiotics doctors use and the drugs they prescribe are often dictated by the doctor's relationship with the drug company's salesman. The degree of paranoia one has dictates where one falls in medicine, with the cardiac surgeon having the greatest amount and the dermatologist the least."

4. "In strange towns, if you need a doctor, call the local medical society. In most cases they can recommend someone board-certified and right for your problem."

5. "To see what *doesn't* change, get copies of Cushing's *Biography of Sir William Osler* and Osler's *Book of Aphorisms,* which is written in rhyme. You learn more about medicine than in most books published about the subject in the last hundred years. I would also recommend, for learning about the changes in medicine, that you subscribe to the *Harvard Medical School Health Letter.* Dept. NYBB 79 Garden St. Cambridge, Mass. 02138. It costs twelve dollars a year, is written for the layman, and covers subjects like ulcers, diet and exercise, heart problems, and cancer. Informative and concise."

6. "Doctors should have a sign in their office, for their own benefit, saying, 'Is it a medical decision or because of the payment on the house?'"

7. "Jump rope for exercise, if for any reason you cannot play sports. Jumping rope tones the body completely. It exercises the heart. It's cheap. It's portable. Best yet, several minutes a day will improve your health, your physique, your ability to do your job. Several minutes of jumping is equal to double that time jogging, a set of hard tennis, or two hours walking a golf course. And it's over so fast you don't have time to be bored."

Dr. Peter George turned me on to jumping rope. I believe it has saved my body from dropping into my feet. When I travel on business or pleasure, my rope is packed in my bag. After five minutes I feel better, stronger, ready for the day or evening. At home it becomes a game. I jump rope, and my daughter chants at me:

> *Lincoln, Lincoln, I've been thinkin',*
> *What the heck have you been drinkin'?*
> *Looks like water, tastes like wine,*
> *Oh my God, it's turpentine!*
> *How many bottles did you drink? One, two, three,*
> *    four, five, six . . .*

Currently, I can get to five hundred before breakfast. And my daughter thinks she's got a little kid for a daddy.

"I believe doctors," said Mather Stevens. "I know it's one of my failings, but I want them to be the Almighty. But the important element in choosing a doctor is to find one concerned about you. Maybe for the wrong reasons. That's why I always go through my alumni directories, school and college, finding a doctor when I need one. Then I call the old classmate, sucking him into the situation, and ask him to make a recommendation. That's one easy way to get a response. The other way, which says a lot about the nature of medicine today, is to have an unusual ailment or disease. Then you get doctors all over you, for the research possibilities.

"I almost had something like that a few years ago. I'm the twenty-seventh ranked court tennis player in the world. It doesn't matter that there are only about a hundred players in the world. It's the original game of tennis, the true sport of kings, played inside with a net and rackets, a combination of squash, tennis, shuffleboard, and God knows what else. There are only four courts in North America; a very clubby sport. Anyway, I got hit in the left eye with one of the balls, which looks and feels like a soggy baseball. I think I was in shock, but I kept yelling in the emergency room, 'I'm the twenty-seventh ranked player in the world, *do* something. Save the eye, save the sport.' They paid attention; they thought they had a world-class athlete. They didn't know that all they had was a world-class divorce lawyer."

I was walking with my Philosopher-King from his office to the club where he played court tennis. "I don't know why I believe doctors so implicitly," he said. "I have a friend who is one of the most creative bankers in America. In terms of getting new business, that is — not creative in questionable practices. At any rate, he has always been mistrustful of doctors, very much of the I'm-from-Missouri school. He wants second and third opinions. Anyway, one of his pet peeves was Dr. Benjamin Spock. He felt that Spock's books had ruined a whole generation of children by encouraging parents to be permissive. As it happened," Stevens went on, "my friend was on the board at Case Western Reserve Medical Center where Spock was also a board member. My friend used to enjoy the trip to Cleveland for meetings, flying out in old Caravelles with the exit in the underbelly of the plane.

"Once on his way to a meeting in Cleveland, my friend took his usual seat next to where the stairs would drop down, so he could be the first off the plane. The flight was ruined for everyone by the presence of two children flying alone who threw things, screamed, fought, misbehaved, and made circumstances miserable for the other passengers. My friend was ready to kill when he arrived in Cleveland, and, ready to descend the plane's ramp, he was shoved aside by the brats, who raced down the stairs first.

Walking across the tarmac, my friend saw the children racing toward a tall figure waiting for them beyond the normal section where people were allowed to stand. 'Grampa, grampa,' the two kids screamed, and my friend, getting closer, could see them jumping into the arms of their grandfather, Dr. Benjamin Spock. Quickening his pace, my friend walked up to the doctor, confronted him, and said, 'Doctor, I have to tell you that my flight was made abominable because of those two youngsters. I assume they are related to you. They should be punished severely. They should never — I repeat, *never* — be allowed to fly unattended.' My friend turned on his heel and walked to the cab.

"On the ride into Cleveland his irritation increased, the slow burn turning to flame. Finally, at the board meeting, he demanded that Dr. Spock be dismissed as a board member of Case Western Reserve Medical Center. His motion was adopted."

"What's the moral?" I asked Mather Stevens.

"Beat your kids when they deserve it," he said. We moved on toward Stevens's esoteric sport.

# 8 INDISPENSABLE: THE SMART LAWYERS

Wall Street and finance were *the* business of the 1960s. The stock market collapsed in 1968–70 and has never really recovered. It is clear that with escalating fees and revenues and the growing myth of indispensability, the legal profession is *the* business of the 1970s. It will be with us, growing like a malignancy, into the 1980s and beyond. I must admit to a prejudice here. I suspect any institution that makes itself indispensable the way the legal profession has made itself indispensable. Two stories illustrate part of the problem:

Last year I accompanied a client, a widow, to her lawyer's office in preparation for the liquidation of her husband's estate. We sat in a small conference room in the early afternoon. The lawyer asked us if we would like anything in the nature of coffee or soft drinks. For some reason, both the widow and I were thirsty. We asked for Cokes. A secretary arrived with two Coca-Colas, set them down with paper cups, and said to her boss, "Which client do I memo for the Cokes?" She was serious. The attorney was serious also. He said, "Make it C1747." I decided that when the day came that I couldn't buy a Coke for a widow it would be time to hang it up.

Last week I had lunch at the top of my building on the thirty-eighth floor, a dining club with wraparound windows looking out over the city. I often write at lunchtime, taking a notebook to a booth or a table for one. It is good diversion, and I have the ability to concentrate even in a crowd, especially if the crowd is an unfamiliar, anonymous one. Actually I pretend that my table is in a cafe in Paris in 1921. If the Lost Generation could write in those circumstances, nursing a glass of wine and watching the people go by, so could I.

I was conscious last week of three men sitting at the table next to me. It was obvious that they were attorneys working on opposite sides for corporate clients. For five minutes, as they drank Bloody Marys, they discussed various merits of their clients' cases. Then for an hour and thirty-four minutes they talked about the quality of life in their respective cities, how long it took them to commute, which town had the best restaurants. After coffee, one of them said, "Well, the meter's ticking. What was this, an hour and forty minutes?"

"Round it off to two hours," said another. There was a brief battle for the check, with the hometown lawyers victorious. "What's the difference;" said the out-of-town man, "we'll *both* charge it off."

As they were leaving I looked up and said to them, "Gentlemen, I couldn't help overhearing your conversation. I work for one of the corporations you're representing, or rather one you *were* representing. Let this be a lesson to you for the future. Never assume that there are no ears in public places."

I admit to tremendous satisfaction hearing them sputter and apologize and offer excuses until I asked them to leave and let me finish my lunch. This was a meager blow for restoring legal responsibility. And perhaps these two stories are not typical of the profession. Yet today there are four hundred forty-five thousand lawyers in America. And according to the IRS figures, the gross legal product (fees paid to lawyers) in 1950 was one point three billion dollars. By 1974 that figure was almost *twelve* billion and is certainly higher now. Corporations can deduct legal costs as a business expense. All *we* can do is make funny gestures at lunch.

We are at the mercy of the system that has made litigation as much a part of our lives as sleep.

Of course, there are Smart People ways to cut down the odds and tip the scales of justice in your favor. One thing I have done is to buy shares in Commerce Clearing House, over the counter, at the time around 12½. This company produces the major product for law libraries, the updated changes in tax laws that are clipped into volumes and constantly used for reference. With the ever-increasing government and legal bureaucracies surrounding us, Commerce Clearing seems a natural to benefit from our misfortune. The company has a remarkable financial record. It has been paying dividends since 1936, has over fifty-six million in cash against less than three-quarters of a million in long-term debt, and has a current assets-to-liability ratio of better than three to one. On lower earnings it has sold in the past as high as thirty-two, and, as I see it, demand for its product has got to grow. At any rate, as the lawyers would say, *"Caveat emptor,* let the buyer beware." And also, *"Volenti non fit iniuria,* to a person who consents, no injustice is done."*

Everyone needs a judge on his or her team, an old-time judge with experience, who has seen everything and knows what justice is really all about. I met *my* judge, my legal Lamplighter, in the locker room of the club where I play squash. Of course, I knew who he was when he came in. Everyone knew the judge, a chief justice of the criminal court in my city for fifty-two years. He undressed in a cubicle opposite mine, and, as I watched him, I saw he wore garters to hold up his socks. One garter was green, the other red.

"Gee, Judge," I said to him, "I bet you've got another pair at home just like those."

He looked down and laughed. "You would think so, young man," he said, "but as it happens, they were given to me by the crew of my destroyer during the war. Green and red. One for

* As of April 7, 1979, the price was 22 bid.

starboard, one for port." The judge paddled off to the steam room in his paper slippers. He was wrapped in a large bath towel. He looked exactly like a Roman senator, his fringe of white hair circling his head like two apostrophes. The judge lived at the club. He was a widower, and everyone made it easier for him there than would have been possible at his home. The judge held court in the steam room, telling stories, commenting on politics and the news, philosophizing. When he could take no more of the heat, he would shower and receive a massage and a sunlamp treatment. Then he would continue his seminars at a table in the locker room, nursing a martini, straight up. One day after he had left the steam, one of the lawyers who remained there said, "There are dozens of stories about the old judge. Some years ago an off-duty policeman was in a downtown bar. He was solicited by a homosexual who took a stool next to the cop. In front of the judge the cop testified, 'I was having a beer, Your Honor, when the defendant took the stool next to me, reached his hand over, and placed it on my Johnson bar. He also told me what he'd do for me if I went to his apartment and what it would cost. I arrested him for soliciting.'

"The alleged homosexual was called," the lawyer went on. "He swiveled his hips up to the bench. In a lisping accent he said, 'One thing I'd like, Your Honor. I'd really like a speedy trial.'

"The judge looked at the defendant and without hesitation, with a mimicking lisp, the judge said, 'Guilty. Is that speedy enough for you?'"

Everyone in the steam room laughed and agreed that the judge was a great character. I asked the judge later if the story were true.

"Not only is it untrue," he said, "it's not funny. I never joked in court unless the joke was favorable to the defendant. It is true," he said, wrapping his towel tighter around himself, "that I made comments from time to time that might have been unusual. I remember a drunken lady who was hauled before me once. She said to me, 'Judge, I can see the love light in your eyes.'

" 'Madam,' I said to her, 'those are two cataracts. Enjoy your night at the expense of the public.' "

It is unusual today to be able to spend time with people who are convinced that they know what is best for others. The judge is one of those people. He is opinionated and not afraid to suffer the consequences of those opinions.

"Tell me we're reaching for the great society," he says. "I was on the bench for fifty years and I'll tell *you*. This society is as phony as a three-dollar bill. Britain went down the drain because of the highest motives. It was the refusal of their highest intellects to look at hard facts. The social order today has a tendency to attribute all people's faults to the way they were brought up. Nature is neither that perverse nor that generous.

"I was born in 1892, so I've got a foot in the last century. Even by the 1930s office space went for only a dollar per square foot. Legal secretaries worked five and a half days a week and made fifteen dollars. At that same time, in the 1930s, the Feds across the street were paying file clerks *forty to fifty* dollars a week. What has ruined America is big government. And progressively we have the paradox of democracy: the right of society to be free. We carry it to illogical extremes, like the tyranny of the environmentalists. They are able to halt progress in energy exploration indefinitely. The American Civil Liberties Union would be protecting Hitler if he were alive. Some problems are not soluble within the framework of freedom for all. Eventually it could lead to revolution, when the people cannot stand taxes and inflation. The utopian society the liberals want is hogwash. They all remind me of Pollyanna's gravestone. Written on it is, 'I'm glad I'm dead.' "

Rags-to-riches stories of other generations can be boring and predictable. But the quality that crosses all lines, that all Smart People who are successful possess, is that they have worked their hardest. They universally agree that there is no substitute for this hard work. But the judge tells me that "if the current generation had to peddle, the way their grandfathers had to peddle, there would be a whole lot fewer problems in America." He can sound platitudinous. But the philosophy comes from a man who has sat in judgment on over twenty-five thousand cases ranging from grand larceny, divorce, and libel to murder.

The judge has the magic shared by all Lamplighters. People are attracted to them. You are caught by their words or actions. You may not agree with what they say. But you remain to listen and admire their independence.

Unexpected acts recruit Smart People. One day I asked the judge to come out and play golf with me. Many of his cronies had died in the last decade, including three friends who had made up a foursome for many years. He was excited about playing, even if he had to ride in a cart. What surprised him was how many young men rode in carts rather than walking. "In another hundred years," he complained, "Americans will have no legs. They'll move about in electric wheelchairs. Over those years only their mouths will have expanded in size." The day produced some surprises. The sun was shining and there was little wind. "This is a golf day an old man dreams of," the judge told me. "You can avoid using a shrink if you get up in the morning, look in the mirror, and acknowledge your faults. Don't cry about it. Do something about it. That's why I always adored golf. You must remember how much like life it is: it's the next shot that counts."

On the tenth hole the second shot is blind, over a hill and down to a well-trapped green. The caddy is supposed to stand on the hill and signal whether or not the previous foursome has vacated the green and it is safe to hit. We were waved on by my caddy, and we hit our second shots. Cries immediately came from over the hill. When we arrived at the source, one irate golfer was screaming at us, "What kind of morons hit when we're still playing out the hole? Who the hell let you on the course without knowing the rules?"

The judge listened to the tirade for a minute, then jumped out of his cart. He walked over to the man, who had to be at least thirty years his junior, and said, "This was clearly not our fault, sonny. We were waved on to hit. The fact that our caddy under-valued our abilities is unfortunate, and we do apologize for the inconvenience. But if you persist in this useless harangue, I shall be forced to punch you in the snoot." The judge was deadly seri-ous, and the golfer backed off, later apologizing and claiming the golfer's defense, that he had been chipping for a birdie when we hit into his group. On the way to the showers, after our round, the judge told me, "If there has been a phrase or motto that char-acterizes my life, it has been, 'Don't take shit from anyone.' A useful motto in a fragmented society."

We played golf only that once, but it was enough to endear me to the judge and to make me the recipient of his well-flavored opinions and reminiscences over the last eight years. Many of his stories and memories I have jotted down. They have become what I call "Conversations From the Steam Room." Here is a sampling:

1. "Civil liberties cases have been the biggest boon to this country's criminal element since Prohibition. No cases during that period were thrown out because of illegal seizure, I can tell you."

2. "Prohibition institutionalized crime. It taught them organi-zation."

3. "From do-good laws we proceed to disastrous results. Well-intentioned labor laws were enacted to stop the abuses of child labor. Now the same laws exist to protect the labor barons and racketeers. As for criminals, I never met one in my life, and I've met thousands, who didn't have a true and abiding fear of the hot seat."

4. "What does the bench demand? The bench demands com-mon sense. And it demands a person who is grounded in the fundamentals of common law. Roscoe Pound was one of my he-roes, probably the finest legal mind of our age along theoretical lines. 'The law,' Pound said, 'must be stable, but it must not stand still.'

"A good judge must adapt his morality to the circumstances.

His philosophy has to be adapted to the world around him. There was a time in the early 1950s when there was a rash of ambulance chasers suing for sacroiliac injuries. It seemed that all my cases for days were one dubious sacroiliac injury after another. Finally, one of these shyster lawyers got up and said, 'And what is a sacroiliac injury?'

" 'It's a pain in the ass, sir,' I interrupted. 'Sit down on yours.' Common sense, if you please, on the bench. We need common sense. Speaking of that, I take great issue with the Socratic method used for cases in law school. This method is not indispensable to the law. No good legal rule ever emerged from argument. Socrates wasn't a goddam attorney; he used the method for his own purposes. Right-of-way is the oldest rule of law. It wasn't evolved by the Socratic method. But the tragedy of law today is that it's oriented to the gold standard."

5. "There are no functional courts anymore, few civil trials. It is a mistake to think that all courts are for criminals. I always worried about the taxpayers and tried to dispense justice without waste. My successor has five psychiatrists on his staff.

"God, the trouble with the world is that it gets bogged down in petty detail. My father ran a small store with thousands of screwups a day. But he'd never allow it to get him down. He'd say the first phrase he learned in English, 'The hell with it.' People have got to be taught to disregard trivia, to rise above nonsense. Whenever I get bogged down and feel myself being dragged along with the crowd, I read Oliver Wendell Holmes, Jr. I read Dickens and Thackeray. I think of Holmes's language: 'Certainty generally is illusion, and repose is not the destiny of man.' That does it for me, the language."

6. "Some advice to young people who want to be attorneys: Remember, you're not a lawyer until you can say no to a client. Knowing that, I would spend six months before I went into practice, going from court to court listening to trials. You will never get as good an internship. Indeed, I would recommend this also

for anyone contemplating litigation. You should know what to expect from the American legal system. The surprise if you go in unprepared could kill you.

"I would also advise new lawyers to take jobs with the government before they enter private practice. The government dominates our lives today, and it is essential to know how the high-powered games are played in the IRS, SEC, FCC, and the other bureaucratic corridors. The final thing I'd advise young lawyers is this: Don't get married before you practice for a few years. Pay scales are outrageously high in our big cities. But the first years of practice require a monastic dedication that can make a career, but ruin a marriage."

I saw the judge recently, sitting in the main lobby of his club, his back to a dying fire. He was watching young couples walk by him on the way to a mixer, a cocktail party. "You know," he said, "young attorneys today are not steeped in the fundamentals of common law. But the big difference in this generation of attorneys seems to be their lack of involvement with the community, their selfishness, if you will. They are turned inward, worrying about their families and themselves."

Then he talked to me of other lawyers he had known, other judges, famous people whose friendships he prized. At one point he paused and watched several young women go by, giggling, anticipating. "H. L. Mencken said to me once," the judge sighed, "injustice is relatively easy to bear. What stings is justice."

The judge backed his chair closer to the fire, closer to the warmth.

Mather Stevens is more than my Philosopher-King. He is also my legal Maven. Several years ago he called me and said, "The County Bar Association, the biggest in the state, is stuck for a speaker to talk before Tip O'Neill, who is featured at their annual dinner. I volunteered your name, for a special reason. I want you to see the legal profession operating when they're among their own."

He picked me up for the black-tie evening, and we took a cab to the hotel. The County Bar Association included lawyers in all the outlying districts of the community. "You'll see all the country lawyers," Stevens told me. "Everyone who brings law to the people who don't know a thing about smooth corporate attorneys or six-figure divorce specialists."

Stevens left me alone to wander the huge ballroom where drinks and hors d'oeuvres were served to four hundred guests. My rainbow heart pin is particularly effective in crowds of strangers. Any number of women in long dresses and orchid corsages asked me about it. Lots of lawyers asked me also, but immediately lost interest when they found out I was not a judge. Many of the lawyers in the county are courthouse lawyers, deal-makers, with white socks and big cigars. I wandered from group to group, grabbing an occasional chicken liver wrapped in bacon and an occasional Scotch and water. I stayed and nursed my drink whenever the conversation sounded interesting.

"Did I ever tell you the time Jocko met the president?" one lawyer was asking his cronies. They shook their heads no. "Well, after being introduced, Jocko says to LBJ, 'You play gin, Mr. President?'

" 'No,' Johnson admitted. 'Never played gin. Only canasta.' Jocko left the president flat, turned on his heel and muttered, 'Then I can't make any fucking money in this place.' Johnson loved it, and he and Jocko became great buddies."

Another lawyer was saying to a small group of political friends, "What's he pissed off at *us* for? We never did anything for *him*."

By the time dinner was served, the men were all feeling like Mr. Justice Holmes, and the women were all Madame Queens, wives of city councilmen. It was a scene out of a Daumier lithograph. I was at the head table, on a dais looking out upon the crowd. All the judges were at the head table also, along with the master of ceremonies, a witty clerk of court with a five handicap in golf, and an empty chair waiting for the Honorable Thomas P. "Tip" O'Neill, Speaker of the House of Representatives. A Superior Court judge was on my left. A Circuit Court of Appeals judge was on my right. Drunken lawyers literally stood in line below us, waiting to pay homage to the judges, to press their flesh, to ask to be remembered to their families. The judges smiled and nodded and acknowledged the fealty as their right and privilege. Wives came up also, some urged by their husbands, some needing no urging. This went on, up and down the head table, all during fruit cup, bean-and-barley soup, roast beef, and imitation baked Alaska. It was the most extended mass apple-polishing I have ever witnessed, worse than the military on inspection day with a general expected. I went on after a forty-minute tribute to a retiring judge. By the time I was introduced, the crowd was too drunk and having too good a time to pay attention to anyone, much less someone who was going to tell them about getting a novel published. Cigar smoke hung in the air about ear level. My opening was, "Ladies and gentlemen, do you know the difference between a rooster and a lawyer? No? Well a rooster gets up in the morning and *clucks defiance.*" No one even paid attention to the insult. Halfway through my charade, Tip O'Neill walked in to a standing ovation. I was all finished. After he ended his speech, O'Neill came over to me. "Kid," he said, "I'll follow your act any time."

I went after Mather Stevens, wanting to kill him on sight. "You were a riot," he told me. "When you and Tip were together, all I could think of was that joke about the Pope and Sidney Goldberg. You know the punch line: 'Who's that fat guy up on the dais with John Spooner?' "

On the ride home Stevens told me, "That's the legal profession. And it's a hell of a lesson for you. Most people who are lawyers come to it by accident. On my twenty-first birthday I was doing KP in the army and realized that I was totally unsuited both for being a subordinate and for being a superior. So willy-nilly, I figured law school was a safe route. I wanted you to come tonight because every myth should be explored first hand. The mentality of the County Bar Association can show you that life is business as usual, despite ethics committees, despite Watergate.

One of the advantages Mather Stevens has is that he looks like the consummate snob, but is really a humanist, gentle and liberal in the best sense of the words. His favorite books are Gibbon's *The Decline and Fall of the Roman Empire*, John Barth's *The Sotweed Factor*, and the *Flashman* series by George MacDonald Fraser. I include the reading list because of something my legal Maven taught me long ago: "Find out what people's favorite books are. I always ask my clients that question. It tells you a great deal about who they are and what they think." It is a worthwhile Smart People technique for you also. You can tell a lot about others from the books they mention. Unfortunately, we live in a time in which, too often, people cannot name a favorite book because they haven't read one in years. Smart People read.

My legal Maven has explained to me the hostilities that surround the legal profession. He has suggested ways to choose lawyers with an eye toward holding down the cost of services. "We [the large law firms with fifty to two hundred lawyers] all increasingly use paralegals to solve many of our day-to-day problems. The paralegals are assistants trained in specific tasks who ease the workload of the attorneys. Their time is charged against the client, generally in the fifteen-to-twenty-dollar-per-hour category. A young lawyer will bill from twenty-five to forty dollars an hour. My charges as a partner run at a hundred dollars an hour, with the biggest divorce attorney in the city getting a hundred and twenty-five dollars. A superstar, someone who might do a job for the president of the United States, charges his time at about three hundred per hour. My year's billings last year were for approximately fifteen hundred hours. But I read a study recently claiming that the average lawyer's meter ticks for from sixteen hundred to twenty-four hundred hours a year. Of course, you don't collect for every hour. I've been a master in lots of cases for a flat thirty dollars an hour. And we do a good deal of pro bono work for which we're not paid at all. A firm needs fifteen to twenty partners to maintain a healthy library, overhead has escalated so much. To stay current with loose-leaf services, federal reports, state reports, and tax bulletins, not to mention other expenses, our overhead per partner now is between eighty and eighty-five thousand a head."

"Does that excuse the endless time cases take up? Especially if they must go to court?" I asked. "Obviously the public pays through the nose for your growing overhead."

"Well, there's justification for what you say. My rule of thumb for the lay person would be $(a)$ use a lawyer only when you must, $(b)$ if your lawyer's advice doesn't make sense, it probably is bad advice, and $(c)$ if you need a lawyer, ask another lawyer to recommend one. Always ask someone in any profession about his peers."

"Unfortunately," Stevens went on, "we are a profession remembered for our mistakes. People's feelings about lawyers are dictated by experience, same as with stockbrokers (pardon me) or proctologists. In divorce cases, a lot of people change lawyers because they're dealing with unhappy situations. They can't change their husbands or wives. So they change the attorneys.

"So many new lawyers feel, 'God, I did great in law school but I'm nowhere in practice.' Many people who go to business school have already had practical experience in business when they get to the graduate level. Practically no law student has ever had legal experience. As for the courts, they are paralyzed by constitutional decisions. Civil cases take a back seat to criminal cases, and the wait before you're called can be endless. I maneuver a lot to get judges I like. This is perfectly allowable. And I have a trick. I really pay attention to what a judge's opinions have been. Then I rephrase the judge's opinion when I appear before him, knowing he's going to eat it up. It helps to know the foibles and prejudices of judges beforehand."

My legal Maven has several Smart People hints for dealing with lawyers.

1. "Check rates at the *start* of your problem. Don't wait for your first bill. Ask what fees everyone in the law office receives: paralegals, associates, partners. And find out approximately what the feeling is about the overall cost of doing your job."

2. "Find out if your lawyer is on any big case at the time you consider retaining him. Prior commitments can put you on the back burner."

3. "Your own lawyer can frequently give you lower-than-usual rates. Presume upon friendship in this case. The guilty conscience of a friend can keep your bill down. As a part of this, check your meter as the case progresses. 'How are we doing on cost?' You don't want any surprises months later."

4. "I hate to say this, but it's true. Don't let lawyers push you around. The squeaky wheel will get the grease. So be a nuisance if you have to be. You'll be noticed that way."

5. "Does your lawyer keep good records? Does the firm charge you fifty cents a page for Xeroxing? (It costs *them* ten cents.)"

6. "Tell your lawyer everything. In divorce actions, your opinions provide the trick that can get at the weaknesses of your husband or wife."

7. "Above all, make sure your attorney keeps your disclosures private. Make sure that your information is confidential and kept that way. I live by an old Chinese proverb that, translated, says, 'In a closed mouth flies can't get.'"

"If I were to come to you cold, looking for an attorney," I asked Stevens, "and I frankly told you I was shopping around, how would you hook me?"

"First of all, I'd ask in the initial interview about your home life, your kids and their names. And, of course, what your favorite books are. Since no one else would ask the client that, you'd be curious, and you'd be back. When you came back, in the first two minutes I'd ask you about your kids' health and I'd ask after them *by name*. It's never failed to get me a client, especially women who are already anticipating getting custody."

After further chat I said goodbye to my Maven. Stevens smiled. "By the way," he said, "my best to Scott, Nicky, and Amanda."

Knocko del Rossi, my legal Roughrider, is always on stage. He wears a three-piece suit that inevitably seems small on him because his belly protrudes from under the vest. The belly is always circled by a thick black belt with the double G symbol of Gucci, shining at the prospective client in polished brass. Knocko del Rossi weighs two hundred and fifty-seven pounds and always carries at least five hundred dollars in cash on his person. He keeps the cash held together by rubber bands, small bills on the outside, the heavy stuff on the inside. Knocko is the sort of attorney you don't see very much any more, the fixer, the dealer, the man who can take care of anything. Years ago, a Knocko del Rossi would have run for office to consolidate his power. Now, the scrutiny of the press is too intense for people who know how to deal. So Knocko runs his constituency from two places: during the day, a cafeteria opposite the courthouse, and at night, the Hideout, a bar around the corner from the court. Knocko owns twenty-five percent of the Hideout, a workingman's bar where every drink is a dollar, and, on Friday nights, linguine with clam sauce is served free to anyone.

Although Knocko del Rossi is my age he seems older, older, I suppose, because he operates like a father figure. To everyone who seeks him out he says, "Everything's gonna be all right. I'll get the facts and everything's going to work out." I met Knocko during basic training. We enlisted at the same time, and he was chosen, on the bus ride to our first base, to pass out lunch money to the recruits. He organized a poker game in the back of the bus, won a hundred and thirty dollars, and loaned the money back to the losers. Fifteen dollars would repay ten borrowed. By the time the bus got to Fort Dix, New Jersey, Knocko was in business. He had his customers, he had lined up the bruisers to back him up, and he had the confidence of the sergeant who picked him to supervise the rest of us. In our basic training company, Knocko was platoon guide and I was one of his squad leaders.

There were a number of Puerto Rican recruits in our company — residents of Puerto Rico, not stateside city kids. They were frightened, innocent, and expecting the worst in the U.S. Army. They talked in Spanish. In the latrine after lights out, they polished boots and cleaned rifles for other soldiers who paid them for doing the duties the others were too lazy or indifferent to do themselves. "No comprendo," was what the Puerto Ricans said constantly, whenever the noncoms would tell them anything. At reveille one day, while we were lined up in the company street at five-thirty in the morning, our exasperated first sergeant announced, "And as for you Puerto Rican personnel, there will be no more of this 'no comprendo' shit. From now on you all speak English. Do you read me?"

"No comprendo, sergeant," yells Knocko del Rossi, stepping forward. The sergeant took Knocko to the company commander's office, where del Rossi defended the Puerto Ricans' right to speak Spanish and to have orders repeated slowly. The sergeant was transferred to another company, and Knocko had his brass polished, his rifle and boots cleaned, and his bed made for free by the Puerto Ricans for the remainder of basic training. "And they all sleep with their bayonets under their pillows," Knocko told me. "If the noncoms came after me they'd have to get by the Latinos first."

It seemed so out of character for Knocko to go up against the establishment that I asked him about it. "You've got to get the markers out in life," he said. "You have to build up a network of people who owe you favors. Then living can be easy. My father has been a clerk of court for forty years," Knocko said. "He told me that he once went to a fish store in his neighborhood and asked Mr. Katz, the owner, about what he did with day-old fish. 'I sell it to my friends,' Mr. Katz replied. 'What?' my father said, surprised. 'Sure,' Katz said, with resignation in his voice. 'If you can't sell rotten fish to your friends, who *can* you sell it to?'

Knocko was full of stories from his father, whom he made appear to be the source of all wisdom and humor.

Knocko and I stayed in touch after the army. He went to law school then, and I can remember meeting him for dinner in Chinatown. He told me what kind of an attorney he wanted to be. "I'm going to stay in the neighborhood," he told me. "I lived in a three-decker house growing up. We didn't mow the lawn, we swept the concrete." He laughed. "Everyone in the neighborhood was poor. I remember one time I was sick with the virus. There was no food in the house, no milk. The local congressman, Spagnuolo, came by with sacks of groceries. He was our savior (as well as being my godfather). That was it as far as I was concerned. When I grew up I wanted to be the savior of the neighborhood. You remember the army? Christ," Knocko said, "that was the first time I was ever away from home. I didn't know enough to have a shaving kit. I wrapped my razor and soap in a facecloth."

Knocko del Rossi has the wisdom of the poor boy who wishes never again to be poor. "I love trial work," he says. "In a courtroom I'm an actor, an advertising man. Preparation is the one essential in trial work. Preparation, and knowing the judges. I'm a romancer of judges in the best sense of the word. No money passing hands, nothing like that. But a lot of romance: golf games, dinners, an occasional junket to Vegas. When I know I'm coming up against a judge who doesn't buy my act, I get a continuance, picking days when my boys sit. I don't mean the judges are in my pocket. What I do mean is that you know who likes you and who doesn't and who'll bend over to give you a break. Those are the guys on your Christmas list."

Why do I need a legal Roughrider?

"Basically," Knocko says, "you need me to cut through the crap." And that's true. Your legal Roughrider is better than anyone else for dealing with impossible bureaucracies.

Knocko solved three problems for me that no other lawyer could have done so efficiently and inexpensively. Almost everyone who works in police stations, in firehouses, and in federal and local government buildings grew up in a neighborhood not unlike del Rossi's. Knocko knows them all. Several years ago I was asked to assist the widow of a client of mine in obtaining Veterans Administration benefits due her on his death. I went to a friend of the widow's at a large law firm for assistance. Several paralegals worked on the case for seven months, charged the widow seven hundred and fifty dollars. Finally the widow received a form from the VA that said, "Claim rejected. No indication that death was service-related." I took the widow to Knocko del Rossi. He had a sister-in-law in charge of benefits at the Veterans Administration. In two weeks the widow began receiving three hundred and seventy-five dollars a month in benefits from the government plus payments awarded because of the delay. *And* interest. Knocko charged the widow two hundred dollars and said to me, "The easiest two C notes I ever made. My sister-in-law takes the right form to the right desk and waits for it to be signed. The big law firms are wired to no one but other big law firms. They mail everything; they know nothing."

Two major law firms assured me a year ago that they could do nothing to extend the visa privileges of an au pair girl from Finland living with us. Knocko got the visa in two days, *plus* an eventual work permit. His charge was eighty-seven dollars and fifty cents, which included half a case of Johnny Walker Black for the immigration man at the Federal Building who had lived as a boy on the middle level of Knocko del Rossi's triple decker.

The third case of Knocko's effectiveness involved a friend of mine who had a neighbor with two German shepherd dogs. The shepherds were let loose at night and developed a nasty habit of baying at the moon during the hours between two and four A.M. My friend complained as politely as he could. Then, when the barking continued, he called the police. The local dog officer forced the neighbor to curb his shepherds at night. Directly after this police intervention my friend and his wife were awakened regularly at three-thirty A.M. by the phone. Answering it, my friend would hear fifteen seconds of a human being imitating the bark of a German shepherd.

"What can I do?" asked my friend, a pacifist by nature. "It's driving us crazy. We can't sleep. I'll be damned if I'll move, but the guy next door is a nut. Also I can't prove it's him. To boot, he's an auxiliary policeman, so the cops are indifferent to my complaints."

"Will you pay for a solution?" I asked my friend.

"Of *course* I'll pay," he said.

So I called Knocko, who laughed for several minutes. Then he took down the particulars, including the dog owner's phone number and place of employment (he was an engineer). The very next Thursday night the dog-owning engineer dropped his wife at the front entrance of a suburban steak house. Then he drove around back to park his car in the crowded lot. As he locked his door he suddenly found himself lifted off the ground by both elbows and, with his arms pinned, carried quietly across the lot to a high fence. He was pushed up further, unable to resist, unable to see in the darkness, and hung by his raincoat collar from a hook, high on a fence post. Two men, seeming like giants to the engineer, had carried him across the parking lot. A third man now stood in front of him. "We'd just as soon put the hook through your neck as your raincoat," the third man said. "You've got this one warning. No more pets bigger than turtles; no more phone calls after midnight. You've got a brain; love thy neighbor." They walked away. The engineer ruined his raincoat getting down, then ran to his wife after vomiting in the parking lot. My friend had no more trouble from his neighbor. Some time later he received a bill from Knocko del Rossi with this memo: "Tax advice — four hundred and seventy-five dollars."

How do you find a Knocko del Rossi without serving in the military with him? Go to any courthouse. In any city or town there are hangers-on who pass time around the courthouse the way hobos meet in train yards and retired shoe men sit in brokerage offices. You'll recognize these people instantly.

They are respectable retired old-timers who adore politics and the law and cannot stand being away from their cronies. They have been policemen, court officers, clerks in records offices, assistants to legislators. They live to gossip, run errands for lawyers and politicians, and swap stories of murderers, thieves, and judges. Ask them, "What lawyer fixes things best? Who solves problems around here? Who would you recommend to a stranger?" The hangers-on always know the answer. And they always know the right people.

## THE MICKEY THE DUNCE ROUTINE

Knocko del Rossi is the best user I know of the Mickey the Dunce Routine. "Most people love to hear the sound of their own voice," he says. "You've got to know when to play Mickey the Dunce, when to keep your mouth shut. People love to hear themselves talk. If you say, 'I didn't know, Officer,' 'I didn't know, Your Honor,' 'I didn't know, Doctor,' 'I didn't know, baby,' these are all very effective Mickey the Dunce ploys.

Use the Mickey the Dunce Routine after you have run a stoplight, were late with your alimony, have built an addition to your house without a variance, or have come home drunk. You use the routine *after* you have done something you probably shouldn't have done."

Knocko also has business lunches at restaurants of *his* choice. "I'm having a Beefeater martini," Knocko says. "Have a drink yourself, the deal will go smoother if we're friends."

"Okay, a Bloody Mary," says the person Knocko is negotiating with. Then the waitress brings Knocko a glass of water on the rocks in an old-fashioned glass. A twist of lemon peel floats on the water. Knocko orders three of them during lunch, and he allows himself to be charged by the restaurant at martini prices. Knocko also has at his disposal three telephone numbers that belong to three women whom he uses as special agents. They kick back a percentage to him in old bills. "The ability to *deal* in life," Knocko says, "cannot be restricted by what seems popular or unpopular at the time. There is no dirty pool. There is only, Do you make out or not? Are you pushed around or not? Are you screwed or not?"

Knocko taught me about another Smart People tactic: the Hundred Club. He wears in his lapel a small diamond pin that says "100." The Hundred Club exists in at least fifteen states and was founded some twenty years ago. Members contribute two hundred and fifty dollars a year to provide financial assistance to the families of policemen killed in the line of duty. The club's motto is "We care for those who care for us." It is difficult to join the Hundred Club unless an influential member pushes you in or unless you save the life of a policeman.

Del Rossi had personally finished a case of St. Pauli Girl beer at the bridal dinner of a client from the Highway Authority. He topped that off with some champagne followed by a bottle of Sambuca, a particularly potent Italian liqueur served with coffee beans floating in it. Weaving home in his Mercedes he almost collided with a burning automobile parked on the soft shoulder. His sudden stop blew a tire on the Mercedes. Cursing the other car, del Rossi jumped out and ran to attack the driver. Instead, he dragged the already unconscious man from the front seat and, sobering fast, pulled him a furlong away before the man's car exploded. The other driver was an off-duty police captain. He provided Knocko with the diamond lapel pin and life membership in the Hundred Club. No member ever gets a ticket. It gives you a nationwide identity with the police. Any member can always get off with a warning and a handshake in almost *any* state for *any* offense short of child porn. Look into it. But continue to avoid Sambuca.

I sat with Knocko del Rossi at lunch in his cafeteria recently. From the window where we sat we could see the white granite courthouse. During our spaghetti carbonara, Knocko gave over four hundred dollars to five separate people who came by our table, made a touch, and left. "I've got markers all over town," he told me, "with poor people, people in trouble. But it comes back a thousandfold." I tried to tell Knocko about a stock that might interest him. "Eat your carbonara," he said. "If you can't sell rotten fish to your friends, who *can* you sell it to?"

I have a rule that I have adhered to when recruiting lawyers: I never hire a lawyer I cannot understand. I tell myself, as you must tell yourself, "This stuff is *not* incomprehensible. I can understand what I am told. I am paying attention. If I hear nothing but jargon, this is not the lawyer for me."

The legal profession has developed its own language; lawyers try to appear to be magicians. But law is no different from any other subject. If your lawyer cannot communicate with you simply and directly, fire him or her. When I consult an attorney, I ask that he justify his recommendations. As a stockbroker, I explain *why* I'm buying a stock for a client. This is only reasonable; it's *the client's* money. Lawyers know very little more than you and I do. Make them disclose their thoughts. If they say, "It's too complicated for an explanation," fire them. I also tell every attorney on first meeting, "I would like, as we go along, a detailed explanation of what you are going to do. Then, as we proceed, what you indeed *are* doing." This keeps them on the track and aids you in preventing that feeling of helplessness. It also establishes immediately that *you* are in control, not the attorney. It also might be wise to say at the beginning of your relationship, "I have two thousand dollars to spend on this problem. Let me know when I've spent five hundred, then when I've spent a thousand, and so on." It's your money. You must control the cost as much as possible.

As I have mentioned before, there are two qualities that all truly Smart People share. One is that *contrast* is a prime ingredient in their lives. Smart People must change battlegrounds occasionally to keep themselves fresh. They also have dimensions that go beyond what people see in them on first meeting. This sense of contrast they all maintain.

The second quality the Smart People have in common is an old-fashioned virtue: they all work their tails off, and they have worked hard since childhood.

In any discussion of law as it affects our lives today, we also have to think of politics. It is not a necessity to have a politician on your Smart People team, but the laws that shape our lives are nudged along by our politicians. Particularly since Watergate, there are many questions about the quality of politics and the moral insensitivities of the people who practice it. We all care about our future; we all think about our past. As an aid to defining how we have lived, how we will live, the lucky person has a politician on his Smart People team. Selfishly, recruiting a politician serves many practical purposes. A politician knows key people who can help you. A politician's power can rub off on you. My legal/political Smart Person is my Summa in this area. He is the Honorable John F. Collins, consulting professor of urban affairs at MIT and a two-term mayor of Boston. He personally turned around one of the most blighted and decaying cities in America and gave it life, a sense of purpose, and a renewal plan that is the envy of every major city in the country.

Smart People put a large premium on experience. You cannot learn life from a book. Sam Goldwyn used to say, "I bow down and kiss the feet of talent." The more you can absorb by sitting and listening at the feet of Smart People, the more you can avoid the inevitable mistakes that crop up in everyone's life. John Collins and I have a business relationship that, I am pleased to say, has developed into friendship. It is difficult to write of friendship without the friend's objecting to a view of himself that may not be what he believes to be true. For this discussion then, I'll take purely the Smart People side and talk about the control of power, the vision of how a city should be, and the arrangement of a life after the peak of power is passed.

I went to Mayor Collins's home recently to spend a day discussing his particular views of politics, the law, and motivating people. Cape Cod in the winter is a surprise. The towns, packed with tourists and summer residents in season, seem almost deserted. Some smaller towns look like abandoned frontier villages, where the settlers have moved on because of hostile Indians or crop failure.

John Collins lives with his wife, Mary, in an enclave of attractive houses, a lively neighborhood of scientists from Woods Hole, active businessmen, secret heavyweights. Set on a hill, the Collins house looks out on the water, toward New Bedford and the Elizabeth Islands. It is a place of escape in the best sense of the word, surrounded by the elements, a spot of peace and renewal. I waited in Mayor Collins's living room, sipping a Scotch and watching sleet batter at the windows, seeking angry entry. He received phone calls like tribute, from politicians, businessmen, clients. The floor was stacked with books, newspapers, briefcases full to bursting. People checked into Cape Cod by telephone, giving news, seeking reassurance. Finally, he shut off the calls and talked to me.

"Two things have affected my life deeply," he said. "Number one is the fact that I grew up dirt poor in the middle of the city. For many years I never knew anyone who made more than thirty dollars a week. Because of this I believed, and still do, that no one is going to make my ship come in but me, and that anything worth having in life is worth working hard for. Ambition is not a bad thing in a child. I know it kept me going. I wanted to be mayor of Boston for as long as I can remember, and yet, if you ask anyone in my high school class, they probably would say that they never would have expected it. Because I was always so quiet. But inwardly I had my eye on the apple, on the future.

"I went directly from high school to law school. Life began early in those days; there was no slowing down the process for years of preparation and courses that you'd never really need or use later. So desire was one big influence. The other was that I got polio in 1955 and really lost most of the use of my legs. Because of that I figured I had to work harder and think harder than anyone, to achieve my goals. Running for mayor the first time in 1960 I was a decided underdog. Because of my physical difficulties, just in getting around, I was worried about appearing weak to the voter. I figured I couldn't make anything look difficult; I didn't want anyone nervous about my ability to perform. Let me tell you, when you have to concentrate every fiber of your being on walking half a dozen steps on crutches and on making it appear casual to the observer, changing the face of a city is a snap. Everything in life is deciding how badly you want something. Then, doing it or not.

"When I was first elected mayor, Boston was a deteriorating city, physically and emotionally. The political hack system had always predominated; there was really only one building in the city over ten stories. Well, I set out to do two things in office. First of all, I wanted to prove that every Irishman in politics wasn't either dumb or dishonest. And that a city other than Chicago could be efficiently governed. Then I had to change the face of the city, the only major U.S. city with no building boom. The only way to do this was to involve business, the private sector. And, since I had been the underdog, business didn't know me from a hole in the ground. Well, I know about time pressures, and I figured I had to do the job fast because I never was going to win any popularity contest."

He laughed. "I had been in the Massachusetts legislature. I'd argue cases in the morning for my law practice, go to the legislature in the afternoon and then to committee hearings. Then I'd have dinner and go back to my law office until nine or ten. That was four nights a week and, of course, all day Saturday.

"The people I picked for my mayor's team were essential. My people didn't have to be the smartest. Degrees are generally meaningless anyway. I had two criteria: My people had to be good, decent, honest people. And they had to be loyal to me. The biggest mistake in government today is the hiring of whiz kids who look good and sound fine but who do nothing. They're all illusion and no substance.

"As mayor I had to be tough. I'd come in at nine-thirty in the morning, not early. But what they didn't know was that I'd have taken home two briefcases full of work and read until two or three in the morning. I also had an assistant who looked at every single piece of paper. If it seemed like one department had awarded a two-thousand-dollar contract for having an empty lot cleared out, and there was room for some funny business, I'd call in the department head. We'd discuss big things at first, like Jack Kennedy's candidacy or the state of the city. Then I'd say 'That lot you're clearing in the South End. The price looks a little high to me.' That would be enough. They couldn't believe that I'd bother with such small detail. It kept everyone on their toes.

"'You're here,' I'd tell my department heads, 'because you're the best person for the job. Look around at one another. If anyone does anything dishonest you reflect on the mayor. You are disloyal to me, and to everyone in this room, and you're destroying the faith of the city. No one gets second chances, and I don't want any wives crying on my doorstep.' They all said after that, 'If Collins catches me, he'll castrate me.' And it worked."

John Collins got business out of the grandstand and into the ballgame, as he intended. His master plan went for renewal of fifty percent of the city of Boston. His plan was not to go after individual sections but to envision the entire city changing simultaneously. It was a radical plan, but it was successful. Today, almost ten years after the end of John Collins's second term, every important change in Boston is the product of his vision, from the uptown Prudential Center to the new City Hall overlooking historic Faneuil Hall Marketplace and the most attractive and impressive waterfront area in America.

We went out for lunch and, on the way, drove around to see

how the ocean looked in winter. Collins talked about America in
the present and how he saw our future.

"You know I didn't particularly enjoy the trappings of power,"
he said. "I saw myself as the manager of people's money. You
hear from the fringe people when you are in power. Eighty percent of the people who work for a living don't have time to write
a mayor about the quality of education. *These* are the folks you
have to make the tough decisions for, ignoring the ten percent on
the right and the ten percent on the left. It's tough not to care if
you're loved or not, but just concentrate on getting the job done."

He continued, as we drove along the deserted beach front,
"Every man should have more than one life. It keeps you young
and alert. I've really had three lives. My work as a lawyer, before
my polio. Then, as mayor. And my career since then. Teaching,
learning every day.

"I'm not optimistic about America. There is a leadership vacuum which is the fault of the post–World War II parents in this
country. There is only the illusion of performance. Old ideas of
doing what's right and working hard have been replaced by the
idea that work is to be shunned, that people have a preordained
right to life without sacrifice. 'Do your own thing' is the most
insidious cliché of this century. No one values any freedom other
than a mocking, uninhibited personal freedom that does not realize it has a cost. We want every privilege without discharging
our responsibilities. Kids of hard-working parents only say, 'Don't
pollute the natural state.' That leads to no jobs. The elitists all
apologize for the fact that their parents made money."

We arrived at the restaurant, and John Collins worked his way
laboriously on his crutches to the front door. As we moved into
the warmth he said to me, "Every morning I get up and look in
the mirror. I say to myself, 'You're the smartest son of a bitch
you're going to meet today.' Then I go out and try to use my
experience to help the quality of life in this country." A man came
up to us, reminding Collins that he had been in the FBI, and had
known the mayor years before.

"Of course, Bob," said the mayor. "After OCS. Right after the war."

"You've got a great memory, Mr. Mayor. We miss you," the man said. Other people came up to us, patting him on the back, shaking his hand. One woman said, "God bless you, John."

"How about that?" he said to me, obviously pleased. "How bad can life be, if God blesses you?" He smiled and we ordered lunch.

# 9 SMART MONEY

I asked Henry the Red, Philosopher-King, about making deals and about discounts in business. Red Henry never answers questions simply. He always goes for the phrase that will live or the story that illustrates the theme.

"You want to learn about discounts and deals?" Henry asked, gathering his thoughts. "A woman goes into a grocery store and asks the owner the price of a pound of sugar. 'Eight cents,' says the grocer.

"'*Eight cents!*' says the lady. 'Across the street the man is charging *six* cents.'

"'So why don't you buy it from him?' says the grocer.

"'Because he's out of it,' answered the lady.

"The grocer smiled in triumph. 'When *I'm* out of it,' he said, 'it's only *four* cents.'

"But I don't want to philosophize about money," Henry the Red said. "You've got to have it. Period! I'm a nogoodnik if I have guests at my house and I excuse myself to watch Walter Cronkite. It's rude. But I have a friend who did some business with J. Paul Getty. He was over at Sutton Place, Getty's palace outside London, and in the middle of cocktails, Getty excused himself. My friend was left alone in a room the size of Bridgeport, Connecticut, and a butler came in to ask if my friend required anything.

" 'Mr. Getty left so abruptly,' my friend said, 'Was there anything wrong?'

" 'Oh no, sir,' said the butler. 'Mr. Getty excuses himself every day at this time to watch his favorite show on the telly.'

" 'What's Mr. Getty's favorite show?'

" 'Oh sir, it's that animal adventure,' said the butler, smirking. ' "Daktari." ' "

Henry the Red knocked his pipe into an ashtray. "For the rich," he said, "anything is forgivable."

Like it or not, money is how we keep score. I have distributed three hundred and sixteen questionnaires to Smart People of my selection around the world. In addition to the questionnaires, I have spent time (dinners, lunches, tennis games, cocktails) with over a hundred and fifty other people during the last year, and I have asked them all, "What are the two most important things in life?" Money and health were the two elements mentioned by virtually everyone, with money receiving the slight edge. Shaw in *Man and Superman* said, "Lack of money is the root of all evil." I believe it, for money is my business. In the investment world it is the by-product of fear and greed.

Wall Street is the bottom of the barrel these days, both as perceived by the public and as acknowledged by itself. A seat on the New York Stock Exchange sold a few weeks ago for sixty thousand dollars. In 1968, a decade ago, seat prices reached almost *six hundred* thousand dollars. Fear and greed.

A brokerage boardroom is the mirror of the public's soul, a reflection of how we view our times. We have forty stockbrokers sitting in our boardroom watching the mystery of the tape flashing by. The prices trigger happiness and sorrow, the same prices for all to see, but instantly producing forty different reactions. Customers also sit in the boardroom, but without the excitement of the 1960s. The customers now idle away their days, seeking company, warmth, and friendship much more than they seek the action. Partially from the clients who pass through the boardroom to my yellow-painted office, I have assembled my Smart People money team. My team advises me about taxes, real estate, the health of the economy, and investments through which I can prosper outside of my own field. They take good care of me because life is a trade-off. They expect something in return. What they expect mainly is the essence of Smart People, someone who cares about them. And, of course, someone who cares about their money.

Is my approach unique? It is a fundamental technique that implies knowledge of human nature, knowledge of the fear/greed syndrome that, in my opinion, is the most important lesson for investment success. I'll give you a concrete example. In 1975 Andrew Tobias, writing for *New York* magazine, did an article entitled "How to Invest Your Last $10,000," which assumed that most people in the stock market had been taken to the cleaners in the bloodbath years 1968 to 1974. I won't quote any of the other alleged experts mentioned in the article. But suffice it to say that many of them were extraordinarily pessimistic. Here's what the article said about me:

"'Brutus,' whom I last saw on a Boston TV show wearing a bull's mask over his eyes and a ring in his nose — and who, under his real name, John D. Spooner, reviewed his own book, *Confessions of a Stockbroker*, for the *Boston Globe* — thinks there are some great opportunities in the market at these prices. 'I would not buy the big blue chips that have been knocked down,' he says. 'What I'm interested in is a list of companies that will survive, that are financially viable, that were $20, $30, $40 a share, but are now selling from $12 down to $5, paying 8 to 10 percent dividends that are well covered by earnings.' He names companies like Gerber Products, Hershey, Papercraft, Coca-Cola Bottling Co. of Los Angeles, General Cinema (the largest theater chain in America and the largest bottler of Pepsi-Cola), Keyes Fibre ('the premier manufacturer of paper plates, an old New England company'), and Triangle Pacific. Unfortunately, most of these are already more expensive than they were a few weeks

ago. 'If you're already in stocks like these,' he says, 'then sit tight
and add to your position wherever possible.' "

As I am writing this, the gloom-and-doom atmosphere still per-
sists, with the Dow Jones industrial average at 740, about a three-
year low and down from close to a thousand just twelve months
ago at the beginning of the Carter administration. In view of the
bear market and the pervading atmosphere of fear, how have my
investment selections from 1975 fared? Take a look at a comparison of prices of stocks I mentioned in *New York* magazine in
January 1975 with prices in February 1978, when the Dow Jones
was at a twenty-three-month low, and with adjusted prices of
May 1978.

|                        | January 1975 | February 1978 | May 1978* |
|------------------------|:------------:|:-------------:|:---------:|
| *Gerber Products*      | 9            | 28            | 30½       |
| *Hershey Foods*        | 9            | 20            | 22⅜       |
| *Papercraft*           | 7            | 17½           | 18¼       |
| *Coca-Cola, Los Angeles* | 8½         | 40            | 40        |
| *General Cinema*       | 6            | 28            | 35½       |
| *Keyes Fibre*          | 12           | 23            | 30        |
| *Triangle Pacific*     | 5            | 28½           | 33¾       |

In addition, every one of these companies has raised its dividends at least once during this time. Not only did the *worst*
performer double, but the average stock mentioned yielded a
dividend return alone (at 1975 prices) over ten percent. You can
beat the stock market with common sense, avoiding the herd
instinct with patience. It also helps enormously to have someone
handling your money who cares about *you*. And one other element. Do business with someone who can afford to be honest,

* With the high-volume rally that began in April 1978, the Dow was at
837 on May 1, 1978. Since this compilation all the companies mentioned
have either held their prices or gone even higher.

who does not have to act with commission in mind, but rather with *you* in mind.

Here is how *I* would choose a stockbroker if I were not in the business myself. I could call the local branch office of any major member firm of the New York Stock Exchange. I would ask to speak to the manager. "Do you have a terrific stock picker?" I would ask. "Someone who does not necessarily have the biggest business in your office, but a person who has the knack for picking winners?" There are such people. Almost every major broker-age office has someone who is just wonderful at finding poten-tial winners. Once satisfied that there *is* such a broker in that office (again, the question is unusual enough to be answered honestly), I would then visit the office and ask to be introduced to the biggest producer of business.

"Do you use so-and-so's ideas?" I would ask, mentioning the name of the fine research broker.

"I use the best ideas," a good salesman would say, "wherever they come from." I would then open an account with the biggest producer. These people *never* refuse an account, no matter how small. They want all the money they can get. I would choose this biggest producer because he would pick the brains of the *smart* broker and buy me the smart broker's ideas. Why choose the producer over the smart picker? The best analysts are often poor salesmen; too often their business is small, and they are more tempted to sell too soon, before their stocks reach their potential in price. The big producer often gives you the best shot, because the volume of his business allows him to let you ride longer with a stock and also because his ego is usually such that he really *wants* you to maximize your profit. Even if you have only a thousand dollars to invest, the most successful broker will want to build you up so that your account is meaningful — and not only to you. His ego needs the gratification of *your* success.

Within the stock market I can take care of myself. What about other aspects of money — how to make it, how to keep it, how to make it grow. One of my methods in choosing companies to

invest in is to question my Smart People in the world of business.
Picking the best brains can be extraordinarily effective. Here's a
sampling of the brains from which I choose:

The International Golf Club in Bolton, Massachusetts, is the
ultimate company perk, a private playground that used to seem
as frightening to me as the controlled pleasures of Orwell's *1984*. I
was taken there by my financial Summa, Father Abraham, or
Father A., as his friends at the Beinstock Delicatessen call him.

I don't have many clients like Father Abraham. He calls me
and tells me what to do, what to buy, what to sell. Period. "Look,"
he said to me long ago, "if you want the business, don't give me
any advice. I don't want to blame you if you're wrong. I don't
want to be in your debt if you're right. Your father was like a
brother to me and for his sake, when I buy or sell, you get the
orders. Just take them down and we'll both be satisfied. Now,
what kind of discount are you giving me?"

Father Abraham is the chairman of the board of a public company, a shoe manufacturing firm whose sales volume last year
was a hundred and twenty-three million dollars and whose earnings over a recent five-year period look like this: 1973, $1.40;
1974, $1.02; 1975, $1.80; 1976, $2.30; 1977, $2.97. His compensa-
tion last year, including bonus, was two hundred and seventy-five
thousand dollars, and he owns or controls over three hundred and
fifty thousand shares of his stock, which recently sold for eighteen
and a half. I give Father A. a twenty percent discount from our
posted commission rate, a discount with which he is not happy. "I
don't give discounts," I told him. "I manage money and I offer
service, attention, and, I hope, results. There is no fee I charge
other than commission. When I want to be Zayre's discount store
I'll let you know. You want to do business with Tiffany's, don't
expect cut-rate prices."

If this speech sounds arrogant, it is — for a purpose. And it was
spouting back at Father Abraham a lesson he has taught me in
spades. "No one is going to be selfish for you if you are not selfish
for yourself." He told me this the day of my father's funeral. "I'm

generally considered to be a prick," he added, "but being a prick has made me millions of dollars. I give to charity and I love my family. But you have to be tough and you have to demand things and you cannot show weakness in business. Important above all — if you're ever in a position of power, push it for all it's worth. If you want something, *ask* for it. Because once you lose leverage, and once you head down, no one will give you *nothing*.

"It's no mystery," Father A. says, "in the business of business. Sometimes you raise prices and you double your volume. That's when people need you. Never be surprised when you ask for the moon and they deliver it. Don't ever tell me about what you coulda asked for or shoulda done. There's an old expression: 'Shoulda, coulda, woulda . . . didn't.'" (Father Abraham has an effective personal quality, as do most Smart People: contrast. He can switch from the language of the modern business professional to the language of the immigrant hustler.)

It was March at the International Golf Club. There were half a dozen cars in a parking lot that could hold several thousand. The clubhouse was mammoth, seeming like five Holiday Inn lobbies pieced together by a mad developer. By virtue of some heavy consulting done for the company, Father A. had privileges at the club for a three-year period. "Harold Geneen operates like a king," Father A. said admiringly. "Who else but a king could afford to keep a place like this to use for a few meetings a year and to play a few rounds of golf? Flowers grow in some of the sand traps, for Christ's sake. *That's* how much use the course gets."

Father Abraham's family and mine had hors d'oeuvres and cocktails in the bar. Except for the staff we were the only people there. It was as if we had arrived a day after the season had ended. Dinner followed hors d'oeuvres. We ate endlessly, alone in the giant dining room surrounded by tables covered with cloths and set up for guests that would never arrive. We had lobster cocktail, eggdrop soup, beef Wellington, salad, a choice of twenty desserts including chocolate soufflé. After coffee and brandy the

manager and his assistants drove us around in golf carts to inspect the guest cottages, small houses furnished lavishly and waiting for visiting heavyweights from ITT and beyond. Each room
had its own bottles of Chivas Regal and Beefeater sitting on a
silver tray. The manager gave us complimentary gifts wrapped in
gold paper, old-fashioned glasses with the ITT logo on the sides.
When we finally left, there were only two cars remaining in the
lot that would accommodate thousands.

"Why shouldn't one of the three highest paid executives in the
world have his own playground?" asked Father Abraham. "Do
you know that when Harold Geneen had a business conference
recently he sat on a balcony overlooking a ballroom. In front of
him were nine phones, lines connected to all parts of the world so
that people could ask him questions from anywhere, about anything. Six other special lines were at his fingertips. They led to six
assistants on the ballroom floor who sat at a long table. Each of
the assistants had endless data about the divisions of ITT: earnings by subsidiaries, product and sales figures, personnel records.
ITT has over sixty subsidiaries and more than three hundred and
seventy thousand employees. The assistants on the floor had two
jobs. One, to pick up the phone if Mr. Geneen rang and answer
any questions he had about any division. Two, to ring Mr.
Geneen in the balcony if he made any error regarding anything,
during his answers to callers from all over the world. In two and
a half hours of fielding questions, Mr. Geneen never had to call
the floor once. And they never had to call him. Is that man
entitled to his own golf course?"

Father Abraham was driving us home. He put his Seville onto
automatic pilot and took his foot off the accelerator. "Me," he
said, "I couldn't give my life to a company. Couldn't give every
minute, twenty-four hours a day. I like to be with the family
sometime. Twelve hours a day a prick is enough for anyone."

Father Abraham likes to operate with big numbers. He never
buys less than five thousand shares of anything. And he always
buys what highly placed friends tell him to buy. "I buy inside

information," he says. "I lay out fifty to a hundred thou, I want some guarantees. Now the SEC and the government think they're going to legislate human nature. They're killing the country. Let me give you two huge examples of why we're heading down the drain and why you've got to make your pile soon before it's too late."

We were sitting this time in the Beinstock Delicatessen at six-fifteen A.M. This is Father Abraham's club. Every morning at six he meets a half-dozen of his friends, all in their sixties and seventies, all owning public companies or holding stock in public companies to whom they sold out. The men eat scrambled eggs and lox and bagels, drink coffee, criticize society, stab people in the back, and philosophize about the poor suckers who cannot emotionally afford to eat breakfast at the Beinstock Deli at six A.M. The breakfast group is a very exclusive club; women are never allowed, and each member had better be in attendance every day if he doesn't want to be ripped apart by the others. But you can learn more about business in America today in two hours at the Beinstock Deli than you can in two years at most business schools. The combined personal net worth at the table some mornings exceeds a hundred million dollars. And Father Abraham is the spiritual leader.

"Here are two reasons America's in the shithouse," he says. "My daughter works in Kansas City, for the office of Israel bonds. Now everything in Israel is unionized. They're constantly plagued by strikes. Because of the importance of labor there, the bond sales offices *here* are unionized also. The AFL-CIO, if you can believe it. All the workers in the Kansas City office are members of the union, including my daughter. Only if she does something like sleep on her desk can she be fired. Her job is to go out and sell bonds to organizations and individuals, go to prayer breakfasts, run testimonials, sell bonds. She shares an office with a real bomb-thrower, a union radical who is in the habit of drinking whiskey out of a bottle hidden in a paper sack during office hours. He's always trying to get the workers to strike for more money, and the organization can't fire him. He has union tenure. Unless they can prove that he's drinking on the job. My daughter has always tried to reason with him. 'This is a class struggle,' he yells at her. 'And when we go out, you wouldn't dare walk past me on the picket line.' The guy doesn't give a damn about Israel; he just wants to march a picket line and destroy. Well, here's the capper. My daughter was typing a letter to a bank president she had solicited. Her radical co-worker saw her and said, 'What are you doing?'"

"'Mowing the lawn,' my daughter answered, still typing.

"'That's a *clerical* job,' he shouted. 'It's people like you who ruin the unions. Typing isn't in your job description.' He ran over to my daughter and ripped her letter out of the typewriter, shredding it.

"'You're not supposed to type,' he screamed."

"What did your daughter do?" I asked.

"She bounced his whiskey bottle off the point of his head," Father A. told me. "Then she had him fired for attempted rape. There *is* no picket line to walk for attempted rape."

"A funny story," I said.

"A sad story. These are the attitudes today, lack of anything but selfish motivation. It murdered England. Eventually, it will murder us.

"The labor force in this country stinks. They all need remotivation. You cannot get people to put in a decent day's work. They're all spoiled rotten, and, I repeat, that story is not funny. It's pitiful. I get work out of people because I push them, then reward them when they least expect it. I keep them off balance, and I never lose sense of who is boss. There is no democracy in running a business.

"The second story is about the government," Father Abraham continued, "and about how impossible they're making it to operate. I had a drink yesterday, a Tab out of the machine at one of my factories. I'm drinking the Tab, and I see stuck onto the neck of the bottle a label, small as a stuck-on price tag. The label says,

'This drink may be dangerous to your health. It has been determined that saccharin has caused cancer in certain laboratory animals.' Do I need this stuck on a bottle I'm drinking from? Jesus H. Christ, of biblical fame! The idiocy of this government, with capitalism being pushed into a corner. We're going for no growth in this country. And no growth means death. You wonder why the stock market has been in a ten-year decline? Look no further than warning labels on pop bottles."

I have asked Father Abraham if he would ever want to be president of a multinational corporation like ITT.

"Our company," he said, "did a hundred-and-twenty-three-million volume last year. Yet I can still operate as if it's a family enterprise. When I consulted for ITT they gave me psychological tests. They told me I was an entrepreneur, not a manager. 'You're fifty-one percent entrepreneur and forty-nine percent professional manager,' they told me. 'If you ever wanted to make it at ITT, you'd have to reverse those numbers.'

"I told them," Father A. said, "I'm *fifty-one* percent entrepreneur and *forty-nine* percent professional manager, and I'll be goddamned if I'll ever give up the other two points. Small talk is half the battle with me; I love it. For Harold Geneen there is no such thing as small talk. If he goes swimming he has to relate Fahrenheit to centigrade in the water temperature. His idea of a joke is keeping meeting rooms at fifty-eight degrees. 'We don't want anyone falling asleep at meetings,' Geneen says. But he isn't fooling. His business meetings are like stage plays. When my consulting contract was up, they told me I didn't bleed enough, that was my problem. Ha! That was *their* problem. I'd got my stake already."

This is an obvious point, but why would you need a Father Abraham on your Smart People team? Because the petty financial matters of life — balancing a checkbook, assembling your tax information, staying within a budget — get all of us down. With everything that depresses us about day-to-day finance, we need to remember the big picture, economics as a whole. I use Father

Abraham to help me keep the big picture in sight and to explain it to me. That's why he is important. And remember, successful people love to talk about their experience. When you meet people like Father A., ask them questions. This is how *they* keep in touch with their success. By remembering it for *you*.

I have a serious failing. I hate to get out of bed in the morning. Every day I could gladly sleep until noon. But I have forced myself to meet with Father Abraham at the Beinstock Delicatessen at six A.M. at least once a month. I have been saving notes from my financial Summa for some years. A sampling of Wisdom From the Deli follows:

1. "The professional manager is a bore. He needs his business plan and his strategy. He has to translate the strategy into short-term and long-term objectives using reporting data and budgets. Also, the manager has to show consistency of personal behavior so that his employees know how to respond to change. These people say, 'A good executive is someone who talks himself out of a job.' The delegation of authority is everything. Professional managers are constipated. You should spend time instead with entrepreneurs; they go for controlling their own destinies."

2. "What makes a good entrepreneur? Two things: First, the ability to take risks. But, most important, the willingness to make yourself *available*. Buzz around a subject, look for an opportunity. Never shut yourself off, and miss a break that might be coming from an unexpected direction."

3. "Never give your money away to your children in your lifetime. Always keep control. If you don't, if you listen to the lawyers and the accountants, you'll find yourself being led up the steps of the nursing home. 'Watch your step, dad,' they'll say. Never give up your money while you live. And it helps also not to let anyone know what they're getting beforehand. Have the last laugh."

4. "Above all," Father Abraham told me one morning, "never forget who you are and never believe that there are people who won't hate you for it. My banker looks at two things when he

loans money. Integrity first, and second, the ability to pay back. But as to who you are, I have a story.

"It was Christmastime, years ago, on the day we went public. We were in New York, my partner Harold and I *and* our wives. We had got the check from the underwriters. We were truly rich; it said so on the check. So we made copies of the check on the underwriters' Xerox machine so we could always have them to look at and remind ourselves of the fact that anything is possible in America. Feeling great, we all went to "21" for dinner to celebrate. Since one of the best things shoe people know how to do is duke people, we were seated in the middle of the bar, downstairs. As we're joking and laughing and toasting, we noticed the people at the next table. They're smiling at us, three of them, two men and a woman. The men looked typical, like the president of Goodrich or U.S. Steel, Waspy, ex–Yale football players, Greenwich, New Canaan, Grosse Point. The woman looked like, you know, the former Mimsy Albright, blond, superior, divorced twice, tan. We smiled at each other, toasted each other with gestures, not words. It was a great dinner, millions of bucks in the kick, feeling good, at "21" in the bar. The three Wasps eventually got up to leave and passed by our table. I smiled and lifted my glass. "Merry Christmas," says I.

One ex–Yale football player grinned down at us, silly with our champagne. "Or Happy Holiday," he said, "as the case may be." They swept out of the bar, and we looked at each other silently, my partner and his wife, my wife and I. Four Jews who should never forget for a minute who they are because nobody else is ever going to forget it either. And you better learn that lesson young."

You want to know America? Recruit a successful entrepreneur for your Smart People team. Lamplighters make things look easy, at the same time that they seem so difficult for other people. I met Whispering Saul at a Newcomers' Club party when my wife and I moved to a new town. Whispering Saul was dressed as a clown. He was trying to win the prize for best costume. In his quiet way, Whispering Saul is always trying to win. I am not a fan of organizations that have costume parties. As a matter of fact, I have been anti-institution, anti-organization all of my life. But there I was, on a Saturday night in a hired hall, dressed as a half-assed pirate with my wife in similar costume.

It was our first Newcomers' event, one I had been dreading for weeks. "Look" my wife said, "I don't know anyone in this town. You go blithely to work, and I've got to operate in a totally new environment. If we get *two* people out of this organization whom we like, and who can teach us the town, it's a leg up, it's a plus. We'll go as pirates, jump around, look foolish. Who gives a damn? If it's horrible, then it's cost us a night. The human spirit can put up with anything for a night."

It *was* horrible. The other people were smug, self-satisfied couples, thinking they were making it. One set was dressed as A Streetcar Named Desire. Another as Ozzie and Harriet. But it was worth it to meet Whispering Saul, who has become my financial inspiration, my fiscal Lamplighter. One of Saul's hallmarks is his voice. He is so soft-spoken that he makes everyone bend close to hear his words. You must pay attention to Saul; it takes concentration. "You'd be amazed how effective it is in deal-making," he has told me, "It makes everyone play my game. It also secretly annoys hell out of people that they have to lean forward and hang on every word. It throws them off their rhythm when it's their turn to speak."

A man dressed as a giant bunny that night was complaining to Saul about having to borrow fifty thousand dollars to cement a hamburger franchise he was buying. In his clown paint, with a permanent smile painted on his face, Whispering Saul said, "When you borrow five thousand from a bank and you can't pay it back, you've got a problem. When you borrow five *million* from a bank and you can't pay it back, *they've* got a problem. Wherever possible in life, when you want to deal, use the bank's dough. And borrow more than you need."

We became friends that night, the four of us, clowns and pirates. Saul's wife had been the Lady of the Bookshelf, hostess of a children's TV show in Minneapolis. She was a funny and gentle woman, entirely confident in the ability of her husband to produce economic miracles. We said good-bye that night as the two clowns drove away in Saul's Rolls-Royce, a classic 1959 Silver Cloud One by James Young with an ivory antique backgammon board set into a panel in back.

Whispering Saul became a client of mine after I told him that people didn't understand the stock market because it was not a real business, it was a state of mind. Anyone who wanted to trade, pick short-term trends, be in and out was crazy. I told him that you couldn't beat the market on a short-term basis, that eventually you'd create nothing but commissions, ill will, and diminishing capital. "I've lost small monies in my life," he agreed, "to learn big lessons. If you sit in on a poker game and you don't see a sucker at the table, get up. Because you're the sucker."

Whispering Saul is an entrepreneur. He grew up in a small town in Iowa, worked his way through the Wharton School where, he said, notices would be posted: "There will be a meeting of all Christians at Wharton next Wednesday. In the phone booth." After college he sold computers for Sperry Rand, then decided it would be far better to staff the companies buying and making the computers. He founded a personnel company, specializing in the placing of technical people, and he built it from scratch to a volume of eighteen million a year. Then he sold out to a conglomerate on the Big Board for three million cash.

"You know the steps in a deal, don't you?" he asked me. "They are 'conception, confusion, panic, punish the innocent, and reward the nonparticipants.' They sure as hell didn't want to give me cash, but I wanted to have my stake and I wanted to have it young enough to give me flexibility forever. And I was restless. I didn't want an employment contract. I realized that I never wanted to look forward five years and imagine myself in the same place. So, I became a problem-solver. Another reason I took cash, and this was in 1969, was that it is becoming increasingly difficult in America to cash in your chips. IBM would find it tough to go public in the climate that exists today. No more funny money; half the Big Board sells at seven times earnings. Creating instant wealth is tougher and tougher, unless you're that one-in-a-million shot in show business.

"Our mass-media society accentuates the negative element in our lives. The press and television have emphasized the negative so much in politics and in business that the little sucker feels better when successful people are dragged through the mud. The media diminish all the struggle to achieve. No more heroes, tax the American Dream out of existence. Until this attitude changes, if you're hot for short-term gains, don't look at the United States. But *long term*, if you look at a map of the world, there is nothing so potentially exciting as what can go on here."

Whispering Saul's three million has traveled in the last ten years between commercial paper, Treasury bills, short Eastman Kodak at 97 (covered at 49½), the Swiss franc, and back to Treasury bills, with a recent hankering to buy the Dow Jones average stocks heavily (then current DJ level 740). He has the Midas touch to a greater degree than anyone I have ever known. But it is made all the better by his insistence on privacy and the fact that his family gets more than equal time with his business.

"Smart People," Saul says, "put value on things in terms of incremental costs. What does this mean? It means that, instead of taking a winter Florida vacation, I'll spend an extra thousand or fifteen hundred to go to the Bahamas, where you can count on the weather being good. I'll go to a clothing store where I know the owner, where they massage me, instead of saving a hundred dollars a suit by shopping the manufacturer's factories or waiting for sales. In other words, I make *all* of my decisions based on the mental wear and tear. So much in today's world has to be done by you personally that the least complicated method, even if it's not the cheapest, is often the best for you."

Whispering Saul refers to himself in business as a benevolent despot. Since he sold his personnel company he has become a full-time problem-solver for a major bank, stepping in at their request on loans to failing companies. Saul's job is to turn the failures around, or at least to salvage something for the bank that it wouldn't ordinarily have had. In exchange for his services, Whispering Saul receives fees of up to half of what he recovers, or a continuing piece of the action should the company be returned to health. "So many of our major banks," he says, "if the truth came out, are close to down the tubes with bad loans to the real estate investment trusts and third-world countries. You know the definition of ecstatic? Ecstatic is what the dumb banker is who gets all his principal and interest back. But you want to know *the* biggest secret to succeeding in deals? Whether it's buying a house or getting more money from a new employer or beating your financial opponent? *Give the semblance of being aloof.* Your attitude should always be, 'I don't care if it happens. I don't need it.' Even if you desperately do. *That's* the key to winning."

Why is Whispering Saul my Lamplighter? Because he always surprises me with his ability to produce success at every level of life. He buys houses at bank auctions, houses with all their contents. In one old Georgian mansion, before he resold it to the Greek Orthodox Church for a hundred percent profit in nine months, he found a Gainsborough portrait that Christie's moved for three hundred and seventy-five thousand dollars. That was enough to buy five more houses at bank closeout prices. In the house he lives in now, a Gothic mansion with forty rooms, he has live-in help. Three seminary students live in, free of charge, in the servants' wing. In exchange for free rooms, they cut the grass, guard the grounds, and baby-sit. Whispering Saul is about to donate a pond on his property to the town — for which he will get a hefty tax deduction. Then he'll sell the mansion to a local

religious cult, the Islandia Foundation that emphasizes macrobiotics and making slaves of runaway teenagers. "Religious cults
and criminals," Saul says, "they're the people who pay in cash.
But the macrobiotic freaks won't harm the wildlife on the town
pond. They won't eat the ducks. Everyone will be happy, and
that's what I like."

Saul also uses a technique valuable to people who earn large
ordinary income. Saul uses commodities — specifically, U.S.
Treasury bill futures spreads — to move ordinary income from
one year into the next. What is this technique? Simply, it is this:
Treasury bills are short-term obligations of the U.S. government.
You can buy them in five-thousand-dollar denominations, for
periods of ninety-one days, one hundred eighty-one days, or one
year. They generally pay higher rates than savings banks for
similar time periods, and you get interest on them from the day of
purchase until the day of sale or maturity. Treasury bills are
bought at a discount. (For instance, you may pay forty-nine fifty
for five thousand dollars' worth of bills. At the expiration date
you are paid the full five thousand.) Now U.S. Treasury bills can
be traded on a *speculative basis* as a commodity, the same way
gold or soybeans or wheat or corn can be traded speculatively on
commodities exchanges. "Spreads" are a sophisticated technique
that needs a Smart Person watching the pot for you. The tax
strategy for spreads is this: A broker knowledgeable in commodities sells short *x* amount of U.S. Treasury bill futures for Saul's
account. At the same time he also *buys* a similar amount of
Treasury bill futures contracts. This is a spread. It limits the risk
because he is going in both directions at the same time. The
technique would be similar to simultaneously going short General
Motors and buying Ford long. Saul explains it to me this way: "If
you buy Treasury bills, the income you receive from them, the
*interest*, is treated as ordinary income. The government treats
the trading in any commodities futures the same way it treats the
underlying commodity. Thus, a loss in U.S. Treasury bill futures
taken by anyone is considered by the IRS *so far* as an *ordinary*

loss against income. Assume you're doing really well this year
financially. You want to move twenty-five thousand of ordinary
income from this year to next. You put up approximately a
twenty-five-hundred-dollar margin to do this. There is risk on a
spread, as in any commodity transaction — and here particularly
if there is a credit crunch with interest rates going to twelve or
thirteen percent. But a shrewd commodities person can recognize
a loss for you one year, establish a new position for the *new* year,
and be nimble enough to wind you up with a profit overall on the
entire deal. Commissions are heavy, risk on spreads of twenty-
five thousand probably can be as much as three to four thousand.
*But* if you can put up twenty-five hundred, knock twenty-five
thousand off your income, and still have a legitimate crack at an
overall gain, the risk for high-bracket people is peanuts."

Can you knock twenty-five thousand dollars or more off your
ordinary income with Treasury bill spreads? Not any more you
can't. The IRS threw this technique out as a legitimate strategy in
December 1978, making the trades *capital* rather than *ordinary*
items. For moves like these my advice is that you deal only with
large member firms of the New York Stock Exchange who have
sizable commodity departments. Again, a call to the manager of
these offices is essential. "Do you have," you ask, "a specialist in
commodities? Particularly Treasury bill spreads? Is he wired into
any computer service that signals interest rate curves?" If the
answer to *all* these questions is yes and if you have large capital
gains, it may be worth a trip to that brokerage office. Trading in
any futures is not like buying a hundred shares of Farfel Electronics. Make sure you understand what you are doing, and make
sure your income is substantial enough to handle the risk.

I once went to a YPO meeting with Saul, where he was delivering a speech. YPO, the Young Presidents Organization, is a
unique group of chief executives operating nationwide. Requirements for membership are these: age, under forty; company sales
in excess of three million dollars; and more than fifty employees.
Smart People should know at least one member of YPO. The best

place to recruit a YPO member is at a health club or athletic facility where you are the *social* equal of the Young President. Such an acquaintance can give you access to information at the highest levels and entrée for yourself and your family to jobs, investment advice, and free consulting. Your friend in YPO can get favors for you through this elite network of highly placed people.

If you know a young company president who does not belong, urge him or her to look into it. (The YPO office is in New York.) It can ultimately benefit *you*.

If your friend decides to join, he will be forever in your debt. You will have placed him in a position to be exclusive. *Everyone* loves that.

Whispering Saul is the treasurer of YPO's local chapter. His speech was about money and success. It contained many of his favorite hints, several of which are worth passing on:

1. "Never go into business just to go into business. You have to set your goals. Be like Abraham Lincoln, who always had long-term goals. Make sure there's a need for your business; then do it."

2. "I call myself a benevolent despot because I motivate people to work hard for me. But when you motivate people, no matter how kindly you act, *always have an ulterior motive*. This is part of planning. Where do I want to be in a year? five years? *ten years?*"

3. "Who influences you in life? People who have taken an interest in you are the ones who influence you. Think about this. It's important."

4. "I've bought companies no one else could have bought, because I always look for the opponent's weak point. On one deal, when we were two hundred and fifty thousand dollars apart, the president asked, 'What's going to happen to the company car?' I knew he wanted to retire to Florida, and I said, 'We're going to buy it and give it to you.' That was what he really cared about,

his Cadillac. He didn't care about the quarter of a mil; he wanted his perk. Look for the weak spot, human frailty."

5. *"Don't be afraid of the absurd.* I saw a house I wanted a few years ago. The owners were asking four hundred and fifty thousand dollars. There was rust on all the drainpipes. And the roof leaked. I felt the price would scare most people away. People would be afraid to make an offer. I bought that house for a hundred and ninety-five thousand. Low-balling is an attitude. Don't be afraid of it."

6. "When you're in business you have to forget emotions. Remember this when you're faced with firing personnel. The trauma of dislocating people's lives is not what they tell you. Early in my career, I agonized for a month about letting someone go. While I agonized, the man came in and quit. 'The son of a bitch,' I said to myself, 'quitting on *me.*' Since then I've always acted when I knew it was *best for the business.*"

7. "The day of the twenty-five-year pin is gone. You cannot get long and gracious service out of employees. The kids of the sixties who waffled on life are coming back into the system, and they really don't want to work for employers. They want to work for themselves. Franchising is going to boom again. And if you do it well you can create another McDonald's. This is an area I would recommend investing in."

I walked to the bar with Whispering Saul after the speech. "The most important element I forgot to say," he told me.

"What's that, Saul?"

"It is primary not to hedge if you want to be truly successful. To act is everything, *if* you have your plan. Everything I've ever achieved in life, if I had thought too long about it, I wouldn't have done it."

The young presidents crowded around the bar, offering each other deals.

Never judge personal lives when you judge one of your Mavens. Think only of their expertise and what they can provide for you.

Business travels on its stomach. Lunch is often the best time to recruit Smart People. Buckley, my bond Maven, is sensational at lunch, especially on days when he has lent the key to his apartment to a friend. This puts Buckley in a jovial mood because he knows that someone owes him a favor. Favors owed to Buckley the Bond Man can eventually be translated into hard dollars.

T. J. Buckley is five feet nine inches tall and has a mass of black curls that endeared him to everyone when he was an altar boy in Saint Ann's parish, Medford, Massachusetts. A large sign dominates one wall of his office. The sign says, "If they hadn't invented whiskey, the Irish would rule the world." Buckley is an expert at lunch maneuvers. He choreographs lunch with his clients to the extent that you think you're watching a Broadway musical. At his regular restaurants the maitre d's love him, the waiters love him. He gets pampered and makes sure *his* customers feel the same way. There are people you meet in life who can get away with anything and people eat it up. Buckley has a little-boy grin and a mischievousness that makes him easy to forgive. For instance, several months ago, one of Buckley's favorite restaurants was featured in newspaper accounts of negative inspections by the Board of Health. The inspections were politically inspired but generated a lot of unfavorable publicity, citing roaches, rat droppings, and greasy water in the sinks. Before the publicity, Buckley's favorite restaurant was generally considered to be the finest in town. The day of the bad news, Buckley had had a private room reserved for six of his best accounts. Buckley gave the waiter and the maitre d' continual grief about the cleanliness of the establishment. "Never again will I come here, Mario," he told the waiter. "This is it. The place reeks."

The old-time waiter, a pro, was distressed. "Oh, Mr. Buckley, our place is immaculate," he wailed. "That report was a put-up job." Nevertheless, Buckley continued to give everyone a bad time. He left with his clients after lunching, with endless assurances from management that cleanliness was next to godliness and that their restaurant was above reproach.

The next day, Buckley reserved a private room for eight for luncheon. Before he arrived, he went to a joke shop and purchased a giant rubber fly, hiding it in a paper bag. Buckley gave the same grief to the maitre d' as the day before, telling him he could no longer eat in a place that endangered his customers' health. At the luncheon table, Buckley raked Mario, the waiter, over the coals. Mario kept apologizing, taking personally the Board of Health's citations. "Well, never mind," says Buckley, "we're here, and we may as well make the best of it. I'll order. Let's see," says Buckley. He had the rubber fly on the table covered by a linen napkin. "I'll have half a dozen oysters," says Buckley, "then a salad with Roquefort, the small filet, rare and . . ." He hesitated while Mario stood poised and eager to serve. Buckley then whipped the napkin off of the rubber fly, authentic in every detail, only blown up a thousand times. ". . . And," he said, "a small plate of shit for my fly." That lunch maneuver got a two-million-dollar bond order for Buckley from one of the largest insurance companies in the world.

Needing a bond, or debt, expert at all in your life represents a departure from patterns of the past. The truth is that most middle-class Americans have become much more sophisticated about their investments in the last ten years, sophisticated because so many have gone to the cleaners in stock and commodities markets and the term "sophisticated investor" now means someone with his money in daily-notice accounts at the savings bank.

"People don't care about the stock market anymore," said Henry, the old Philosopher-King, to me recently. "Companies can sell for two or three times earnings and nobody gives a damn. Our lives are too surrounded by trauma to care about the long term. We want *today*. Pleasure today; profits today. Tomorrow the Arabs could double the price of oil. Tomorrow the Israelis could drop the bomb on Damascus. No more in our lifetime can you give a thousand dollars' worth of IBM to your granddaughter and have it be worth twenty-five thousand by the time she gets to college. The average guy with a little money wants to buy a U.S.

Treasury note paying nine percent or better. That used to be unheard of. Brokers wouldn't tell you such a bond existed, let alone sell you one. No commissions in bonds. But today it's the *current yield* that counts. What you receive automatically while you wait. Capital gains are a snare and a delusion. Something that the *other* guy *used* to get."

The major retail brokerage firms are looking to manage every aspect of your financial lives. Increasingly, they are unwilling to take a chance on gunslinging brokers who tend to bury customers in stocks that never double and commodities that go down the limit six days in a row. The new Wall Street wants brokers who sell products that the customers can *live* with: annuities, tax shelters, managed programs that the firm stands behind. We are looking toward the day when stockbrokers wear uniform blazers and disposable shirts and offer only products under the company umbrella of special merchandise . . . at high commission rates. I am doing a quarter of my gross production in corporate, municipal, or tax-free bonds. Speaking in St. Maarten a short time ago at a four-day convention of stockbrokers, *I did not hear one stock tip.* Not one story on a company being advanced as a "sure thing" or "the next Digital." If *stockbrokers* aren't talking about the market, what the hell are the customers talking about? That's why you need a debt expert today. That's why I have Buckley the Bond Man.

The first time I saw Buckley, he was grappling on the floor with a margin clerk who had mistakenly emptied a file into a paper shredder. The file contained Buckley's tax returns from 1970 through 1973. All those years had been under audit and all of those audit results were now under appeal. Buckley believed in direct action because for a long while his hero had been John Mitchell. Before he had become attorney general, Mitchell had been the number-one municipal-bond attorney in America. "John Mitchell is incredible on detail," Buckley had been told. "If he ate a bowl of spaghetti, he could describe to you every individual strand."

At a bond traders' convention in Boca Raton, Buckley dogged John Mitchell, following him everywhere, waiting for an opportunity. Seeing him cross the lobby alone on Saturday morning before breakfast, Buckley jumped over a couch and stood in front of Mitchell, as the lawyer knocked his pipe into a heavy crystal ashtray. "Mr. Mitchell," Buckley said, "I'm an admirer of yours. You're tough. You're smart. You have a big reputation. What's the most important lesson you've learned in the bond markets?"

Mitchell glared at Buckley, then decided. "You cut your losses fast," the lawyer said. "*Selling* anything is the key to success. Buying is the easy part. Always remember: If you know you've got to eat shit, you don't want to do it in nibbles."

Thereafter, Buckley became a master at profit taking and at keeping losses to a minimum.

Bonds in recent years have provided record returns, in the yields they offer and in the degree of safety they possess, in relation to the instability in stock prices since 1968. Triple A corporate bonds, the highest quality, have been issued with coupon rates of as much as nine and three-quarters percent. Municipal, or tax-free bonds, have been brought to market with returns of as much as *eleven percent*. This would be equal to a twenty-two percent return for an investor in the fifty percent income bracket. When the U.S. government, in recent memory, issued notes paying *nine percent* and maturing in five years, the public stood in line for blocks around Federal Reserve buildings to plunk down one thousand to five thousand dollars for the largest government-guaranteed return in history. Government issues are, of course, the highest quality of all. If the government falls or fails to pay back its obligations, you'd better melt down your candlesticks into gold or silver bars and be prepared to fire on your neighbors with a shotgun. Because nothing will be worth *anything*, except to be a survivor.

With savings banks paying slightly over five percent and with this source of income fully taxable, average people are flocking to the debt market as never before. Buckley offers several kickers to remember as a primer for buying or trading debt securities:

1. "There are *no* state or local taxes on income from any U.S. Treasury debt issue. This is obviously a major plus for investors in states that make you pay heavily for the privilege of living there."

2. "For estate purposes, there are bonds designed specifically to provide money for estate taxes. These are called 'flower bonds' and generally they sell well below par — that is, below full face value, which is usually a thousand dollars per bond. The government will accept these flower bonds at full face value in payment of federal estate taxes. Thus, even if you paid seven hundred dollars per bond, the IRS will give you a thousand dollars' credit per bond. Tremendous savings can be realized from utilizing this method, and any smart bond man has several 'flowers' to choose from at any moment."

3. "Try to buy corporate bonds at par or below. Buying bonds below par means buying them at a *discount*. (Buying *above* par is known as buying at a *premium*, a habit to avoid whenever possible.) If you buy a bond paying eight percent that comes due or matures in 1990 and you pay a thousand dollars for it, you own the bond at par, and it pays you eight percent per year in interest, usually in semiannual payments until you get back your thousand dollars in the year 1990. If you pay nine hundred fifty dollars for the bond (quoted in the newspapers as '95'; *you* add the zero to obtain the true dollar value), you have bought your bond at a discount. Your current yield will be *higher* than eight percent — actually, eight point four two percent — because you bought your bond for *less* than a thousand dollars. Also, when your bond matures in 1990, you will have made a long-term capital gain, the difference between your cost of nine hundred fifty and the pay-off price of a thousand.

"*Try* to buy bonds at a discount; always look for an edge, however small. As a bellwether of the bond markets, for a beginner *or* a seasoned bond player, watch one bond listed on the New

York Stock Exchange bond list: the American Telephone and Telegraph eight point eight percent debentures, maturing in the year 2005. These bonds are heavily traded, rated triple A, and can be your clue to interest rates and other bond prices. When these bonds sell at a premium, or over a thousand dollars per bond, be very careful in your bond selections. Bargains will be difficult to find. When these Telephone debentures sell *under* a thousand dollars (that is, at a discount) quality debt issues should be plentiful."

4. "Look for relatively short maturities if possible. Five to ten years, especially in tax-free bonds. The skittish quality of financial markets will not change in our lifetime. If you own only bonds that mature in ten years or less, you cut down the potential for disaster. Owning bonds that come due beyond the year 2000 increases the chance of volatility in bond prices and increases the possibility that your heirs will inherit the problem."

"Bond traders live in a world of their own; they hang together," Buckley the Bond Man tells me. "But we're shooters socially. The fraternity is wild, much wilder than the stock guys. Because nobody in the real world knows what the hell we're talking about. It's a great advantage. The first place I worked, the president of the firm took me to lunch and lifted up a glass of water. 'This is the company cocktail,' he said, taking a large gulp of water. I quit in two weeks when I found out that most of the traders got absolutely *faced* at lunch. On *real* alcohol. The more you are one of the boys, the more business you can do. We take care of each other."

Bond traders operate away from the public. Every day at lunch and long into most nights, the traders at the brokerage houses entertain their opposite numbers from banks, mutual funds, municipalities, and insurance companies. These institutional traders buy and swap hundreds of billions of dollars' worth of bond issues every year. Several major insurance companies can be buyers of at least *a hundred million dollars a day* of various debt issues. Buckley the Bond Man does seven hundred thousand dollars in commission business a year. His share of that is around twenty percent, or a hundred forty thousand a year before taxes. He does not own one share of stock. He has never owned a share of stock. "None of the bond people buy stocks," he says. "They don't understand anything without a coupon attached."

As with most Smart People, Buckley likes to philosophize. "Of course, we socialize a lot," he says. "The bond guys are like lepers. We stay together, suffer together about eighths and quarters and obscure issues that nobody ever heard of. Sure, we try to screw each other on price all the time. But that's business; that's a given. We buy distress merchandise and try to vulture the bonds out to high Episcopalians in the trust departments. But those guys are the worst thieves of all. Of course, it evens out, the screwings. But the freebies are essential. We give basketball and hockey seats, and baseball boxes, so we get paid back in commissions.

"The only thing that's tricky is the presents. You've got to be careful. Hey, you think we're any different from the corporations abroad? To do business you've got to come across. Our stuff is peanuts, but you've got to come across or you get shut out. The watchdogs can never understand that. That's why they make twelve-five a year and get their kicks screwing things up for others. But presents you can *touch*, that's difficult.

"There was a guy a few years back did all the buying for one of the biggest cities in the state. You know, for the city employees' pension fund, stuff like that. To get a hundred bond order, you'd have to take him to the Ritz for a three-hour lunch, take him to the Bruins. For two hundred bonds, you'd have to deliver booze to his house or bring him office presents: a leather desk blotter, Cardin shirts, a Mark Cross suitcase. For half a million bonds and up, he'd want to go to New York for the weekend, massage parlors, the whole bit. We'd put it all on T and E (travel and entertainment) and bury it somehow. The expense account. But the guy pushed it too far and we got the bastard. One night at a

Bruins-Montreal game, he must've had sixteen Narragansetts. Kept sayin' how he loved Ken Dryden, the Canadien's goalie. The drunker he got, the more he talked about Dryden and the funnier he sounded. Funny *strange*. Well, I had to take him home.

"He lived with his widowed aunt, Mrs. Caruso, who had a mustache and dressed in black, but I never thought anything about it except what a pushy pain in the ass he was. He's passed out by the time I get him home, so I got to pull him out of the car and drag him up the front porch. Suddenly, he wakes up, grabs me, and tries to kiss me on the mouth. 'Got to have you, Kenny,' he's mumblin', I swear to God. He was wild for Ken Dryden. Well, we had the sucker after that, two million bonds a week and never a peep. Lasted for a year until he moved to Florida with some stockbroker who left his family and turned queer after Xerox collapsed in '75. Taught me a lesson. You can never live high off the tit for very long. Something always screws up. Never think *anything* lasts forever. Especially when you get to the point of saying, Where has *this* been all my life?"

Buckley the Bond Man has no private, retail accounts. But he'd be tickled to accept them if you walked off the street and asked. *Most* professional bond people would be happy to do business with you. All you have to do is ask. Be polite. Be charming. Go into Goldman Sachs, or Lehman Brothers, or Shearson Hayden Stone, or First Boston, or Salomon Brothers and ask to speak to an institutional bond trader. Tell them you represent major family money and you're looking for a personal expert to help manage the debt side of your portfolio. No real pro will refuse you. Buckley never would. He'd be flattered that his reputation had spread to the public. With returns available on bonds ranging from a safe eight and a half percent to much higher yields with some risk, anyone with funds to invest today needs a bond Maven. It should make a tremendous difference to the management of your personal money.

However, I am afraid that if you have only a thousand dollars or less to invest you will get a cold shoulder from Buckley and

bond people like him. What do you do if you have a thousand to
five thousand dollars to invest in bonds? When Telephone eight
point eight percent bonds, maturing in the year 2005, are selling
under par, buy them. This way, your money is secure unless
catastrophe hits our economy and our financial markets. Your
return will be almost double savings-bank levels; you'll also have
liquidity and, most likely, a capital gain when and if interest rates
come down. And you don't need a broker's advice. All you need
to do is to watch the daily listings on the New York Stock Exchange bond list. Buckley, or people like him, *will* do business
with individuals privately. But you should have a minimum of
fifty thousand dollars to invest. And, as in dealing with any Smart
People, it would not hurt to have something to trade.

For years, Buckley has booked a private dining room, once a
month at noon, in another of our city's finest downtown restaurants. He books a table for eight, in a room where, supposedly,
Joe DiMaggio proposed to Marilyn Monroe. Six of the customers
who join Buckley represent three insurance companies, two
banks, and one investment management firm. The seventh is a
state official who has influence on the State's purchase of bonds.
Cocktails are served from noon to one, luncheon from one to two-
thirty, coffee and brandy the rest of the afternoon. Seldom does
anyone go back to work, and often the same group stays on for
dinner. T. J. Buckley is the master of revels. The food and wine
are superb, the conversation dwells for very short periods on
money markets, then lapses into low subjects. Recently, Buckley
gave a monthly luncheon on a rainy day, and, because of the
dreary weather, extended cocktails for an extra hour. The restaurant management always goes along with his schedule changes.
They like Buckley's business; the old professional waiters, all
men, love his banter and his gratuities. "By three-thirty," Buckley
told me, "everyone in the room was juiced. The state official says
how much he'd like a woman that afternoon. I excuse myself to
take a pee, leave the room, grab my raincoat, and run like hell to
the subway station nearby, which is always loaded with hookers.

I find one, a young blonde with thigh-high boots, and we run back in the rain to the restaurant. I take her up the stairs," Buckley went on, "and I tell the owner, the maitre d', several waiters, 'My sister.' I bring her in the room, shut the door, grab her by the tits, and everyone cheers. Seven guys representing institutions that control over *twenty billion* in assets cheering the arrival of a young hooker in boots. Well, the state's man goes at it right on the floor with everyone watching. Then Walter, the waiter, starts banging on the door (I had stuck a chair under the knob). I opened the door a crack and showed Walter a glimpse of a fifty-dollar bill. Walter is a dignified gent, about sixty-five, been at the restaurant forever.

" 'No, no, Mr. Buckley,' Walter says. 'Come out here.'

"I slip out the door, sure that Walter is shocked and wants the hooker proceedings stopped immediately. I push the fifty at him, but he shakes his head.

" 'I don't want the money, Mr. Buckley,' Walter says, 'But . . .' He hesitates and whispers at me, 'But instead of the fifty, do you think I could take a crack at the *girl?*' "

Buckley smiled at me. "That's the new equality," he said. "Knowing how to lay it on the help."

Billy the Shooter is my financial Roughrider. His motto, which he utters repeatedly, is "Every once in a while, the blind hog gets the acorn." He uses this to call curses upon those people who have just struck it rich, people he considers dumber than he is himself. Billy the Shooter knows all the angles. And he is always just on the verge of making it big. But his sense of humor gets in the way. He finds it impossible to let the people on the other side of the deal know that he is really serious. And the people on the other side of deals have lingering suspicions that Billy really, deep down, is contemptuous of them. Which, deep down, is correct. "The best way of getting people to respond to you," Billy says, "is *overkill.* Give them something to remember."

Billy the Shooter lives by this code. He is the greatest practi-

tioner I know of building a career using the OPM technique.
Other People's Money. For a long while it was his grandfather's
money. This money allowed Billy to be sent to the finest schools,
including Le Rosey in Switzerland, where he developed contacts
that would serve him a lifetime. Much less wealthy than most of
his classmates, Billy developed skills to make sure he was always
included on the fanciest holidays, in the fanciest circles. Among
his talents is the ability to caricature, to capture faces in a char-
coal sketch quickly and accurately. He is also a superb skier,
racquets player, and horseback rider, skills that lead to his being
in demand as a partner and companion in special places of the
world. All free for Billy the Shooter.

Street-smart Smart People are essential to your ability to survive in the modern world. This is true whether the street is called
Main or Fifth Avenue or the Champs-Élysées. But there is another dimension to Billy that necessitates his inclusion in the
group of Smart People. He is an expert in an area where we all
need an expert. You cannot speak knowledgeably about the
world today unless you have access to information about the
Middle East. Almost a third of Billy's classmates at Le Rosey
were Arabs. He has hustled throughout the Middle East, successfully and in grand style. But only a Roughrider can give you the
true picture, for it is a picture seen not only from palaces, but
from the marketplace.

"The key is to get friendly with the Arabs early," Billy told me.
"When I was fourteen I was sent away to school. It was lucky I
was a big kid, because the Arabs have buggery on their minds
from the word go, the rich ones especially, because they can buy
it. I didn't publicly dump on the Arabs the way so many of my
classmates did. I was everyone's buddy. Holidays were so much
better that way. Morocco for Easter is a hell of a lot more interesting than Evanston Township, Illinois. When I was a kid I was
invited to Kuwait to visit a friend. You know they've got the
largest Cadillac dealership in the world in Kuwait? Kuwaitis
don't do a goddamn thing. They get the Palestinians to do all the

work. Anyway, I went hunting on my first visit. Not with weapons, but with falcons. You know a falcon can cost as much as a hundred thousand dollars? And did you know that the falcon has to attack his prey from above? Other birds in the Middle East try to fly above the hunting falcons — all by instinct, you know. If the birds can get above the falcons and do-do on them, the falcon becomes useless, impotent. He will not hunt anymore if he has been do-doed on. It's a fact. The falcon then has to be put away; the shame has been too great. The shame!"

Billy the Shooter wears a small gold earring in his right ear. And he wears custom-made suits that make him look like the ads for the international division of the Morgan Guaranty Trust. Until you spot the earring. He carries a black thorn stick bought in the New Caledonian Market at Bermondsey, outside of London. The cane has a spike at the end of it, originally intended for use on icy winter sidewalks. Billy the Shooter uses it to draw pornographic pictures on pavement. He does quick sketches of genitalia in front of historic buildings and moves on after his drawings are done.

"What do you want, cocktail knowledge of the Middle East?" Billy asked me.

"A painless introduction" I said. "Not about Kissinger's traveling entourage, but the real scoop."

We were sitting in the bar of the Regency Hotel on Park Avenue. Billy was wearing black tie, dinner jacket, and pink flannel trousers. He looked like a Charles Dana Gibson drawing of a young dandy, except for the gold earring in his right ear.

"First of all," he said, "there is only one thing that counts in the Middle East. *Access.* When money was forming there, funds were divvied up, so much to Britain, so much to the United States, so much to France. Now there's a coterie of middlemen, White, Weld types, bright MBAs whose wives don't mind if they travel three hundred and sixty days a year on private planes. There are about thirty strong middlemen in the Middle East who can provide you access. One of them from Saudi Arabia is the most visible. He has several children at Le Rosey. One son had an eighteenth birthday this year, and his father sent him a present: two American women for his delectation. They were put up at the Palace Hotel in Gstaad for the winter. Two women for the kid's birthday delectation.

"These middlemen provide the access. Why go for it? Money, that's why. Money you cannot believe. Because they are talking about *building countries from scratch.* They are talking about putting in the entire telephone network of Saudi Arabia, for instance. Or every road in Kuwait. You are talking forty- and fifty-year contracts for *billions* of dollars. Ralph Parsons, the management contractor, was just hired by the Saudis for a twenty-eight-year contract involving an estimated cost of ten billion dollars. That's why the Middle East is wide open. It makes the American frontier look like a Punch and Judy show."

Billy the Shooter kept ordering brandy. He knew who was paying. "What lots of people in the West don't realize is the tragedy of Lebanon. Beirut was one of the most beautiful cities of the world. It was the trading center of the Middle East, and the Lebanese were the greatest middlemen in the world, classic merchants. Beirut should have been one of the three most important financial centers in the universe. Everyone needs a place in the Middle East to get drunk and get laid. Beirut was that place. One of the most memorable trips of my life was ten years ago when an Italian princess whose portrait I was sketching took me to Beirut for a weekend. Middle East Airlines was like the magic carpet. It was Lebanon's airline. You got personalized matchbooks on your seat, Dom Perignon every time you opened your mouth, gorgeous stewardesses who would be your slaves. We land, we go to the St. George Hotel on the water, where we have a suite. Now Italian princesses make love like no other women in the world. Because they really believe they *are* princesses, and that they can turn you into a frog if they choose. That night, at the Casino du Liban, I won continually at chemin de fer until the princess took me off to an exhibition involving goats, fresh fruit, little boys, and old

women. But it's all gone now. Muslims, Christians, Palestinians
. . . a delicate balance. You upset the balance . . . no more Beirut.
In America no one knows what that means. But it means the heart
is gone from the Middle East."

Billy noticed a couple sitting in a corner. The woman looked
like Ali McGraw. "Send them a bottle of Dom P.," Billy said to
the waiter. To me he said, "A classmate of mine at Rosey was Ali
McGraw's first husband. You can put the bubbly on the tab. The
company pays for it, right?

"Now Jordan," Billy went on, fortified. "Jordan is a terrific
country. Not much oil, but the Middle East pipeline passes right
through it. It's the original 'hills skipped like lambs and the
mountains like rams' country. Jordan is the Old Testament. Except that King Hussein is *the* man of the 1980s. There are more
Palestinians there than Jordanians. Hussein is very benevolent.
But occasionally he orders his pilots into the air (he's a great flyer
himself) and wipes out a few thousand Palestinians. Just for the
exercise. Then, before he was married, for two months a year he
went to Palm Beach and balled his brains out. I've been out with
one of his Florida ex-honeys. He took her to the movies in Palm
Beach, where he would buy *six rows* of seats. Four bodyguards
fan out around the king and his date. My lady friend is always in
*Town and Country*. She says Hussein is one of the great lovers of
the world. He's my man of the eighties, but I'm more optimistic
for him than for Jordan. Trucks of produce go from Israel to
Jordan daily across that pathetic stream, the Jordan River. Trade
flows continuously across the King David Bridge. They trade
even during the Middle East wars. Nothing stops commerce. But
the solution for the Middle East, in the back of everyone's mind,
is *to give Jordan to the Palestinians*. That country will be the
sacrificial lamb."

Billy the Shooter's thumbnail sketches continued, amid occasional requests for the piano player to do songs from *Guys and
Dolls* and *Pajama Game*.

"Saudi Arabia," he said. "Forget it. I got bedbugs in Jeddah at the Kandara Palace Hotel. Even your Lavoris is confiscated at the airport for its alcohol content. All the Western colony lives for in Saudi Arabia is to wait at the spot where they drop the Paris *Herald Tribune* once a day. The best trivia to know is that back in the thirties, Aramco was drilling in the desert and, after seven wells, had come up with nothing but dry holes. They decided to give it one more shot before abandoning all hope. Then they drilled Old Number Eight, the most famous well in the world. And that sucker is still flowing.

"Iraq. Baghdad is the worst, and the Iraqi Arabs are the worst of them all. They've got some oil, not much, and a hell of a lot of tribal dissidents. I sum up Iraq in one phrase, 'Where there's a Kurd there's a whey.'

"Syria. It seems that everyone in Syria is named H'sad, and they all look like Abe Beame. They're not as smart as the Lebanese. There's a thriving Jewish community in Damascus, and all the money in the country goes for defense.

"Kuwait. They're about to have the greatest port city in the world, Kuwait City, being designed, naturally, by Americans. I once won the tennis singles championship of Kuwait on the terrific courts of the Kuwait Hilton. The people are remarkably organized, and although no liquor is allowed publicly, they all drink like hell on the sly. A lot of Kuwaitis used to go to Beirut and play the American stock market through a Merrill Lynch office there. The only problem was that if the stock went down, the Kuwaitis would not pay for it. They're great smugglers, very smart, and used to be scared shitless of the Shah of Iran.

"But to sum up the Middle East, I'll tell you one story that explains a lot. I had just been in Cairo after the Six Days' War. Believe it or not, I had been delivering a hooker named Mary from the Phoenicia Hotel in Beirut to a banker in Alexandria for a fee of twenty-five hundred U.S. dollars. That was in the days before the flight to the Swiss franc and the German mark. After the delivery I was in Cairo. There was one plane leaving that day for London. I had to be on it, and my hotel forgot to wake me. I had forty minutes to get thirty miles, through Cairo and along some of the most impossible roads in the world. I kept throwing more and more Egyptian pounds to my cab driver who kept his slipper to the floor, through police, through pedestrians. With the airport in sight, and me bouncing off the roof of the cab," Billy went on, "I was holding six months' pay for the cabby in Egyptian pounds in my fist. We round a bend at eighty kilometers. There's a shepherd and his sheep directly in our path. 'Stop,' I screamed. But the slipper stays on the floor and *Bang*, we put the shepherd to pasture about a hundred feet over the car. My cabby also takes several sheep with him, and he gets me to my plane as the doors start to close. 'You killed that shepherd,' I told the driver.

" 'What is one shepherd, my lord, against your missing a plane? Six months' wages pay for many shepherds.' *That's* the Middle East."

Billy the Shooter went over to the piano to sing "Wunderbar" from *Kiss Me Kate* and to ogle the woman to whom he sent the Dom Perignon. "I'm about to go dancing," he told me, "so I'm going to sum up Billy the Shooter's maxims for the successful life:

"1. The great skill at being ruthless is to always leave them loving you.

"2. Make sure you know a second language. Make sure your children learn a second language. Internationalism is more than ever the wave of the future.

"3. Contacts are essential. But use your access *only* when absolutely necessary. You can't waste these people on frivolous requests like getting your nephew into college. Save access for *yourself*.

"4. Try never to get anyone pissed off at you."

Billy got up. "I have also learned," he said, putting on his opera cape, "through bitter experience, this rule: Anything that flies, floats, or fucks, you must never buy, only *rent*."

Billy the Shooter, fingering his one gold earring, went off to dance.

"I have a lot of rich friends," Mather Stevens told me. "But, unfortunately for their character, they have been rich through inheritance, waiting so long for what they call BDs. Beneficial Deaths. My father never accumulated money. But we lived well, and he believed that you owed your children the best education. So we all went away to school, and my father, I remember, told me as I was leaving for boarding school at age twelve, 'Eat with the rich, but play with the poor, who are capable of joy.' The lines are by Logan Pearsall Smith, an essayist you should read.

"I've tried to live by what my father told me, and I, too, spend my money on things I love. I don't accumulate it. A few years ago," Stevens went on, "before I was a partner in my firm, my wife and I went to Delray Beach, Florida. We were guests of my brother and sister-in-law who had the use of her parents' winter home for ten days. The house was in a development of mostly retired people, some of the thousands of folk who move to Florida to play golf and grow old among their contemporaries. The second day we were there, we received a call inviting us to Palm Beach. The call was from another attorney who was trying to recruit me for his firm, a high-powered corporate shop whose senior partner was fond of saying, 'We believe in small offices and big houses.'

" 'I heard you were down here,' the lawyer said. 'Come over and play with the *rich* people. I want to show you granny's house. Bring your tennis rackets and swimsuits.' He called them swimsuits," Mather Stevens told me, adding, "My first day at boarding school, another new boy came up to me and said, 'Hello, I'm Franco Hapsburg. I'm a bathing enthusiast.' Can you believe it? Well, we pick up the speech of those we admire.

"At any rate we went to Palm Beach to granny's house. Granny turned out to be the lawyer's grandmother-in-law. She lived in a Moorish castle built for her as a wedding present in 1918 by her husband who was a timber baron and whose name you would know. Granny was one of the Palm Beach matrons who had elderly retainers and lawyers who would fly down in wool suits from Chicago for the day and relatives who drooled and groveled every time she said, 'Time for a cucumber sandwich and some tea.'

"Well, it was a big production for her attorney grandson-in-law to have my wife and me for the day. We came through Checkpoint Charlie at the end of her gravel driveway about ten in the morning, after the ride past the palaces that lined the ocean drive. Everything that day was geared to let me know that such luxury was waiting for *me* the minute I jumped law firms. We played tennis on granny's grass court, we swam in granny's marble pool, we were served luncheon in a garden full of the statues of Rodin and the like. Granny came by to inspect us, had a sherry, sniffed, and was helped into her 1950 Cadillac for the afternoon ride to the Bath and Tennis Club. There she played bridge every afternoon with friends who complained about times that had forced Mrs. Marjorie Merriwether Post to scatter broken glass on top of her walls to discourage trespassers.

"The problem with the day was that, as it went on, the lawyer recruiting me became drunker and drunker. He was abusive to his wife and increasingly revealed his bitterness that he was the grandson-in-law of granny and not the actual son. We ate dinner at the Everglades Club, and our host became drunker, louder, and ruder. His wife leaned over to us during the salad course and whispered, 'I apologize. Of course, I'm going to dump him.' It was frightening after dinner. The lawyer, knowing deep down that he was blowing Palm Beach for himself forever, drove around the parking lot of the Everglades Club at forty miles an hour with us in the back seat. He bounced his car purposely off parked Mercedeses, Silver Clouds, and the occasional Bentley. 'Send the bills to granny,' he was yelling until he locked bumpers with a vintage black Lincoln, and our day in Palm Beach was over.

"My wife and I drove back slowly to Delray," said Mather Stevens. "We stopped for a nightcap at a roadhouse, a dive called the Porpoise, on Route 1. We each had a beer and played an electronic tennis game, feeding quarters into the machine. Several people were giving us the hairy eyeball, and one young man in faded jeans and a tee shirt that said 'Gators make better lovers' drawled at us, 'Picking up some local color, folks?' We finished our beer and left the Porpoise, driving by the pickups and second-hand ragtops in the parking lot.

" 'The only thing we haven't done today,' my wife said, 'is go to a progressive dinner party in the suburbs: you bring the casserole, I bring the strawberries Romanoff.'

" 'It's a terrible curse,' I told my wife," Stevens said. "We're doomed to wander from palaces to hovels, misunderstood everywhere. It's no favor to anyone to look like you're rich when you're not."

# 10 FUTURE SMARTS

You'd better realize that our future is going to be even less personal, more automated, more expensive, and more encumbered by bureaucracy, inefficiency, and indifference. This situation is not going to be helped by your flattening your stomach or increasing your daily run to twelve miles or whittling your real estate person's commission down from three to two percent. Your future depends on recruiting Smart People and making them respond to your needs.

Everything will change in the next fifty years: our economy, our technology, our life-styles, our life expectancy. What will *not* change is the fact of our needing human contact to get us through the nights, the days, and the facts of an increasingly impersonal society.

Recognizing that you *cannot do it alone,* that Smart People techniques work, can assure you a more comfortable future, a more successful future. It can also ensure a present that is happier, because it encompasses other people who are working for you — while you provide something for them as well. Not only will your life be made easier and more successful, but you will be assured that you do not have to live it anonymously. You do not have to do it *alone.*

"One thing about the future," Henry the Red told me. "You'd better teach your children to seek professions that will always be in demand: medicine, the law, dentistry. Because the government is going, little by little, to make it impossible to pass along money. But if you can *sell* something, you'll always be able to get along. The good salesman will always make a living. No matter how our society is structured.

"You talk about salesmen," Henry the Red had said to me at lunch recently on the first day of the shad roe season. "My uncle Sumner, called Summy, has to be the greatest. He used to peddle ribbon, all kinds of ribbon, to department stores in Connecticut and Rhode Island. For dozens of five-and-tens, varieties, family businesses, Summy the ribbon man was a sign of the holidays to come. But for years he had tried to crack Sears, Roebuck without success. 'Those guys won't deal with a little Jewish peddler,' he complained, after attempting for the fiftieth time to sell an order to the Sears ribbon buyer. Knowing that he had the best ribbon in the East, Summy reasonably was steamed. Steamed enough to call the chairman of the board of Sears, Roebuck to complain. 'I'm going to make a civil rights issue of this,' he told the chairman. 'And the fact that you discriminate is going to be plastered all over the front pages of the newspapers.' The chairman, not wanting a fuss over a small matter, passed the word down the chain of command to the ribbon buyer: 'Give Summy an order.'

"The buyer was furious but agreed. When Uncle Sumner next came to call, the buyer, pompous and self-righteous, said, 'All right, Sumner. Here's your first order. We'll buy enough assorted ribbon from you to measure from the tip of your nose to the tip of your penis.'

"Very seriously, Uncle Sumner wrote down the order, thanked the buyer, and left. Three weeks later a hysterical Sears, Roebuck buyer called Uncle Sumner. 'What the hell's going on here? There are three truckloads of ribbon in our parking lot, and the drivers are showing me the signed order memo. What's going on?'

"Calmly, Uncle Sumner said, 'I'm reading your order to me. You wanted enough ribbon to measure from the tip of my nose to the tip of my penis, right?'

" 'Right,' said the buyer from Sears.

" 'Well, you son of a bitch,' said Uncle Sumner, 'the tip of my penis is in Minsk!' "

Uncle Sumner is a survivor. As long as there are salesmen there will always be survivors.

E. B. White has written in *One Man's Meat*, "The future . . . seems to me no unified dream but a mince pie, long in the baking, never quite done." The main message in this book is that it doesn't matter what the future will bring. Human nature does not change through history. There will always be bigotry, envy, greed, fear, generosity, and love. There will not be utopia. We shall still need goods and services and friendship from others. The Smart People concepts and techniques will always be necessary and appropriate. They will provide the key to any future for ourselves and our descendants, whether it's on Mars, on an asteroid, or in Boone, Iowa. Life will still involve, more than anything else, the solving of trivia, the day-to-day problems that face us.

The big picture — wars, détente, shortages, diplomacy, politics — concern us all peripherally. The selfish living of our lives will always depend on how we relate to other people, what they can do for us, what they are willing to do for us. And what we can offer *them* to make them respond. I work in a business where predicting the future is a daily routine that has become so boring no one really pays any attention. And not only boring, but almost universally wrong. The truth is that so-called experts can never take into account accidents, acts of God, and individual initiatives that change the course of history. Everyone seems to know that events and personalities in the Middle East will have the greatest influence upon our lives in the next several decades. Americans are whipped into frenzies about energy crises, the Israeli position, the Arab demands, the power of OPEC. Smart People have to step back and not blindly swallow news stories. Smart People must keep their own perspective.

I have a story about perspective. It involves the Middle East, the area of the world that can have more meaning for you and me than any other. Why? Because peace or war in the Middle East involves our major source of energy, and the energy issue involves the balance of power in the world. Ripples of tension there make us all nervous. But when you can see famous people who influence history up close you can understand the absurdity and the irony of this history. You want to worry about the Middle East? Listen.

I was in New York recently, staying at the Regency Hotel at Park Avenue and Sixty-first Street. When I came in from dinner one night, it was almost midnight. I had had several drinks and a good deal of wine. The elevator doors were beginning to close as I reached the narrow hallway where they were located. Ordinarily I wouldn't have done it, but I jumped into the closing space as the doors were shutting. Everyone already inside looked at me with surprise and I grinned at them, apologizing. The atmosphere was immediately tense. There were three others in the elevator besides the operator and myself. A tall man jammed his hand underneath a tan trenchcoat. A tall blond woman looked at her companion, as if to ask if she should be worried at my intrusion. The third person, shorter than the woman, was Moshe Dayan. I was surprised myself. There was an imminent crisis at the time, about settlements on the Golan Heights. Sabres were being rattled. Not really knowing what to say, but wanting to establish that I was a friend, I smiled some more, gave my floor number to the operator, and said, "How are you, General?"

The elevator stopped at their floor. Dayan looked up at the blond, over at me with a brilliant grin, then back at the blond. "*Vunderful*," he said to me as he moved from the elevator with his party and, "*Vunderful*," once more as the doors slid closed.

What is the Middle East crisis compared with the immediacy of a blond?

You think there's any mystery about life or politics or celebrities? Smart People make sure that they understand humor and that they understand character. If you do this too, then the future will take care of you. Perhaps if we can combine the best of man's sensitive nature and his scientific curiosity we can approach the ideal. As Fritjof Capra says in *The Tao of Physics*, "Science does not need mysticism and mysticism does not need science, but man needs both." *Vunderful!*

The Arthur D. Little complex at Acorn Park, Cambridge, Massachusetts, looks very institutional, like a large high school specializing in the industrial arts. The complex houses an international consulting firm, concentrating on solving problems of government and industry. There are row upon row of compact cars in the parking lot, VWs, Volvos, Plymouth Volarés, Pintos. The planners of the future work here. They know that the gas guzzlers are dinosaurs and that, as experts with their eyes on the future, they must not cling to the remnants of the past. Visitors to Arthur D. Little are not free to roam corridors. They must be announced at the reception area and escorted to their destination. Arthur D. Little is a think tank, a consulting complex where much of the work done is classified top secret. Last year's sales were one hundred and forty-six million dollars. A lot of secrets.

General James M. Gavin is my future Summa. He has just retired as chairman of the board of Arthur D. Little. I have always believed that a military man, or a former military man, is a necessary part of your Smart People team. The conventional popular war is forever denied those who might have sought it, gone forever in our thermonuclear age. Wars have called forth much of the great literature and myth of history. I have believed that any true understanding of life has to include a knowledge of what motivates man to go to war, what moves him during war and after the peace. James Jones's *From Here to Eternity* I would certainly place on any high school or college student's required reading list. I have even written a military novel myself, satirical in style. Written about the peacetime army, it is called *Three*

*Cheers for War in General,* the title a quotation from Mussolini which I used ironically.

In searching for ways to plan my future, using the Smart People doctrines, I have found it necessary to plumb the past. James M. Gavin's book *Crisis Now* affected me immensely. Here was a military man, the father of modern airborne warfare, resigning from the army over future policy. Here was a military man, a hero, who very early was criticizing our involvement in Vietnam. This was a man who knew the past and acted on his view of the future. I obtained an introduction to the general through an old friend of mine, a former employee of Arthur D. Little and the greatest left-handed pitcher in Harvard College history, an achievement he modestly derides.

General Gavin (a three-star general) stands like a soldier. His grip is hard and dry, and he looks straight into your face, making you feel you have just flunked inspection. People open up to you if you come to them well recommended. Smart People almost never come to new situations, countries, or people unprepared. My left-handed pitcher had given me a buildup, and I felt I could comfortably talk to a general even though my active duty had been done at a rank lower than private first class.

"You know this man is a legend," my friend told me. "Jim Gavin was an orphan. He carried coal as a kid in Pennsylvania. For twenty-five cents a day. He went as far as the seventh grade in school. That was it. Enlisted in the army as a recruit, then took competitive exams to get into West Point and became the youngest division commander since the Civil War. He planned the airborne invasion on D-Day and virtually invented the modern helicopter tactics used with infantry. He was also ambassador to France, appointed by John F. Kennedy. I remember that I went to a military reservation, Fort Leonard Wood in Missouri, several years ago on a consulting job. The general was with me. While we were on a tour of the place, an old sergeant came up to us. There were tears in his eyes. 'I was with you at Normandy,' the soldier said. 'And General, I've carried this picture around with me for thirty years. Could you autograph it, please?' The sergeant produced a wrinkled, yellowed photo taken just after the 82nd Airborne jumped into France.

" 'I'll be glad to sign it, Jerry,' the general said, his eyes moist. Also, he called the man by name," my friend told me. "After all these years, I've never forgotten it."

The general's office is utilitarian, almost spartan. But his style reflects the contrast always apparent in Smart People. Several paintings hang on the wall. They are scenes of Normandy — an oil of the bunkers facing the white cliffs of Dover, by a Nazi artist; D-Day at night, with parachutes and planes and search-lights in the sky. Then there is a postcard on the wall, a picture of Buddha.

"Isn't he serene?" asked the general, who appreciates the need of man to relax, to remove himself from stress. "I've been devoted to many things in my life," he told me, "but hard work and the sense that life and society must change are probably the two most important things. One of our biggest problems is the unwilling-ness to work for what we want to enjoy. On the other hand, so many millions of Americans are moving upward, into the middle class.

"My wife and I went to the movies last Sunday afternoon. Most of the women at the theater were wearing fur coats. And jewelry. So much wealth in this country! Europe has never been able to understand this. I am an optimist about the future because of the flexibility of our spirit and, the most important element, because of our technology, which will lead us into a new age. New knowl-edge is unlimited and ever-flowing."

The general went to a small blackboard covered with formulae. "Weapons used to work for years," he said. "Now they are obso-lete in a week. But the 'Methuselah Prospect,' as they call it, death from wars and famine, does not really worry me. Our technology and abilities to be creative will overcome it." We spent a long time discussing writing, war, America, and the problems of retirement. Several of General Gavin's philosophies of life emerged:

1. "Reading gives almost more pleasure than anything in life. My house is filled with books I have read, and am reading. Thomas Jefferson had a library next to his bedroom, and he had the books arranged according to what he would read at different times of the day. Complex subjects he read in the morning; lighter subjects, late at night. The Book of Psalms always comforts me. And Shakespeare — all of it, but particularly the histories. Henry the Fifth, at Harfleur:

> *Once more unto the breach, dear friends, once more;*
> *Or close the wall up with our English dead!*
> *In peace there's nothing so becomes a man*
> *As modest stillness and humility:*
> *But when the blast of war blows in our ears,*
> *Then imitate the action of the tiger;*
> *Stiffen the sinews, summon up the blood,*
> *Disguise fair nature with hard-favour'd rage;*
> *Then lend the eye a terrible aspect.*

"And then Napoleon's speech before the Battle of the Pyramids in Egypt: 'Soldiers, you are about to fight the rulers of Egypt. Reflect that from yonder monuments forty centuries look down upon you.' You can never be bored while you're learning, while you read."

2. "You should search for excellence in your life. This was what was so admirable about Jack Kennedy. I received an invitation from the French recently to a reception at Versailles for President Carter. It said, 'Dark suits for the men.' *Dark suits!*" the General snorted. "When President Kennedy was there, it was in white tie and tails. He looked as a president of this country should look. Now it's a disgrace. You *must* search for excellence."

3. "You must exercise your body. I shall be seventy-one shortly,

and I keep a bowling ball in my car's trunk. I cross-country ski, I play golf and paddle tennis. I jogged years ago when it was embarrassing to jog. You have to keep reaching; *we* have to keep reaching to penetrate the unknown. And a man should never really retire. To do that is to die slowly."

4. "Take risks. I cannot conceive of a life without risk, or a future unless we risk the processes of change. Without risk, you atrophy as a person. A nation atrophies the same way."

General James M. Gavin predicted our disaster in Vietnam. He recognized the importance of the Middle East, the shift of power to this area, long before the energy crisis. He has seen the best and the worst of times. This Summa of the future understands technology. And he understands people. Yet he is an optimist. When Summas are optimists, and you believe them, you find the strength to carry on. In his book *Crisis Now* (co-authored with Arthur T. Hadley), General Gavin quotes Walt Whitman. The lines describe the general's attitude and his hope:

> *Long, too long, America.*
> *Traveling roads all even and peaceful you learned*
> *From joys and prosperity only.*
> *But now, ah now, to learn from the crises of anguish,*
> *Advancing, grappling with direst fate and*
> *Recoiling not.*

All through my school life I tried to avoid science and math. I thought that all scientists were boring, one-dimensional people and that anyone who hadn't majored in English in college could not possibly be of use to me. In college my friends and I called physics and math majors "meats." I saw them as caricatures of people, steaks from which protruded undeveloped arms and legs, the little arms holding slide rules. But I admit to a glorious rebirth in this regard.

My industry is an information industry, and the prime way information is distributed today is through technology. I never knew how the light bulb operated or the principles of flight or how the telephone worked. I never really cared, as long as I had their services. But every day in the stock market I use my quotation machines which give me prices, news, projections, even World Series scores and the time of day. And I receive endless computer printouts of customer statements, credits and debits, investment analyses.

One day a summer neighbor, a physicist-inventor was talking to me about his experiments into life on other planets. "I think I have a truly elegant hypothesis," he said.

"Elegant?" I questioned. "That's a strange word to use in relation to science."

"I see that your education has been sadly neglected," he said. "There are three important things in scientific theory: beauty, simplicity, and elegance. We use these words constantly."

"So do I," I said, "but I never thought . . ."

"That's your problem," the physicist-inventor said. "Any living of a good life should include the understanding of life. In principle I understand *all* of life. A friend of mine years ago had a date with a young lady. After a movie they parked in an open convertible. The sky was full of stars and the mood naturally romantic. Looking up, my friend said, 'I am the only man in the world who knows why a star shines.' He had developed the theory that very day."

My next-door neighbor in the summers has given me many seminars since then. He is one of the most respected inventors in America in the field of optics, a gentle, wise man who is still a ranked senior tennis player. He lives a life filled with discovery and wonder. He is André Simon, my Lamplighter of science and the future. His house, next to mine, looks out to sea. Two telescopes, one mounted inside a rooftop observatory, are trained on the heavens. Twice each summer, Dr. Simon has star parties for the children of the community, to introduce them to astronomy and legends about the constellations.

It is the function of *your* Lamplighters to excite you about subjects or people about which you may have previously known little. All of us have had teachers in our lives whom we remember fondly — Miss Anderson, who taught sixth grade with a sense of humor; Mr. Newsom who was gassed in World War I and taught us to love poetry; Frederick Merk, in college, with his course on the westward movement, nicknamed "Wagon Wheels." All of your favorite teachers, I would bet, instilled in you a love for something new. That's what your Lamplighters should do for you as an adult. André Simon changed my perception of the world of science and mathematics.

Simon played tennis with me one day. He hit flat shots, corner to corner, and moved to the ball in gliding movements, seemingly without effort. He played in yellowed flannels, an affectation he reserves for games with people he can beat with ease. After we had finished, we sat down on the grass underneath a shade tree. "You don't think about discovery in business," he said, "and yet discovery is with all of us daily. If everyone thought consciously, as scientists do, life could be a lot better for everyone. Discovery is part of living a life of beauty. At one point, Sir Isaac Newton was congratulated on *his* discoveries. Newton said, 'To myself I seem to have been only like a boy playing on the seashore, and diverting myself in now and then finding a smoother pebble or a prettier shell than ordinary, whilst the great ocean of truth lay all undiscovered before me.' Tell me," Simon said, "is that not poetry?"

## HUNTING GIANTS

That day, Simon told me about a lifelong game of his that he called Hunting Giants. This game consisted of knowing where various people he had always admired lived and, when in their vicinity, stopping to see them without introduction.

"What about invasion of privacy?" I asked.

"Famous people are always flattered by true fans," he said. "The key is to approach them knowledgeably. How else are we to learn?"

He told me about his wartime experiences traveling through England and then through Europe after D-Day. He worked on the development of weapons systems, but was allowed to wander with a noncom driver because his clearance included the notation "Needs to work independently. Thinks well alone. Let him do what he wants."

He went on drives specifically to hunt giants — once finding George Bernard Shaw in Sussex and later discovering Richard Strauss outside of Munich. Both giants were pleased to meet an American scientist who admired them and sought them out.

Simon tells the story: " 'I have lived long enough,' Shaw told me, 'to see high drama become Betty Grable in a bathing suit at the USO.' Our meeting was brief, but just before we parted he looked at me sharply. 'I find it difficult to believe that America has scientists,' Shaw said, 'but I suppose it's just as well.'

"Strauss was glad of the visit but terribly sad," Simon went on. "He wanted to talk about music and beauty, and he was able to see neither in Munich in 1945. 'A man can outlive his money,' Strauss said, 'and even outlive his sense of beauty when surrounded by *this*.' He waved his hand, indicating all of Germany. Giant-hunting has given me several of the great moments of my life."

None of us spends enough time sitting under shade trees in the summer talking about giants.

André Simon has been married to the same woman for thirty-five years. She had been his lab assistant.

"My parents' friends," I said to him one day, "all seemed to have had miserable marriages. Yet none of them were divorced. They stayed with unhappy situations until they were old enough to be comfortable with each other. Our generation divorces at the first sign of trouble. Can science ever help us with human relations?"

"It's curious," he said. "There are many fewer divorces among scientists than among other people. A main reason is that scientists often marry scientists, or at least marry persons attuned to science. We make more compatible marriages because we can always fall back upon areas of common interest when confronted with problems.

"As to improving human relations? The key for myself and most of my fellow scientists is that *life* can be improved. The genetic improvement of man has got to come. There are millions of people on the planet who now have no chance. Millions who can't get even enough nutrition to have a decent brain. The paradox is that we should be working to strengthen, perhaps change the human race. But experimenting with genetics is undemocratic; people react with fear when the subject is broached. Natural selection has brought us to where we are, and it's fascinating to think about where we came from. We are a beautiful mechanism, and it would be fine to believe that no one had anything but altruistic thoughts about the rest of the race. But, as long as genetics is equated with Dr. Frankenstein. . . ." He shrugged. "One of my favorite writers is Saki. Because of his surprises and his sardonic sense of humor. Saki said, 'A little inaccuracy sometimes saves tons of explanation.'

"Of course," Simon went on, "science tries to live up to the facts of life. But occasionally we push and shove to make size twelve feet fit into size ten shoes. Ptolemy, I'm sure, cheated a little to make things come out right. Also in genetics, I'm convinced that in Mendel's original data on the crossbreeding of peas, something was fudged. Not purposely, mind you. But Mendel's experiments came out with such perfect results. He was a very likeable man, Mendel. I've always thought that his gardeners fudged for him because they liked him so much, and that's what made things come out right."

André Simon is fascinating to me, as all Lamplighters are. He makes me *think about things,* not just about people or bills or whether General Motors will declare an extra dividend.

"Science is divided in most people's minds," he tells me. "Take a drop of water. Why is it spherical? Blow it up to study it and you're a biologist. Blow it up a little more and you're a chemist. A little more, you're a nuclear physicist. But nature doesn't know about these divisions. Science is different from technology. Science holds your feet to the fire and our natural curiosity leads us on."

"Would you say that most scientists are naturally optimistic?"

Simon thought a moment. "I think we are less emotional than other people," he said, "but not necessarily optimistic. One of my best friends, who helped to evolve the trigger mechanism for the atom bomb, claimed to be the foremost pessimist in Europe. He tells the story of an experiment of his in thermodynamics. He was teaching a class in Germany at the time and was getting a point across. He took two thermodynamic containers, large vats actually. He filled one vat with good Rhine wine and the other with an unpleasant material. Then he took a pitcher full of each and emptied the pitchers in the opposite vat. 'You see, class,' my friend told his students, 'thermodynamic change has taken place. Now, all life is like this experiment. The unpleasant material has ruined the wine. But the piss has not been improved one bit.'

"Scientists have a sense of humor," Simon added, "but it tends to be quite precious, ranging from practical joking to games with numbers."

Simon has recommended books for me to read, after I specified that they be books that would stimulate without intimidating. He recommended Stephen Weinberg's *The First Three Minutes*, a book about the origin of the universe; Robert A. Heinlein's early science fiction novels, *Glory Road* and *Stranger in a Strange Land*; and the underground classic, *A Canticle for Leibowitz*, by Walter M. Miller, Jr. "If these books make you think," Simon says, "that's the point. If any of them makes you say, 'Aha,' then you've stumbled on one of my most important discoveries: the "Aha!" Theory. All inspiration is the result of hard work in your subconscious. Your subconscious is capable of anything. You are constantly feeding material into it, integrating everything you perceive and think about. Perhaps after years, you suddenly say "Aha!" and a problem is solved. But your subconscious has been working on that problem. Perhaps for a lifetime."

"Someone told me once," I said, "that one 'Oh shit!' is worth ten 'Atta boy's.'"

"You call it what you want," the scientist said, "but my Aha! Theory is always being used by me. And for important reasons. Particularly for my mental and physical health."

"How so?" I asked.

"The harder the problem you work on, or work toward," he said, "the healthier you tend to be. If your subconscious is working toward solving something, working toward a goal, it seems to be marvelous therapy. Your systems know instinctively that they have to keep functioning because you're *willing* them to function as you work hard toward solution. There should be no such thing in life as a final goal; there must always be something beyond each success. Or else there is only death. Einstein said, 'The most beautiful thing we can experience is the mysterious. It is the source of all true art and science.'"

The day my science Lamplighter told me this the temperature where I live was over one hundred degrees in the shade, setting a record for the end of August. "I'm solving the heat problem in one way already," he told me, getting up to leave my sun deck and return to his house.

"How's that?" I asked him.

"I've cut off my long white flannel tennis trousers at the knee."

If you ever invest in the stock market you need a science and future Maven. My Maven is that rare scientifically oriented person who loves money and the acquisition of things. His name is Dean. But everyone calls him Dean the Machine because, among other things, he can do anything with computers. Dean lives in California, in Marina Del Rey, just outside of Los Angeles.

"I want to live inside one of the Wonders of the World," he

says. "I can't get into the pyramids; the Colossus of Rhodes is gone. But Marina Del Rey pumps with life. It's a terrifying look at the future, and I want it to recognize me as one of its own when it branches out to conquer the world."

Marina Del Rey is a phenomenon, a rabbit warren of expensive apartments and condominiums, pleasure cubicles devoted to the swinging Southern California life-style of boats and surfboards, pastel automobiles, white wine, grass and coke, stewardesses, divorced freedom seekers, searchers for life before real life. Dean has Dymo tapes plastered on his doors, on his night table, on his mirrors. They are his reminders of what the world means to him. Here is what some of them say: "Take the time." "Do it. Do it all. Do it now!" "There is less to this than meets the eye." And, "Vulgarity is the garlic in the salad of charm." Taped to the telephone receiver in his bedroom is the phrase, "Fuck you, nameless fear." He placed that message on his receiver after he was divorced, when he felt terrified calling new women for dates.

Dean the Machine is surrounded by people in Marina Del Rey. And he is also convinced that he doesn't care for them much at all. "But you can ask me any question about computers," he says, "and I can give you an answer. After all, I am a priest of the new religion. All of my fellows who came into computers in the early 1960s were in the vanguard of the future. Didn't we wear the uniform? Sandals, jeans, and beads. Didn't we speak the language? Didn't we join companies and get stock options at two dollars and sell our holdings in the sixties, seventies, and eighties?" The brotherhood of the computer age talks conservative politics and big bucks. "You've got to understand. We don't talk about saving the human race. We talk about running it." They are a cocky, arrogant lot, the priests of the new age. They are not very likable. Dean the Machine has only one strong memory of childhood. When he was nine years old, his mother took him to Palm Beach to visit a great uncle who lived in a white stucco palace by the sea. Dean was ushered in to see the old man, who, as Dean tells it, looked like a cross between John D. Rockefeller and Martin Peyton of "Peyton Place."

"What do you want to be, boy, when you grow up?" the old man asked Dean.

"I don't know, sir," Dean answered.

The old man was annoyed. "Well, boy, what do you like to *do*?"

"I like to take radios apart," Dean answered.

"Then there's only one thing you must do," said the man. "You must grow up and go to the Massachusetts Institute of Technology."

"The old man's age and the setting, in a solarium in Palm Beach, made me think of him as a wizard," Dean said. "So all during childhood and adolescence, MIT was my dream. But, unlike most dreams," Dean said, "it came true."

"When I was at college," he continued, "there was no great opening of the heavens. I jumped into practical mathematics; theoretical math was too weird. And for fun we'd do things like welding streetcars to their tracks with thermite and drinking ethanol with orange juice. But emotionally the heavens did open. One day when I was walking across the Mass. Avenue Bridge, coming back across the Charles from Boston to my fraternity house, a crowd of fifty or so people had gathered at one end of the bridge. I pushed my way through the people and saw that a man was standing outside the protective railing lining the bridge. He was yelling, 'Get back, I'm going to jump.'

"Well," Dean continued, "I had had a few beers, enough for false courage, and I stepped forward, coming close to the man.

" 'Stop right there,' he yelled. 'You come a step closer and I'll jump.'

" 'Go right ahead and jump, asshole,' I said to him. 'Nothing will happen because I'm a Red Cross instructor and I'll jump in after you. You won't drown no matter what you do.' I moved another step closer and he jumped. What could I do?" Dean said.

"The crowd had all heard me. I climbed over the railing and jumped after him. Now this was October and the water was goddamn cold. I had to fight the guy all the way. He was screaming, 'You're young. You've got everything to live for. You don't know anything about anything. Let me die.' He fought and struggled all the way to the Cambridge side of the river where the police waited with two ambulances. One for me. One for him. The papers gave the rescue a big play, and a month later I got a medal from the Boy Scouts on the "Today" show, hung around my neck by Hugh Downs. And if it wasn't for a few beers, I never would have done it. Later, when I was back at school, I went to the police and inquired after the man I had saved. They checked and told me, 'He was institutionalized and hung himself with gimp from the arts-and-crafts shop.'

"All I could think of after that was what the man had said to me in the water. 'You know nothing about anything. Let me die.' I had thought he was an old man, sick of life. He had been thirty-six. In a funny way, from that time on, I began putting more faith in my studies of the computer and less faith in people."

I met Dean the Machine at a party in the Hollywood Hills where he was playing the piano and I was playing my castanets. When we were talking later in the evening, he asked me about finding a literary agent for a book he was writing, and I asked him about semiconductor companies in which to invest. Of course the trade-off is one of the best ways to recruit Smart People. I found an agent for Dean's book (which has yet to be published), and he became a client as well as my scientific Maven.

Of course, for your purposes, the more Smart People within driving distance the better. However, ninety-nine percent of my business is done on the telephone. I never really have to see my computer Maven. It's enough to have a conversation with him once a month, just to help me keep abreast of developments in his field. In the last five years, Dean the Machine has advised me to buy Intel, Wang Labs, Amdahl, Storage Technology, and Analog

Devices. They have all been tremendous winners. How does he always seem to know? Dean the Machine describes it this way:

"There is a cult built up around the computer. All of us involved in the early days, late 1950s, early 1960s, had a reverence for the computer itself. We got an emotional charge from all the electronics, the hardware, the clean rooms with air conditioning. There was also a feeling that what we were doing was somehow slightly inhuman. Of course, lay people contributed to this with their fear of the machines running amok, making mistakes, and a dread that there were no people behind the systems, just more technology. This is one reason why computer scientists are not theoreticians. Nor are they Einsteins who scribble formulae on toilet paper and need tending or they'll die of malnutrition. We understand the world," Dean said, "and we're rather cheeky about it. Most of my friends are politically conservative. Technology is now fundamental to our economy, and it will remain so. We're not only going to show you the way things will be; we're going to line our nests while we do it."

Somewhere among your Smart People you have to have your share of bastards. There are various ways of getting things accomplished in our society. One of them is not running in popularity contests. There is a certain something Dean the Machine loses by not caring about people. "But I get people to respond through fear," he says. "I'm a prick, and it gives me satisfaction that they know it. You know how our lives are being transformed?"

We were in Dean's boat, The Ragman, cruising off Catalina in June. He had three teenage girls aboard, girls who looked like cheerleaders at Hollywood High. They were his crew for the day, thrilled to be on the water with an older man who bullied them. Finding them was simple. Dean is a legend in Marina Del Rey. He has the best boat, fastest car, freshest grass, biggest television screen. He always knows the answers. That day on the boat, he talked about the future, holding the wheel and sipping a Lucky

Lager. "Remember when hand calculators cost several hundred dollars?" he asked. "Now you can buy them for under ten bucks. And they do more work more efficiently. Now we have miracle chips, postage-stamp-sized silicon chips that have in them more power than the room-sized computers of a decade ago. These chips functioning in minicomputers are your future. Computers in the home will be the way of life — paying your bills, filling your bath, waking you up, tending you while you're sick, starting your car, telling you when your wife is ovulating or if she's cheating on you. There is no stage of existence at which the computer will not be functioning. If I were a mayor or city councilman in any town in America I would advise holding public lectures on the silicon chip. You may as well meet your master." Sailing back, the girls brought Dean seven Lucky Lagers. He never said thanks for any of them. He received them as his due.

On my last visit to California I had talked with Dean the Machine about favorite books. He had mentioned several about the Arctic, saying, "I only dwell on what I'm into now. Years ago I would have said *Huckleberry Finn*. But it's not years ago, is it?"

I recently got a letter from Dean. It was the first letter I have ever received from him. It said, "I forgot to mention a favorite book, Dickens's *A Christmas Carol*, but not because of the obvious reasons. Really, it's for one scene that remains one of my most lasting memories. The committee soliciting for charity, filled with holiday mirth, and merry to the point of being silly, arrive at Scrooge and Marley. The solicitors ask Scrooge, 'How much may we put you down for?'

"Scrooge replies, 'You may put me down for nothing.'

"The solicitors break into rapture. 'How noble, how generous,' they exclaim. 'You wish to remain anonymous?'

"Scrooge roars back at them, 'I wish to remain alone.' This exchange," Dean writes, "has clung to me through almost twenty years of therapy. Scrooge gave the only acceptable response that I can contemplate for myself. But Dickens," Dean added, "used this scene to introduce Scrooge as a figure of ridicule worthy of pity.

"Acchht! If we only knew. Love, Dean."

Speedy Sachs is my Roughrider of the future. He is a heavy-weight consultant whose claim is that he can master any subject in forty-eight hours. What makes him a Roughrider and not a Maven is that he gets sidetracked onto trivia, which he considers much more important than the big questions like how to find effective substitutes for oil and gas or how to end starvation in the world. Speedy would much rather spend time figuring out what kind of paintings Picasso would paint if he had been born in the Renaissance, or what influence the crossbow might have on modern limited warfare. Speedy makes a lot of money every year and always spends slightly more than he makes.

"Anything else is un-American," he says. "Besides, all my money goes for experiments in improving people's lives. I start with trying to improve mine. I'm a gentleman. You know what a gentleman is? A person who owns an accordian but who doesn't play it." Speedy Sachs is in his middle fifties. He has had three wives and is, as he describes it, working on the fourth. "When it comes to love," Speedy adds, "a gentleman is someone who puts half his weight on his elbows."

Speedy is very dapper, with close-cropped hair that turned white in his early thirties. He dresses exclusively Brooks Brothers. "In the year two thousand," he says, "there will be a Brooks Brothers look. It is a uniform that says to customers, 'I do not compromise according to fashion.' Customers trust it. And I'll tell you something, there will always be customers."

There is nothing salacious about Speedy's nickname. He was a track man in high school, a hurdler. He received a liberal arts education, took a Ph.D. in applied physics, and has worked on such projects as the first stage of the Minuteman solid propellant ICBM. He was on his consulting firm's first mission to China the year after Nixon's initial visit. He called me out of the blue several years ago, after I had appeared on a television show discussing my observations about the stock market and calling it "an Alice in Wonderland business." He invited me out to his house, with the stated purpose of investing some money.

Speedy Sachs lives in the country in a contemporary cedar and stone house. A metal plaque is set into the wall near his front entrance. The plaque reads, "If you are close enough to read this and you have not been invited, you are already under observation by trained German shepherd attack dogs. Start walking backward. Very slowly. Whistling Kate Smith's version of 'God Bless America.' This is no joke."

Speedy greeted me at the door dressed in gray flannel slacks and a tweed jacket with elbow patches. He held a German shepherd on a leash. "Big Brother won't hurt you," he said. "He knows you're going to make me money." Speedy had named his dog after the ultimate leader in Orwell's *1984*. That day began our business relationship and our friendship. Speedy was pleased that I did not consider him a nut for his digressions into trivia. "Who's to say what's more important than anything else?" he said. "That's why I could never stay married. No matter how bizarre the woman was, she somehow ceased being bizarre when she knew I made a hundred and eleven thousand dollars a year. She wanted a Steuben glass collection or fifty Jerry Silvermans or summers in Biarritz. You know why life isn't going to be very different in the year 2000? Because *people* are going to be the *same*. Technology will make life easier and possibly even more fun. But people will not change. And Brooks Brothers will not change. Ties a little narrower or fatter perhaps. But that's about all."

Speedy Sachs's last wedding had been in France, a good example of his approach to life. He had flown with his fiancée to Paris. And he had also provided a ticket for a Unitarian minister from Bucks County, Pennsylvania, a childhood friend.

"I got married last week in Paris," Speedy announced to me.

"That's terrific, Speedy," I said.

"But where?" he asked.

"Where in Paris?" I said, dumbly.

"Yes. Where would one get married in Paris?"

"Maxim's?" I said.

"No," he said seriously. "There is only one place to get married in Paris. Notre Dame."

"How the hell could you get married in Notre Dame? You're not a Catholic."

"Easy. The minister, my fiancée, and I walked into Notre Dame, down a side aisle of the cathedral. He performed the ceremony there with a delegation of nuns from Hamburg, Germany, watching us and holding their rosaries. Then we went for a wedding picnic in the Bois de Boulogne, paté, cold chicken, champagne, and pears. Then I gave the minister fifty bucks for his church and his ticket home to Bucks County."

Speedy Sachs is always experimenting with his life. He doesn't change the way his contemporaries change, eating dried fruit one year, jogging the next, wearing leisure suits and love beads one year, taking up TM the next. Sachs experiments daily. But better yet, he is an originator.

"You know," he tells me, "most of the progress of civilization has been accomplished by people who are not formally educated, people who don't know that they *aren't supposed* to do certain things. Edison was an applied researcher. 'I want you assholes to try everything,' Edison said to his assistants as they searched for something to use as the filament in the light bulb. Progress is created by people who don't know any better. Christ, I didn't know I was alive until I was twenty-eight, when I finally got out of school. For the street kids of Brooklyn, for the truly ambitious, they're halfway into careers by then. Edison also said, 'genius is one percent inspiration and ninety-nine percent perspiration.' I'm sorry to harp on Edison. But he looked so goddamn good. That's why I willed my hair to be white, to look like Edison. Concentration."

Speedy's home reflects his ideas of future dwellings. "One thing you should strive for," he says, "is a place of escape, a place to renew the soul, a place of survival if necessary, a place you can defend. The dwelling should be as trouble-free as possible, with backup energy systems, solar panels for collectors, wood stoves with a source of wood handy that you can cut yourself. Kerosene lamps, coal supply, candles. I have an M-1 carbine so I can protect my turf. At a hundred and fifty yards I can hit anything I can see."

"You expect to have to defend your turf?"

"Not necessarily. But I think I would welcome the change of pace. I always regret that I taught stateside in World War II. War appeals to me. My blend of coward, opportunist, and chicken shit usually does great in combat."

Speedy has a picture window that looks out on woods and a small pond, a wildlife sanctuary. That is, the window *would* look out on the pond, if Speedy had not painted it black. He painted it black several years ago and uses the window for a movie screen. On the screen he shows films of the sea, with a sound track of the surf crashing onto rocks on the Pacific coast of California. "I do all my work here," he says, "all my thinking. The sea calms me, allows me to pierce deeply the womb of any problem. Thus, I have the sea without suffering the damage that an ocean environment inflicts upon a house."

Speedy Sachs has a machine on the floor of his bedroom. It is a negative ion machine that he turns on every night before retiring. He claims that, if he goes to sleep in a foul mood, the negative ions react positively on his sleeping system and he wakes up optimistic, full of piss and vinegar. When he awakes, Speedy pushes a button next to his bed and lies nude on top of the covers. Above his head a sunlamp rests on a track. The button activates the lamp, which travels on the overhead track up and down over Speedy's body. At five minutes, a bell rings, and Speedy rolls over while the lamp's rays go up and down his back side.

"If you keep learning something every day," Speedy Sachs says,

"you will create your own future, as I have tried to do. One thing
I have, as you can see, is books. Knowledge. I believe in *toilet*
books, not in coffee table books. Toilet books are for absorbing, in
a quiet spot good for concentration. I believe, for instance, that
all homes in the next century will be built with bidets in the
bathrooms. Most Americans seeing bidets for the first time pee in
them or use them to wash their feet. A bidet is an invention
created to clean yourself after bowel movements and other bodily
functions. A necessity for cleanliness. 'So we beat on, boats
against the current, borne back ceaselessly into the past.' That's
Fitzgerald and that's your future. Not *1984*. Not *The Greening of
America*. Not *Future Shock*. Communism is generally left in college corridors."

Speedy has designed the furniture in his house himself. All of it
is assembled in sections with wooden pegs and can be disas-
sembled for moving in minutes. When I was there, a cat walked
through his living room. Picking up the cat and smiling, Speedy
said to me, "I built this cat from parts."

He made one of the first black boxes in America, for duplicat-
ing the sound of push-button phones so that long-distance dialing
can be toll free. "I don't use it much any longer," he told me,
"since penalties became too severe. I only built it for amusement."
While I watched him he called the Tel Aviv Hilton, asked the
time (10:47 A.M.), and, saying he was in Room 672, ordered
bagels, lox, and cream cheese from room service. "Women love all
this," he told me. "Then we get married and they find out I'm
serious. No one can take too much of this reality. But I'm hoping.
I'm always looking for Eve, just as I assume they are looking for
Adam."

I try to stump Speedy Sachs, to pose questions that he cannot
answer. I'm always disappointed. Last year I stopped by to visit
him, needing answers to two literary problems. He was listening
to the radio, to the "Latvian Heritage Hour."

"How can you listen to that?" I asked him.

"I love it," he said. "Everything they sing sounds like an alma mater. What freebies do you want today?"

He reminds me that I get bits of knowledge from him for nothing, and that his regular fees for jobs can range up to as much as fifteen hundred dollars a day. But he knows that many of his bits go into my books, and he loves anything that smacks of immortality. Besides, I bought him Coca-Cola of Los Angeles at nine in 1975, and the company was taken over last year at forty dollars a share. Some clients remember the gifts of money.

"I need to blow a hole in center field at Shea Stadium," I told him. "A big hole that will terrify thousands of people."

Speedy didn't bat an eye. "Easy," he said. "Except, do you care if you kill an outfielder?" After fifteen minutes in his lab, he brought me an answer. Then I said, "I need a sharp weapon, one that can kill like a sword, but one that prevents your opponent from getting near enough to stab you back. I need something unusual."

"What you want is a *runka*," Speedy Sachs said. "A runka is a long metal spear, pointed at the end, but with two sharp prongs on either side about a foot down from the main point. The idea is to shove the pike through your opponent, but stop him before he has a chance to reach you with his sword. The two prongs do that very effectively. They'd most likely catch on your victim's ribs."

Speedy Sachs is not an optimist about the future, but neither is he pessimistic. He feels that he is a realist and has offered several suggestions to reinforce this view:

1. "To liven up a dinner party and stimulate a discussion with pretentious people, offer this phrase after coffee: 'If you want a higher standard of living, you have to settle for a lower quality of life.'"

2. "Realize that scientists oftentimes paint pictures that the press reports to terrify people. Realize that scientists are really only after results. They don't care about *you*. They just want something to *work*."

3. "The Turks like to attack their problems. The Persians sneer at the Turks because the Persians love problems. They write poems about them. We Americans are so screwed up because we abuse the word. We don't even know the test of the goddamn word "problem." All we want is sympathy and understanding. That's why we'll always have capitalism; we're too dumb for the perfect world. We'll say to the perfect world, 'Don't install one here.' "

4. "The ideal life is probably three weeks a month married and one week not. For both parties. But I've not been able to get any of my wives to take this idea seriously."

5. "I pay attention to the motto I borrowed from a prime minister of India. 'I know I will never understand reality. So now I can concentrate on action, Dharma (duty) and commitment.' "

6. "Several helpful hints: (*a*) Watch the color of your urine. If it is too yellow, drink more water. Your urine should be clear in color, and a lot of water is good for you. (*b*) Pay attention. (*c*) Get your employer to install 'white sound' at work. These electronic circuits, broadcast through any public address system, produce a rushing sound, almost like the sound of surf. It masks human speech and allows you to work more productively, with less stress. (*d*) Learn more than the other people who are doing the job at hand. (*e*) Watch out for hookers with blotchy skin. (*f*) Eat where the truckers eat."

Currently, Speedy Sachs is turning down consulting assignments. Eight years ago he was a speaker at the Cannes Film Festival. Then he flew to Paris with a starlet and several producers. They checked into the Georges Cinq. As he was lying in his tub in his all-marble bathroom, golden light flooded the room from the window outside. Speedy was transfixed. He stayed in the tub for seven hours, until the special gray light of twilight softened the room. He got up from the tub convinced that he had had a vision of what he should do. He wanted to recreate that gray without paint. He wanted to build a light generator, to mix blue and green, red and white, to duplicate the special gray. Experimenting with light, he devised a system to mix any shade of any color, making the mathematical possibilities infinite. "I have small control boxes," Speedy says. "We can sit and create paintings of color for hours on end. And never the same. This is the ultimate art form." He became obsessed with his art form, almost to the extent of losing his sense of humor. So I called him one day and said, "Speedy Sachs, my urine is very yellow."

Laughing he said, "Drink more water," and begged me to pose him a problem he couldn't answer.

Mather Stevens even answers questionnaires with philosophy. "When I think about the future I think mostly about our generation." He rummaged through his desk and handed me a copy of the introduction to his fifteenth college reunion report, which he had written a few years ago:

Dear Classmates:

Has it been fifteen years since we've walked through the Yard at night and listened to Bach pouring out of open windows? Has it been fifteen years since we've gotten drunk at crew races, or smelled the fear in Lamont at reading period, or imagined that a girl in Widener was staring at us? Has it been fifteen years since we've sent a room-mate to Rexall's to buy Trojans, had a beer and onion rings at the old Cronin's, almost flunked Chem 20, played the jukebox at the Casablanca, had 2:00 A.M. English muffins at Hayes-Bick?

Nostalgia has become very popular in a world that has become very small. And the nostalgia seems to center on the era of the fifties and on us, the "Silent Generation." As a class we espoused no causes. We were too young for World War II and Korea, generally too old for Vietnam. Our wars were with the six-month National Guard or the Reserves, or three-year stints in the Navy cruising friendly waters or in the Air Force flying empty skies. We believed in good times and studying, not necessarily in that order. We also believed in, and respected, authority. A real fear of probation existed, and the thought of somehow being "expunged from the records" was too fierce to mention.

When talking to a young radical friend of mine about the fifties, he referred to us not as silent, but as the boring generation. "Your words,"

he said, "were not the words of conversation, but of rock 'n roll songs."
Were we boring? Are we boring? Are we still silent?

Five hundred seventy-eight responses have been received to our
Fifteenth Report, with some $6,800 contributed toward its publication.
There seem to be very few surprises: many messages from doctors and
educators, much interest in community affairs and in leisure activities.
Many words about children and families. The Class of 1959, judging
from this Report, is firmly rooted in the middle class. Perhaps what is
missing is half the story, from the half of the class who never answer
Were we boring? Are we boring? Are we still silent?

Is it only ten years until 1984?

> Sincerely,
> Mather Stevens
> Co-chairman, Class Report

Then Stevens pointed to a framed needlepoint motto on the
wall. "That was sent to me by a client," he said, "a woman whose
divorce I had handled. All she wanted was a decent life."

The quotation was from Joseph Conrad's *Heart of Darkness*:
"The mind of man is capable of anything — because everything is
in it, all the past as well as all the future."

# EPILOGUE:
# THE IMPORTANCE
# OF GOOD-BYES

Henry the Red often tells me that you cannot inherit experience or teach it to others successfully. "Like a wet dream," he says, "you have to have it yourself."

There is a danger in building your team of experts. Occasionally your team becomes too attached to you, too jealous of your time. I had a friend named Zeno who was a restaurant owner. We became acquainted as I frequented his restaurant in my days as a bachelor. Booths in his place gave privacy. Fresh linen and flowers were on the tables, and old-time waiters nursed you through dinner, taking pleasure in your pleasure. Smart People always have favorite restaurants where they get the full treatment, where they know the staff by their first names and where the staff knows them by their last.

Everything seemed fine with my friend Zeno, although little by little I learned from him about the troubles with his summer cottage, the troubles with his children, the fights with his wife. He would bring over a bottle of twelve-star Metaxa to my booth, pour the complimentary brandy, and lay on the problems. Dinners were delicious and the service was the best, but the waters were being muddied by the therapy.

One evening after work, and shortly after I was married, I stopped in at a bar next to my office for a pre-home shooter. I was with a client, and he was just launching into his tale of too heavy taxes, when Zeno the restaurateur came over, threw his arms around me, and hugged. Zeno was big all over, and his upper lip always perspired from the excitement of yelling at waiters and pleasing customers. That evening Zeno was drunk. He sat down and complained, "My partner runs the restaurant tonight. He says, 'From now on we do things *my* way.' It's no good not to be in control. The customers love Zeno, but a partner is no good."

My client soon left, and I was left alone with Zeno. I couldn't break away. Stuck, I invited him to our apartment for dinner and arrived, with Zeno in tow, grinning foolishly at my wife. When you are first married, things that years later would be considered unforgivable are accepted as a matter of course. We sat down to lamb chops and artichokes, and Zeno was full of love. "White bread," he insisted, "got any white bread?"

He had to have white bread and butter with his meal. He had to have ice water. And, although he didn't need it at all, he had retsina, the Greek wine that you drink when you're courting and for which you later lose your taste. We watched him wolf dinner, eating the leaves of his artichoke as if they were hot buttered lettuce. "You ever need anyone taken care of," he said to us, "let me know. My friend, Little Charlie, he takes care of enemies."

Zeno was getting drunker, and sobbing about what friends we were. He jumped up. "Hit me in the stomach," he commanded. "Go ahead. I'll show you what rock is." He demanded that I hit him, and I was forced to give him a halfhearted blow. "*No*" he yelled. "As hard as you can." He grunted as I hit him. Then my wife had to hit him. He hugged us both, lifting us off the ground, loving us to death. Finally, after another hour of kisses, hugs, loyalties sworn forever, and demands that I write down names of enemies for Little Charlie to take care of, we got him to leave.


## THE "YOU'RE TOO GOOD TO ME" SYNDROME

Well, this killed Zeno's restaurant for us, which was too bad. We stopped going there shortly after the artichoke night because he wouldn't leave us alone. And the situation led to a Smart People problem: the "You're Too Good to Me" Syndrome. Beware of this. It involves getting too close to your Roughriders. There is a fine line you must walk with your street-smart Smart People. Once they accept you as a friend, you are *on their team* also. Occasionally, when you're too busy or involved to give them what they consider their due, which is *time*, they can turn on you. Keep a certain distance; know how far to go. Once I had missed a month of going to Zeno's restaurant, it was all over. I was relegated to the back room. No more conversation or soul-searching. But no more free Metaxa or deluxe treatment either.

People out of context make others uncomfortable. This is also a Smart People lesson. Keep your team segregated from one another. Don't give away your secrets easily: your special yard man, your baby-sitters, your antique dealer who saves things for you. Above all, don't invite your butcher to dinner with your lawyer, your orthopedist with your bookie, because you think the mix would be a big success. Keep your team in compartments. Make them feel that they are unique to you. They won't feel that way if they meet the others.

Despite this knowledge, we once gave a dance, my wife and I, inviting all of our Smart People — Summas, Lamplighters, Mavens, and Roughriders. The dance was black tie and began at ten o'clock one Friday night with breakfast to be served at one. At first, it was uncomfortable, the plumbers seeking out the carpenters, the lawyers seeking out one another, the doctors the same, and old acquaintances closeting themselves with familiar faces. My Philosopher-Kings were there, tiptoeing around each other. Henry the Red thought it was a big mistake. "They'll all leave you," he said. "Now the uneducated will think you're using them, the educated will think you're playing Gatsby. You might as well move to a different city after this. It's all over."

Mather Stevens, the egalitarian, thought it was terrific. He came up to me during a polka and held up his glass, "A martini was my Yale College and my Harvard," he said, parodying Melville, and doing a little polka step by himself. "I found someone to fix my front steps tomorrow morning, and I've picked up two clients, one divorce and a will and trust. 'Let us crown ourselves with rosebuds, before they be withered.' That's the wisdom of Solomon," he said, "unadulterated." Mather Stevens's fine blond hair was parted in the middle, and his face had a smile polished on it that said, "I'm going to drink stingers tonight and wear red pants." He jumped away from me and cut in on the wife of the man who plows my driveway in the winter. They leaped away, doing the mad polka of the Philosopher-King.

The dance went on and breakfast went down without a ripple. A collection was taken up to keep the band until three.

Henry the Red was seated at a table in a corner, holding forth to a group of men and women he had converted that evening. I came over to him as the band played "Dixie" and you knew it was near the end of the party.

"I thought you said it was a disaster," I reminded Henry the Red.

He beamed, surrounded by his converts who hung on his every word. No teenage guru had ever been more pleased with his flock, no Father Divine so comfortable with a captive audience. He shrugged his shoulders, admitting he had been wrong. "'Your fathers,'" he said, "'where are they? And the prophets, do they live forever?' That's Zechariah," he added. "Unadulterated."

People eventually left, trouping out in pairs, in groups, some having made lasting connections, some never to see the others again. One of my Mavens of the future shook my hand and walked down the steps. She is an astrophysicist, involved in space medicine for NASA. She turned at the bottom of the stairs. "Thanks for making us feel special," she said.

*That's* the secret of Smart People.

# SMART PEOPLE
# QUESTIONNAIRE

Do you have a favorite story about yourself and/or your profession? (If you do just indicate *YES* and I'll call you.)

Do you have a favorite phrase or motto that would describe yourself and your career or your life?

What quality makes you special, that separates you from others in your field?

How do you avoid (if you do) the trivia of modern life? For example, how do you deal with crowds, lines, etc.?

How much luck is involved in success?

If you're so smart, why aren't you rich? If you *are* rich, is it because you're smart?

Do you pay attention to detail?

What is your favorite book? Why?

How do you get people to respond to you?

Do you have an automechanic you trust?

Who is the smartest person *you* know?

List three hints that may be helpful to the layman in understanding *your* profession *or* your approach to life. For example, keep your left arm straight when teeing off.

If a sense of humor is important to you, what is the funniest thing that ever happened in the pursuit of your career?

Do you have brief advice about accumulating money?

Do you have brief advice about maintaining good health?

Where does sex rank among the important things in your life — high or low on a scale of 10?